Mastering Your Time Share

JOHN C. BOTDORF

outskirts press

Outskirts Press, Inc.
http://www.outskirtspress.com

ISBN: 978-1-4787-8876-8

PRINTED IN THE UNITED STATES OF AMERICA

DEDICATION

I want to dedicate this book to my family and friends that have taught me so much about what is important. To my parents who are now both passed I learned to never give up and always start the day with a positive attitude. To my siblings, Carol, Jim and Robert, we have learned that in the end family is all we ever really have so enjoy your family while they are still around. Make the best of it and life will be better. To the mother of my children Ruth, I am blessed with two beautiful children. I salute our efforts to have raised our kids past college age. They are a wonder to behold.

My daughter Alana, and my son Forrest are the highlight of my life. Through all of our ups and downs, it is my kids I am most proud of. Most of all, I respect their ability to make decisions and accept responsibility for their actions. Lastly to my endless friends I have gathered over the years. I have presented so many crazy idea's and have deeply benefited from their love, support and input. They have stuck with me and together we have seen the value of real friendship. I have been blessed with far more than I deserve, and to God and the world I shall try and spend the rest of my days giving back to the important causes I support. I have learned it always comes back to me in spades and provides a deeper and more purposeful life.

I hope those that get to read this book will find a way to travel the world and enjoy the wonders that come with different cultures and experiences.

DISCLAIMER From Author

This Book was written to provide general information about the time share industry and time shares in general. The Publisher and Author have strived to be as accurate and complete as possible in the creation of the contents within this book. Due to the rapidly changing economy and the changes that routinely occur within the time share industry, neither party warrants or represents that the contents within are accurate in every instance, and both the author and publisher reserve the right to make changes to the text without notice.

Neither the Publisher not the author will be responsible for any losses or damages of any kind incurred by the reader whether directly or indirectly arising from the use of any information or examples contained in this book. The purpose of this book is to educate the reader about the time share industry. This book is not intended to use a source of legal, business, accounting, or real estate advice. All readers are advised to seek professional advice in connection with entering into any type of time share or real estate transaction.

All of our readers are encouraged to seek counsel using their own independent sources and to seek the advice of professional real estate brokers before signing or entering into any type of time share or realty transaction. The reader assumes full responsibility for use of any of the information contained herein. The time share business can be complicated and involves many different types of products that can all be sold at varying prices points, often being sold or bought at significant discount or mark up. Readers can be well rewarded or lose significant sums of money if they do not understand the commitments involved with time share and therefore should seek to be fully informed about all types of related closing fees,

Our sincere thanks for your support in purchasing this book and we welcome your comments.

Table of Contents

INTRODUCING
THE NEW VAGABON TRAVEL SYSTEM
—NEW 2018 PRODUCT

Please visit our Web site,
www.masteringyourtimeshare.com,
for more information on the vagabond travel system .

Foreword

PURPOSE OF *MASTERING Your Time Share*—Welcome to one of the first comprehensive books written about modern time shares. Since you have purchased this book, it is likely you have had a positive (or negative) time share experience or are just thinking about acquiring or selling a time share. This book was written to help you navigate through what is becoming an increasingly difficult maze of options, plans, membership levels, and ownership choices, all with a variety of transfer rights and restrictions that not only vary within the industry but also within single companies.

Our objective in this book is to explore the pros and cons of time shares as a vacation option, as a business option, and as an investment decision, to determine whether it makes sense for you or your family. We will look at how a time share can lower your cost of travel and even lower the cost of your retirement.

Based on 25 years of observation, I can make a strong case that time share experiences and opinions run the gamut from "The worst investment I ever made" to "One of the best decisions I ever made for my family." The answer lies in understanding the vast knowledge and choices that now make up the time share industry. Moreover, its rules, perks, and fine print allow consumers to create very different product experiences. This book was written to help you find and identify whether the newest and fastest growing new time share models are meant for you. The right plan can provide invaluable memories for you and your family for generations to come. The wrong plan can leave you emotionally drained and desperate to stop what feels like a dream gone bad that seems to just bleed you of your cash. We will also discuss the many strategies that can be used to land that special reservation you want.

We will also look into what is needed for the time share industry to create a next-generation model for consumers, examine what are the issues, and how can they be solved. A small portion of this book is therefore dedicated to some industry challenges. We believe these obstacles will get addressed because the time share industry has proven it can innovate, create, and deliver new products and solutions to consumers. We will explore the pieces that are already in place and those that should come into play over the next 10 years.

We will also help unwind many of the important questions and concerns that tend to revolve around time shares, like maintenance fees and priority reservations. We will begin by exploring how software now plays a vital role in your time share success and redirect your thinking into a computer prospective.

We will also take a look at the size of the time share market and how different companies serve different portions of the industry, both globally and in North America. The time share industry is widely acknowledged to have originated in the 1960s from a developer named Paul Doumier, who first saw the potential in shared ownership by organizing a pooled investment plan to build a small ski project in the French Alps. We will trace the evolution of this first time share idea all the way into today's fast-moving "points-based" model that now covers everything from room charges, boating, cruises, luxury homes, VIP event tickets, villas, airfares, hotels, and exotic tours. We will reveal not-so-obvious formulas for getting luxury trips for a fraction of their usual cost.

We have also developed some tools to help evaluate whether your time share is serving your needs and what are the options if it is not. We have provided different models for ascertaining what your time share might be worth, how its value should be calculated, and what some of the pitfalls and solutions available to you are.

Today's time share model is really just a real estate derivative that can allow the owner to benefit in many cases by staying in multimillion-dollar properties every year and pay only a small portion of the real cost of annual ownership. Experiences can and do vary widely. Customers owning time shares from the same company can pay two–three times more to use their time share than other members even within the same company, depending on how the rules are used. We will uncover the keys to staying in some of best properties in the world, and then evaluate the actual cost of ownership.

Time share vacations themselves are not priced evenly, and two similar time share properties in the same location used at the same time can cost eight–ten times as much as each other under different pricing models offered by the industry. The key is to understand local markets and weigh them carefully against what has become several different business models designed to achieve the same thing, a great vacation booked at the resort you want, when you want it, and at the right price.

You will discover, as you may have expected, that not all time shares have the same present or future values. In fact, our research shows that different answers may apply to whether a time share decision to own produces positive economic value and to what degree. It is logical that the same time share located in the same building should offer very similar investment profiles, but because of a complicated maze of rules, actual results for cost of ownerships can and do vary widely because of overriding factors related to booking processes, the time of year, software hierarchies, and shifting marketing benefits and demands. We will unravel this maze and break these rules into simple formulas to help you understand and maximize your current and future time share experience.

We will also look at time share as part of your retirement plan and analyze what your future living and travel goals are for retirement. One of my favorite reasons for buying a time share was not for the vacation; it was for work. I used my villas to entertain my clients, write important business plans, and find a way to organize many needed "time-outs" in the middle of what was, and continues to be, a busy professional life.

We will also examine what is going on in the fast-growing luxury time share market. How can a family use the luxury time share market to replace or complement their existing vacation portfolio? What are the cost benefits? The answers may surprise you and provide a whole new way to balance high-value family real estate assets used for vacations. We will discuss strategies to dramatically reduce your family vacation cost while still maintaining your desired vacation lifestyle year in and year out at some of the world's most luxurious villas and homes.

Finally, we will address the future of time shares, see what the tea leaves suggest is about to happen, find out how future retirements will use time shares, and where the market(s) will head. We believe the time share industry has a lot more to run before the industry slows down. We predict three new trends will greatly impact the future of time shares.

The time share business is now impacting over 60 million baby boomers who will start to retire in 2017 at the rate of 75,000 people per week for the next 19 years. The housing and time share industry will then face over 92 million millennials heading into their peak earning years without our goal of "owning a home" in many cases. We predict our housing models will need to shift over the next 20 years with an increased focus on retirement and millennial housing, forcing the industry to address temporary housing means and determine if the time share industry can respond to this shift. Lastly, how can time shares help address our retirement population needs since 75% of Americans are unprepared to retire? We will analyze these issues and propose how and why certain inevitable changes will also likely drive changes in the time share industry.

We believe since the time share is a proven model, dramatic new housing products will emerge over the next 20 years under the time share banner. Time shares have actually set the stage for significant change with not only vacationers, but also with millennials and retirees whose housing needs of the future are more aligned with shorter-term housing. While the 30-year mortgage may never go away, the time has come where living in any one place for 30 years is all but over. Welcome to what will likely become not only time shares for vacations, but also for retirement, business, and the new 1-year time shares of tomorrow.

Dedicated to Mother and Kids.

Glossary of Time Share Terms

A Down-Trade Exchange—This is when an owner chooses to deposit his or her time share into an exchange pool and gives up more economic value than what the trade was worth; i.e., a two-bedroom villa for 1 week in Hawaii in exchange for a 1-week, one-bedroom in a much-cheaper location requiring half of less of the points given up. This is fairly common because the owner wants another location, time of year, etc., and the exchange is for only one trade, and the exchanged unit provides enough utility value to make a one-time down exchange worthwhile in a single instance.

An Up-Trade Exchange—This is when an owner is able to exchange their week for a week that is more valuable. This occurs when a lock-off owner is able to exchange their 1 week for 2 weeks by trading the locked-off unit separately, for example. Trading a one-bedroom for a two-bedroom in a location of similar value would also be an example of an up trade because of the increased economic value gained by the trade.

Banked or Deposit Week—This occurs when an owner elects to postpone eligible travel for a year and move the eligible week or points into the next year. This may be done under certain programs and allows owners to save up for larger trips or to postpone a vacation due to their schedule.

Biennial or EOY— (Every other year) This is a time share or points-based product that is only valid every other year. This cuts the maintenance and usage rights to every other year versus every year. This is ideal for owners seeking to visit high-profile vacation destinations on an every-other-year basis or may complement an existing vacation portfolio.

Beachfront Time Share Index—The Beachfront Index represents the cost of purchasing a home on the beach and comparing the cost to purchasing a year of time share at the beach. We also looked at the annual cost to live in each for 1 year. We put the challenge to the test in Southern California and our index came out at well over 2 to 1. In this analysis we assumed in all cases we would bring $975,000 cash to purchase the time share outright and use the same amount of cash as the down payment for the condo and home example. We then assumed a 4%, 30 year mortgage for the payment.

Category One Time Share—Top 15%—Ultraluxury, top finishes, upgraded luxury furniture, ground-zero locations, high-quality golf courses, ski in/ski out. Usually have excellent dining, recreation, and special amenity packages for the area like boating packages, adventure tours, limos, cars, and grocery service. These time shares rent for $1,000 per night, and more in the high season.

Category Two Time Share—Top 35%—Top-tier locations, well-appointed kitchens, and top-grade washers and dryers, well-run kid programs, great locations, nice pools and amenities, almost always sold out in high seasons. Rental rates of $550 and up for two bedrooms in high season. Some top-tier Category Two resorts are close to Category One because of extended benefits with resort tie-ins like golf courses, restaurants, and shared pools. Many offer tennis and recreation packages like spas, gyms, golf, horseback riding, and other summer and winter sports with shuttle services.

Category Three Time Share—Top 75%—Usually located in a micro-B location within a great city. Could be near ski in/ski out or on or near prime beach locations, and may offer shuttle services in high season. Often older buildings and some have an advantage of larger unit sizes. Usually have smaller amenity packages with either fewer pools or reduced food and beverage services, or none at all. Great family value and provides more affordable vacation price point for families with reduced vacation budgets. Several niche finds in this category that can get close to Category Two time shares in some cases while providing a reduced price point with lower maintenance fees.

Category Four Time Share—Bottom 25%—These are usually former Category Three time shares that are waiting to be sold or repositioned into the market. They often require some degree of deferred maintenance but because of their location they offer low rentals and good value, particularly in high seasons. Some may have higher delinquencies and may suffer from an underfunded budget operating with inadequate reserves. Default rates are usually higher, and they can be very difficult to sell if your deed is titled to a Category Four timeshare. Many of these are in decent shape and are well run but just suffer from design, location, and functional obsolescence. Some will get repositioned back into Category Three time shares.

Developer/Operator—In the time share business, there are many trades involved in creating a top-shelf time share program. In order for the business to grow, new properties need to be acquired which involves a top-notch acquisition team to purchase land and construct the gamut of small inner-city properties all the way to grand scale megaresorts. After construction, the process shifts from development into sales and marketing, and then into hotel/resort management. For these reasons, this book may use the terms *developer* and *operator* interchangeably, as both the developer hat and the operator role are necessary today to be a competitive time share company.

Economic Value—This can be a broader definition of value and equates to some form of monetary gain. Economic value by itself could refer to resale value, rental value, original value, etc., but the general theme is tied to using dollars to define value. Payback models are often used to calculate economic value. We present two different payback models in this book to cover the basic ways it is possible to define return on investment, and in the process, define whether your time share has positive and negative economic value. In other words, it is going up or down in value based on the surrounding economics, and hence, *What Is My Time Share's Economic Value?*

Fixed Week—This is a 7-day timeshare that allows the owner to visit a particular location at the exact same time each year. This was popular 10 years ago, and even today, provides certainly for those owners that prefer to have a locked-in time so they can plan years in advance, if needed.

Fractional Owner—This is a form of real estate ownership that is less than whole, as the name suggests. Often, fractional ownership means multiple weeks that an owner has the right to occupy for a portion of a high season and often includes some flex time for the off-season. This form of ownership can also extend ownership rights for several months and is usually associated with luxury product where an owner shares a property with as few as four or as many as 40 portions of the year.

Floating Week—As the name suggests, this is a time share that allows the owner to pick from certain time periods in which to use the week. These weeks often have names like Platinum, Gold, or Silver, or could be called Premium, High, and Off-Season. This allows operators and owners to price into the time share models certain high-demand times and lets other owners pay less for times that are in somewhat less demand.

Legacy Week—This is also called a "week's owner," usually meaning someone who bought a time share on the traditional "1-week" model where the owner is restricted to booking all 7 days at once. Some of these time share weeks have grandfathered rights which can be valuable, like very competitive maintenance fees relative to the new "points-based" model. While these weeks do not contain many of the newer features of the more advanced and flexible point-based systems now in place, they can provide a valuable contribution to your overall time share portfolio.

Lock-Off Unit—This is a unit that is divisible from the main unit and has a separate entry so owners can share a large two-bedroom unit with an optional third bedroom. The lock-off unit usually contains a kitchenette suitable for small meals and coffee. Popular in the time share industry because it can often be traded for 2 separate weeks because each side has its own key with a door inside the unit that can be "locked off." In general, lock-off villas have very good trading value because of their flexibility, size, and ability to up-split into 2 weeks from just 1.

The Maintenance Fee—The maintenance fee is what a time share developer must charge the owner to maintain, replace, upgrade, and improve a resort. This fee is generally monitored by an independent board of directors with input from all of the stakeholders, including the owners and developer. Even though much of the time share industry has adopted a points-based system, it can be tricky to figure out your actual daily maintenance fee. It is easy to know what your actual fee is by looking at the bill, but it's important to convert your actual bill into a cost per day. It is important to factor in extra days gained via discounts and extra days, as well as making sure your stays reflect also the amount of days you use versus what you may be entitled to. We cover this under the RRC ratio later in the book.

Seasoned Maintenance Fee—A seasoned maintenance fee is one that changes depending on how the owner managed their time share purchase and how they manage their use of their time share account. For example, it is possible for two owners to own a month of time share from the same developer and have different maintenance fees. One owner could have a fee for the year of $6,800, and the other with a fee of $4,800, and both own the same amount of time share.

Additionally, one owner might get 24 nights out of their membership and pay $172 a night in maintenance fees, while the other owner with the exact same amount of time share ownership might pay only $40 a night in maintenance fees. The difference is how the account is managed. One, for instance, may rent a portion of their time share time using the money to reduce their annual maintenance fees, thereby lowering their cost per day.

Payback Models—We use two different payback models to calculate how many years it takes to recoup your time share investment. Although calculating ROIs (return on investment) for time shares involves many variables, we will break down the different methods and help set some standard benchmarks. While clearing an ROI number is not really necessary to enjoy your time share, our models allow you to know what goes into each calculation and could help you assess your time share portfolio. While many other payback models could be used, most are just offshoots of the two kinds of payback models we run here.

The Payback Indicator and our two Time-Share Tools for Calculating Paybacks are:

Payback Indicator—This is the amount of time in years and months your timeshare will pay for itself after factoring in all maintenance costs, your cost of purchase, and your reasonable rental rate that would be charged for the unit/villa if you chose to rent it or you are able to rent it on the open market. This is calculated by figuring out your net rental value per night, and then dividing that annual number into your net purchase price. Paybacks of between 7 to 11 years, assuming inflation of 3%–4% after maintenance fees are in the mid-range of payback indicators. The lower the payback indicator, the quicker it takes to recoup all of your time share investment. I have seen them as low as 2 years and as high as 25 or more.

The RRC Ratio—The Rental Rate/Cost Ratio—Time Share Value over Initial Cost Model—This is equal to what your villa or condo might rent for on a single night if you rented it or what you would expect to pay to rent it divided over your daily maintenance and tax fees. RRC ratios can, and do, range from as low as 1.50 to 1 to over 20 to 1. Most fall into the middle somewhere. This ratio is discussed in multiple parts of this book. Owners with just 1 or 2 weeks will use a regular maintenance fee consisting of exactly what the developer bills you and likely does not have any rental income. Seasoned time share owners that own multiple weeks or even months will be able to net out their rentals, take advantage of seasonal and membership discounts, and will therefore end up with very different maintenance fees per night, often just a fraction of what 1-week owners will pay. This is based purely on how a vacation portfolio is assembled, managed, and used by the owner. In each case, the owner pays the developer the full amount of maintenance fees billed for their membership.

The Opportunity Cost RRC Ratio—This is an extreme stress test for time share investment and takes into account the time value of your money had it been invested. We take on the alternative investment theory and put it to the test. In the process, we address the real question, "Which is more important, making money or taking more vacation time?" Please see the 45-Year Rental versus Owner "Shoot-Out" to see who comes out over 45 years, the renter who invested his money in a tax-free bond and rents a time share every year for 45 years or the owner who purchases a prime 2-week villa timeshare and saves money on rentals.

Portfolio RRC Ratio—This is a calculation that involves taking each day of your time share portfolio and figuring out what your overall Portfolio RRC ratio is using your daily seasoned maintenance fee. This is calculated by taking a representative rental rate on each nightly stay for the year and dividing it by your average daily cost for each day you controlled for that year. Once completed, you add up all of the RRC ratios, and then divide them by the total number of nights either occupied or rented out. This will provide you with your RRC ratio for all of your time shares weighted together. It makes no difference if your days or weeks are with one or more companies as long as your rental rates and maintenance costs are accurate and reflect the season and times you occupy or use your time share.

Stretched Points—The process of optimizing the booking process by converting your time share membership into the maximum amount of nights per year. This could involve booking villa time during the off-season, using premium or bump clauses or points in your membership, trading up a locked-off unit, combining your stay with a promotional deal, using provisional discount clauses, or renting on off-peak days and times in exchange for a longer stay.

Utility Value—Utility value refers to the joy you get from going on vacation, celebrating life while on vacation, and using your time share for its intended purpose: to relax, wind down, and be thankful you are with loved ones and on vacation. Utility value does not have to reflect economic value, although we all recognize a full kitchen is better than a microwave oven kitchen. It makes no difference whether you bought your time share, someone bought it for you, you inherited it, or just bought the right to stay in a special place for a short while. Our definition in this book for utility value is simply how much you enjoy using it.

CHAPTER 1

Why is the Purpose of Time Share? ?

WHY OWN A time share? The decision to own a time share can be very personal and may or may not need to be a pure business-based decision. It may just be a family decision. I believe it would be rather biased to suggest that everyone should pursue a plan to purchase a time share. The answer varies according to what is important in life, what your economic options are, and what alternatives has your life been blessed with that, in some cases, provides vacation home experiences. Some of us did inherit "Dad's" cabin in the woods or the family home in Vail. You may have an entire generation of memories that have unfolded for more than 30 years as you grew up in the family vacation home. In that case, the reasons to own a timeshare may be very different. Just knowing you have alternative choices could be reason enough to own today's time shares. I have also heard from potential time share buyers their vacation home and the opportunity to stay with friends provides all the comfort they need to plan for downstream holidays and vacations. These people are rightfully quite happy with the vacation model they may have inherited from their family.

On the other end of the spectrum, you may not want Dad's cabin in the woods or the expense of owning and maintaining an expensive vacation home. For most of us, though, we may find ourselves wondering after watching a movie or reading a novel set under the "Tuscany sunset," what would it be like to live in Italy one summer. Instead of moving or making life-altering changes to sell the house or quit your job, how about just dialing the 1-800 number, and in 10 minutes, own the right to summer in Tuscany?

How cool would that be? I have seen too many successful people drown their life in the "next deal," only to witness or experience a medical setback, or even worse, see their child make horrible choices, sending the family relationships into turmoil for years or longer. What happened to forgetting about the iPhone and just taking off the most important time there is: family time? Whether time shares make sense or not for you, taking off for personal and family time always makes sense. We need to learn in the United States that it is not only all right to take time off, it is healthy, leads to a longer life, and even improves productivity.

Health of the average U.S. male/female(2017): By almost any standard, Americans are both sleep deprived and vacation undernourished. According to the Centers for Disease Control in Atlanta, the number one killer of Americans in 2014–2015 continues to be death from a heart attack, killing 614,348 Americans, albeit down from over 714,000 in 2013, largely due to increases in technology, preventive treatments, and advances in medicine. Nonetheless, too many Americans are working themselves into a grave. One interesting fact according to www.worldexpectancy.com is the average life span in the United States for 2015 was 78.86 as blended between men and women, with males averaging 76.30 years of age and woman living until an average of 81.30. I find it noteworthy that in Hawaii, according to the same source, the average age for men and woman at death is 81.30. What is it about Hawaii that, all things being equal, would cause someone to live almost 2.5 years longer? It is also noteworthy that Hawaii continues to lead the country as the number one or two spot to travel to for vacation, depending on the year, cost of airfare, and other economic variables. It is like the islands are calling us to relax, and statistics show that people live longer in a more relaxed setting.

Russell Bertrand was a British philosopher who studied society and its connection to working. He noted in his 1932 essay "In Praise of Idleness," that "If society were better managed the average person would only need to work four hours a day. . . . The rest could be spent on pursuing science, painting and writing." I suppose we could add, the right to vacation to obtain the perfect workweek.

The famous economist John Maynard Keyes in writing "Economic Possibilities for our Grandchildren" several decades ago speculated that by 2030, it might be possible for our society to only need to work 15 hours a week. While his logic seemed on track, we know our economy is moving faster and faster with more and more lower-paying jobs routinely filled by retirees. Many of these jobs now require knowledge of high-tech computers, highly automated inventory, and distribution processes that now run everything from fast food to almost any franchised business. Just look at the knowledge needed to work in a Verizon store selling an iPhone. Have you ever seen anyone in an Apple store that is over 35? We are now seeing younger and younger people suffer from heart attacks as stress levels continue to impact us at younger ages. What is going to be the anti-stress solution?

If heart attacks are the number one killer of Americans, it seems logical to ask, what is the leading cause of heart attacks? While several things impact this condition, we know, according to www.webmd.com, that high blood pressure and stress rank as number 4 and 5 out of the top nine triggers for this cause of death.

Ironically, several studies on working productively point to less work as being more productive. In one article written in *The Economist*, the Greeks were mentioned as the hardest-working group of people in the world with over 2,000 hours logged a year, while the Germans came in at 1,400 hours a year working with an astounding 70% increase in productivity. We know in the United States many professionals are working 60-plus hours a week, hitting over 3,000 hours a year, working 51 out of 52 weeks. Adding to this dilemma is the disturbing trend as reported by the documentary *Sleepless in America* that nearly 40% of Americans now average less than 5 hours of sleep per night. While this is higher than other studies we have seen, any amount less than the 8–9 hours per night recommended for adults is negatively impacting our abilities to cope and process everyday life. A very small percentage of the population can get away with 5–6 hours of sleep, and we are still looking for why this is the case for them.

Compounding this lack of sleep trend, we also note that most Americans do not vacation the way they should. Vacations are necessary to relieve stress, reunite with family and friends, and recharge our batteries so we can head back to work refreshed and willing to work hard. Once more, one study has suggested that the more vacation time one takes per year, the more productive one can be during the rest of the year.

The time share industry clearly has a vested interest in telling us to slow down, take a time-out, and in the process, you may become more productive, less stressed out, and as a result, possibly live longer. If you cannot move to Hawaii, then at least head over there and make it a small part of your life. Your heart will thank you, and so will your spouse.

Why time-outs matter: This brings us to what may be the best reasons to own a time share. The calendar automatically forces the overworked and the overstressed to take a time-out. If for no other reason, this is a very good rationale to purchase a time share. As we get older, time seems to move much faster, and it seems, before long, we are planning for Thanksgiving after just putting the last item away from the year before. Most of all, as we begin to "circle the drain," to quote Dick Van Dyke, no one ever regretted taking more time off to be with family and friends. If you asked almost any child as they approach their late teens, what were their most valuable memories, they will more than likely include references tracing back to family vacations. Time share or not, taking time off to go to the Ritz Carlton or choosing to pitch a tent in the woods will get you to the same place . . . taking time to slow down and think about what is important.

Time share ownership forces us to reset the clock, take a time-out, and start preparing for something more important than a business report, an audit, or legal process. This is known as the *family vacation*. If you get one thing out of this book, I hope when you either finish it or put it down for the next chapter, you will stop, discuss a vacation with your loved ones, and then, most importantly, go book it. Remember, just talking about it does not count; take inventory, figure out a time frame, and then plan for a wonderful trip. Just knowing it is on the calendar can make the next several months more fun as the countdown begins.

Can a time share fill other needs in your personal or business life? Can a time share help you in your personal or business life? When we talk about a void, the question arises about what kind of void. We have many kinds of voids during our lives today, such as our careers, marriages, divorces, separations, new employment, job transfers, etc. We also have times in our lives where we might wonder what it might be like to have made that move to a new city and get a fresh start. Perhaps you are thinking of writing a book, masterminding a new screen play, or writing a business plan. Perhaps you have been through a long illness or large business setback and need a fresh start. All of these things have one thing in common. *Where am I going to stay if I decide to make a major move in my life?* It is very possible for the average person to acquire 8–10 weeks of time share per year if you start with a plan.

Yes, hotels are an option but are really not designed for long-term stays. You can find a room on Airbnb but over time, you may want your own space where you can come and go as you please. I have checked into luxury villas and often brought a box of photos with me. I sprinkle them around the room and in a very short time, the place starts to feel like home. You may not be sure how long you will be gone, so signing a 6-month or 12-month lease may not make sense. What does make sense? It is possible that a well-placed time share may be just the answer. The United States alone has over 1,541 resorts (ARDA study by Ernst & Young) available to stay at that are designed for time share owners, with many more on the way.

Many of these are located in or near large cities where tourism, snow, the ocean, golf, sailing, and other attractions bring large crowds for some of the year and, increasingly, year-round. Some of these cities have very large concentrations of vacation villas, and when it came time to create pricing models, they had to forecast the future and accommodate the present. What this means in real terms is that many of these places were running very low occupancies in the off-season, so when it came time to set prices in concrete (in many cases, they cannot change the pricing from 1 year to the next), the large vacation clubs needed to make sure they were load balancing the demand for not only next summer, but for the summer season 100 years from now. As time goes by and inflation hits year after year, many time shares that are now hard to get into will seem like winning the lottery just to get in during the high season. Imagine if you owned a rental house and you had a tenant who wanted to stay for 100 years and the rent could never change. Imagine getting $2,000 a month for life, even when the market for the house goes to $6,000 some 20 years from now. Long-term thinkers see the value in time shares because they are not thinking about the present.

The long-term debate has been great for time share owners but will get better over time, and much better when our country hits an inflationary cycle again. When competition forces dozens of time shares to populate a given area like Hawaii or Hilton Head, the benefit is that one company cannot charge a whole lot more than another or their sales will fall behind the competition. The combined infrastructure cost can also be spread among many more people, lowering the per-week cost for everyone. Competition in the time share industry can be confusing. This is why many programs have so many different names, point systems, value premiums, discounts, and membership rules. It makes it hard at first blush to compare apples to apples. We will help clarify many of these issues in the remaining chapters.

We will examine these time share models in more detail throughout this book. The main thing to remember is we do have some pricing disintermediation among competitors because the overall goal of any time share company is to fill as many villas as possible during any given night. When the industry started converting to a "points-based system" in the late 1980s, most operators had to provide assurances the rental price (price paid in points) would never change and remain constant. This means over the long term, most all valuable oceanfront or ski in/ski out properties have to surge in value because the outside rental world will keep charging more and more every year, causing the spread between market prices and the fixed time share currency (described as in using "points") to widen every year.

In less-desirable locations, a timeshare can be an ideal environment to start or finish a project without paying market prices for rental space, whether it be an office or an apartment. Of course, there are limitations on using any time share as an office as well as for other purposes, but for many, a time share can yield huge cost benefits over more expensive alternatives to get a project done, relocate, start a job transfer, or even unwind during a painful separation or a bitter divorce. A time share can also even help you start life over or create a better rehabilitation environment. Getting over a death where one might benefit from a changed environment can make a big difference for many of us. Lastly, on the business front, we all know laptops seem to work just fine in an office, a hotel, or a time share villa. They just require a plug, and most large timeshare companies now have free Internet, making a time share a perfect office for completing a project.

Is owning a time share an asset or a liability? We will, of course, be looking into this question in great detail throughout the book, but the short answer is, it depends on the situation. Let's start with a commonsense approach to looking at this question. Given the wide array of choices today in time shares, you have to look at the world as one large trading post for a time, and then ask the question, where is time more valuable? Then this question starts to answer itself. Let's take the basic things most people value in a time share. Things like ease of use and booking, pristine location, close to a major airport, political stability, and safe environment weigh in at the top of the list. We also want security within the time share property and in the surrounding city, great space, terrific views, and a well-appointed kitchen with free parking. Secondary factors like pools, tennis, golf, resort settings, and restaurant choices are also important. A good clue to determine if a time share has value is to look at what surrounding homes, apartments, and even hotels rent for by the night that are nearby. If you are in an area where the answer is less than $80 a day, while there may be nothing at all wrong with the area, it is likely that you are not on a major ocean, at the base of a ski mountain, or looking at a golf course. This is just common sense. If, on the other hand, your time share has the above characteristics, and rentals are at or above $700 per night, there is a very good chance that occupancies in high season run at 99% or are sold out, and that there is usually a waiting list of eager customers that will fill any vacancy instantly if a unit becomes available. This means your time share has liquidity, meaning, there is always someone, somewhere, that wants to use it. Finding that person for a rental requires effort, and we will touch on that later in this book.

Remember that in the majority of cases, people purchase time shares to enjoy time with their families and loved ones and to create memories. Times shares are not designed to necessarily be an investment; however, under certain conditions, with certain plans, it is possible to get a nice return on your time share investment in two ways. The first is in savings over a period of time, meaning the spread between what you pay to stay in your time share and what it costs you. The difference is money you would have otherwise spent to rent the place you are staying in. The second is, of course, through renting your time share. It is the combination of these two that can change the time share model from a negative experience to a positive one. The point here is your time share does not have to make you money. If you enjoy it, use it, and like the flexibility in your plan, then you have likely made a wise purchase. Of course, the other extreme is a time share you visited once or twice, is time-consuming and expensive to get to, and offers little in the way of trade value, in which case it may be more of a liability than an asset to your family.

Most time shares will likely fall somewhere in between these two extremes, with possible demand during some of the year, and much-higher vacancies during other parts of the year. Seasonal sports and weather can also play a major role in what has become a shifting demand pattern over time. One example of this would be in Vail, Colorado. In the 1980s and 1990s, it was fairly easy to get a very nice time share in the summer. Summer activities in many ski towns were not very popular in the 1980s. Now, with more attention to the leaves changing, summer sports, the significant rise in cooking and wine events, auto shows, and numerous charity and corporate events taking advantage of lower summer rates, summertime is now very much in demand. We also have an increasing time share population base helping to reduce the off-season to just a few weeks between summer and winter. The Vail Valley located in the Colorado Rocky Mountains is a good example, having earned a very good reputation for summer events, including many regional and national sporting events like soccer, tennis, hiking, training, and, of course, mountain golf courses. Recent summers have shown very high or sold-out time share projects in the peak summer months.

The clue here is to pay attention to your favorite time share locations and ask yourself, would you like to live there some of the time? If the answer is no, then expecting others to flock to your time share to rent, own, or occupy is just not supported by the facts. Demand for locations in prime times is what makes the very best time shares valuable.

The question of whether your time share is an asset is best answered by whether it has created lasting memories and helped provide a safe and relaxing environment for your family. It does not need to pass an ROI test. That said, at some point, all of us want to know our purchase is a better alternative than renting year after year. The best way to figure out if your time share can be viewed as an asset on an economic basis is by running the numbers. We are going to show you exactly how to do it. We start by asking a basic question. If you had to rent your time share to pay maintenance fees or because you need cash, could you expect to get a handful of interested parties to pay a reasonable amount of rent? Alternatively, what would it cost you to rent it at the times you want to occupy it?

If your time share has a high demand for a rental, it is likely more of an asset on an economic basis. If your time share preference is located in a foreign country, has political or safety issues within the country, has fairly high maintenance fees (we will discuss this later in the book), is just not that desirable, it may not be a real economic asset. Likewise, if you have not been there in 4 or more years and it does not have a high-trade value which you use for other preferred locations, then likely, your time share is just a liability and is costing you more than you are getting out of it, both emotionally and in real money. We will discuss options for you later in this book.

What is a time share? discuss the legal structure The time share world of today is evolving very quickly as the industry continues to grow, up 16% from 2013 to 2015, with a combined worldwide economic output reaching $79.5B, according to a study done for ARDA by Ernst & Young (see www.arda.org/foundation). Time share is also referred to as "vacation ownership" or "fractional ownership" and now includes the right to stay in villas, hotels, homes, charter boats, and yachts; take cruises and excursions to the Far East and around the globe; hire chefs; and visit places like the Great Wall of China or the ruins of Machu Picchu in Peru. The industry continues to evolve and also can include air fares and special requests like private events and dinners. Given the public's demand for one-stop shopping, there is no reason not to believe this product offering will continue to grow with services like child care, medical backup, charges to the room for incidentals, all now paid for by your vacation club in exchange for your membership and maintenance fees.

Most of the larger time share companies have now moved to a points-based system, making the addition of new products easy and enjoyable for consumers. The growth in time share is now a complex business beyond just real estate acquisition and development. It requires an ever-changing eye toward the future where the top companies must stay focused on the entire vacation dollar, not just the lodging aspect of travel and vacations. Consumers want more flexibility, product suites, and value packed into their memberships, making innovation more important than ever to capture more and more downstream business. Loyalty plans help create bigger customers and add to top-line revenue because the consumer has seen the value of their vacation plan work and feels comfortable increasing their financial commitment. Some consumers in time shares are now buying four, five, or six times to add to their memberships as needs grow, new products evolve, and demand for new products continues to emerge.

What to look for in a company to manage the future of time shares I often get asked, what is the best time share company to purchase a time share from? While I believe some developers are better than others, most all of the top global operators in business today have something to offer. What is right for one person may be wrong for someone else. Time share companies, like people, have different personalities or profiles that seem to fit some people better than others. The trick is to find the right profile for you. I have seen customers purchase a time share because they just absolutely loved a one-time vacation experience in a certain location at a specific resort, and it happened to be at the XYZ Company.

This is the reason many time share companies have active sales programs on-site, because there is no better time or place to make a sale than when you are on vacation, relaxed, and the thing running through your mind is, "I am so glad we are here," and you are thinking perhaps next year, "We can come back and stay longer." Time share companies pay attention to statistics. They know what works best and what does not work.

That said, to answer the question on time share companies, it is worthwhile to look at what the time share business involves. It is actually one of the most demanding businesses in the world because to offer a truly great product, you have to be engaged in several different industries, all at the same time, and be very good at each one. The time share business, like many other businesses, must continue to grow and innovate in order to attract new customers. Given the complexities of this business and the huge barriers of entry to enter the market, it is very likely we will see the industry consolidate from the top seven brands down to just four or five over the next 10 years. One of the primary reasons will be either the lack of strength in one or more key areas and/or the competitive advantages gained by continued large-scale mergers and buyouts. In Chapter 9, we will cover in detail the 14 things to look for with the time share company of the future.

Fractional ownership versus traditional time share: In today's complex maze of expanding time share products, the industry has shifted from a time share model in some cases to the concept of fractional ownership. In prior decades, a time share week was the product offered in most cases. The difference in fractional ownership versus a time share may not be all that clear to most people. The actual legal difference between the two concepts is very material in a legal sense. *Time share* refers to the right to use "airspace," usually in the form of a villa or apartment. As the time share industry grew and prices continued to rise, the industry needed a better way to "title" the asset and thereby create a legal asset that could be securitized. It is far easier to foreclose on a deeded asset than the right to use airspace. The owner, in effect, is now *everyone* who purchased shares in a project or trust, and collectively, *they* own the assets.

This is not unlike a co-op in New York, where, to this day, to own a unit in a co-op or cooperative asset, the owner must apply in front of the remaining owners, be voted into the building, and then becomes subject to the homeowner rules for that building. Some building co-ops in New York require, for example, that the new owner must pay cash for his shares in the unit or apartment. *Fractional ownership* grants the owner a deed, and while owners do not need to be voted into a time share, they are subject to the rules of the trust or project they invested into. This process of upgrading the title and ownership status was a huge step in helping to grow the time share industry into the multibillion-dollar real estate market it is today and further helped fuel the rise in land prices in pristine vacation locales around the country.

The concept of fractional ownership itself is not new. The first fractional ownership deals for resort real estate in the United States started popping up in the early 1990s according to the Ragatz Associates, and by 2006, there were over 250 fractional ownerships across the country. However, in Europe, the time share concept traces back to the early 1960s when a Frenchman, Paul Doumier, was looking for a creative way to develop and finance a small ski chalet in the French Alps.

Today, there are over 1,700 properties in the United States that involve time share principles, but it is only in the past decade that some of the newer programs offer a deed or "fractional form of ownership" and with it, a title to the property. The main advantage in a fractional purchase is the buyer gets a deed, just like a deed for a home, and this deeded property affords the user the right to occupy the real estate under certain rules and conditions. Fractional ownership of yachts and planes has been around for decades. This form of ownership allows buyers to pool their resources so that collectively, they can share the cost of owning an asset. In resort real estate, many of the top seven resort developers who offer fractional ownership have now expanded the concept to include shares in a property trust, which, in turn, owns all or most of the buildings within the trust. This advancement in the title process is a big step up from owning airspace or the right to occupy and will help advance the industry in the decades to come.

Fractional ownership via a deeded title: This form of ownership usually comes with a third-party management company that manages the flow of funds in and out of the trust for the benefit of all of the owners in exchange for a fee. Many, if not most, of these companies are now public, affording them access to a lower cost of capital to help fund the billions needed to continue to grow their portfolios. When the industry adopted the fractional ownership method of ownership, time shares really converted into deeded ownership, aligning the time share purchase with the real estate practice of buying a house, therefore allowing this form of ownership to offer title insurance, an organized method of transferability, and a securitized method of borrowing and lending against the asset. This has allowed the industry to self-finance by rolling the paper into the pension and hedge fund markets, thus providing a steady source of future capital, a key step that was needed to fuel the kind of growth we have seen in the time share industry over the past decade.

CHAPTER 2

Analyzing the Time Share Resale Market

PERFECTING THE TIME share market and resale process: The advent of fractional ownership has helped the industry perfect the method to buy, build, finance, and trade time share ownership. The rise in software and middleware platforms has also fueled the industry by greatly improving the customer experience, and the ability to track and book vacations, research vacations, and provide a 24/7 communication link between the time share customer and the time share developer. This has brought the industry a long way toward creating a cradle-to-grave customer experience and has provided the consumer a higher degree of confidence that their time share investment can deliver over and over. That said, some more of the pieces are now in place to create the next-generation time share model which can then help address one of the concerns of both the industry and the consumer, namely, how do I resell my time share? For this to happen and as the industry continues to evolve, I believe we could likely see the following trends emerge over the next 10 years:

1. **Creation of a secondary market for financing**: One of today's drawbacks for the industry is the lack of a secondary market to trade timeshares for the consumer market. Today, large bundles of time share mortgages are sold off to Wall Street, and then to pension or hedge funds. The irony is, this paper is good enough to resell in $100M tranches to large pension funds and hedge funds, but not good enough for the world's largest banks to step in and provide a secondary market? Why is this?

   The consumer does not have an easy answer if he/she wants to buy his neighbor's time share unless he or she uses their own financing by using any equity in their home or using expensive credit cards. This has helped, in part, to create a discount market for time shares in the secondary market for owners who may need to sell. We have also seen, at the same time, a steady rise in the cost of time shares year after year in the industry. I am often asked why many time shares seem to trade well below their original values. There are several reasons for this. The first is that we often forget that most time shares are sold with an incentive package that often involves getting some free vacation time as part of the purchase price. While this is generally a win/win for the purchaser and the seller, it still costs money to absorb that vacation time into the sale as a cost. Therefore, the actual price paid for a time share package can be discounted by 10%–20% on the developer side when all of the incentives are factored into the purchase.

So, in reality, a $30,000 time share purchase can really mean you are spending about $24,000 to $26,000 on the time share. The retail value of your incentive, however, can often reach up to 35% of your purchase, or more. My first time share purchase was around $25,000, and I was able to book two business-class tickets to Hawaii from Denver that would have cost me $16,400 for the two tickets, and I got an upgrade to a private beach with a butler at the resort for $250 when I checked in. I calculated the value of the suite was worth around $400 per night in the early 1990s. I got $20,000 worth of incentives to spend $25,000. Many of these types of deals are still around if you know how and where to use all of the incentive clauses. That said, we will likely continue to see the secondary market lag between current market value(s) and the actual resale prices until technology and outside banks enter this growing resale market.

As we see a secondary market develop over time, these resale numbers will gradually improve, and the gap between new prices and resales prices will narrow significantly over time. The only loans that are readily available to a new buyer are packages that are sold from the original developer. The time share industry also has a very large product matrix with prices for a week selling for between $1,000 and as much as $45,000 or more on the secondary market. How can this swing be so wide? The first answer is because time shares come in all sizes, shapes, and types. A week in a five-star resort on the beach is worth more than an inland location in a B- or even C-class building. I have stayed in "value priced" locations that were an absolute bargain, even in Vail, Colorado, for $250 a week. I also have stayed in a four-bedroom villa at the Ritz Carlton in the same town that requires a $200,000-plus membership for a few weeks in the high season in the winter with a retail value of over $9,000 for just a 5-night stay for less than the tax on the villa per day. We have to remember, time shares, like homes and cars, can coexist in the same town, but can have vastly different rental, trade, and resell values.

Primary lenders and banks have been hesitant to offer lending in this market because of what is seen as a wide spread among resell values and confusion on value propositions since resell has been difficult and costly to execute through third parties. Even more confusing is how many of the rights and benefits will actually transfer to the new buyer. Many time share companies retain a right of first refusal and may value the same week differently depending on when it was originally purchased and whether the purchase was a legacy week or a points based week purchased to occupy the same week.. Be sure to contact your time share company to understand the resale rules before you commit to a sale. You want to make sure the sale is duly recorded so in the event your buyer walks from the deal and defaults on maintenance fees, that action will not adversely affect your credit.

In addition, if the sale is recorded through the wrong channel, it could have a material effect on how the original developer and their booking software treat your membership. This transition is why sales can also create different values for the same timeshare, depending on the chain of title and how it passed from one owner to the next. Be very careful to ask your company what their rules on resell are, what the process is like, and how the new owner's status will be effected. This practice can and does vary widely.

2. **The need to develop an electronic marketplace for time share trading**: In an ideal future, we will see an electronic market that will allow buyers and sellers to sell their time shares over the Internet much faster than what happens today. I expect this will take place in about 10 years and will likely initially include only the top 40% or so of all time shares. The reason is it will likely take about $100–$200M to create this platform, which then must communicate with the other large networks in order to achieve real-time functionality. It is not likely any one company has a vested interest in helping to create a one-size-fits-all network; however, as research and development technology budgets rise, we could see a market leader attempt to build their own platform, and then lease out the technology to the rest of the industry. This would likely emerge from one of the larger North American or international companies who have large-scale global computer networks already in place. These changes will also require a number of regulatory approvals to become effective. However, most of the real estate industry is already there with electronic closings now becoming commonplace and legal in most every state.

3. **A resulting reduction in brokerage fees and transaction costs**: In today's environment, we see brokerage

firms offering to sell your time share either for a one-time fee (usually paid up front and not recommended) or with a fee ranging from 15%–80% of the sales price. This cost is too high and discourages trading. The implementation of an electronic network could allow the industry to lower escrow and title commitments through real-time databases that can clear title transfers in seconds instead of the weeks it takes now. All of this is inherent in the industry, creating this platform either as a cooperative venture or from one company that could develop a platform for all to use. We saw the airline industry do this well before the advent of Internet travel sites like Expedia, Travelocity, and Orbitz with the Sabre Reservation system. This greatly enhanced airline travel in 1980s when this platform took effect. This type of electronic network could reduce transfer and brokerage fees to well under 10% and greatly enhance the current liquidity trap that now exists.

4. **The need for resale indexes to create marketable values for time shares**: In order to create a global platform to sell time shares in seconds, buyers will need to have access to certain information in order for a legitimate buy-sell spread platform to exist. This will require converting all time shares, including both prime and subprime time shares, into an index that can value both current and future value and thereby help create some floor-to-ceiling ranges for buyers and sellers to enter and exit the market. We have developed two that can help you place a value on your time share. These are:

The rental rate/cost ratio or RRC ratio: This is the amount of rent you would expect to pay if you either rented your villa on the open market or decided to rent it out expressed as a nightly number. This is then divided by your daily maintenance fee. So, a $500-a-night villa with a $200 daily maintenance fee has an RRC ratio of 2.5 to 1. This number should ideally be 2.3 or higher in high season.

Discussion of the payback indicator: This would be your annual net cash flow after all of your annual night stays are divided by your annual maintenance fees. The annual net cash flow is then divided into your net purchase price, which is net of incentives. So, in the above example, if you paid $40,000 net of incentives and stayed 17 nights a year, your net rental or savings would be $300 times 17 equal to $5,100 per year. Your net purchase price of $40,000 is then divided over $5,100 for a payback of 7.8 years. Ideally, you want to be below 10.0 to start on your payback indicator as this number will change over time as inflation will increase your RRC ratio and therefore, reduce your payback indicator over time.

Time Share Category classes: Since not all timeshares are created alike, the industry will need to create a category class. It is likely at least four classes of time shares should be used.

Category One: 4.5 to 5.0-star luxury villa or home. This would include only the very top vacation brands like the Ritz Carlton Residence Club, the Four Seasons, the St. Regis, etc., or luxury homes that have significant value and are located in top locations. These types of villas or home rentals are likely to reflect the very highest rental premiums of $1,000 a day to $5,000 a day, or more. They also would contain significant amenity packages, both on and near the properties with club, golf, ski in/ski out, and water sports in these examples. These programs often include auto service, private boating, and concierge services like grocery and limousine services.

Category Two: 4.0 to 4.5 star, top location, washers and dryers, top-grade HVAC, an aggressive replacement program, likely runs at 90%-plus occupancy year-round, has a spa, salon, multiple pools, games, activities, shuttle service, near or next to top restaurants, large and spacious units, and state-of-the art check-in or check out service. Likely located in a ski in/ski out, on a golf course, has a prime ocean view, and typically is oversold in high season(s).

Category Three: 3.0 to 4.0 star. These time shares would likely consist of lower-quality buildings, still located in or around the ground-zero locations for vacations. They generally do not compare to the megaresort-style properties situated on 50-plus acres but rather are two- to four-story buildings that may have been converted into time shares because of their location. They also would contain lower RRC ratios, but also would fill a need for families to vacation at more affordable price points. This category would not have the staffing or budgets to refurbish the villas quite as often, and therefore, have longer upgrade cycles. Many of these buildings do not have the curb appeal and landscaping of the top brands but offer a great location and good vacation value at an affordable price.

Category Four: These time shares generally started out as a Category Three property but have slipped, or are in the process of slipping into a state of disrepair and/or lack the funds and personnel to properly optimize the property. They have some degree of deferred maintenance and often have insufficient reserves because their boards, over the years, either did not assess the owners enough, were pressured to minimize maintenance fees, or have or are experiencing higher default rates, forcing a downward cycle in collecting fees. They have much-lower RRC ratios, and can usually be booked at the last minute because they are the last choice for families wanting to get into a prime location due to an event or because of a high seasonal demand in the area, not necessarily because there was demand for a Category Four building. Some of these can and will be sold and repositioned into Category Two or Three properties if enough money is invested into them. The time shares generally sell for as little as a few hundred dollars to a few thousand and can take a long time to sell. In some cases, the owners just walk from these contracts and stop paying their fees. Many of the units are just rented on the open market for very low rates to keep the units occupied.

Maintenance fee default rate: This is a key indicator of how the property or portfolio might perform in later years. This information would be very difficult to obtain at the sales level within a sales pitch meeting but can usually be obtained in a public 10-Q report. A long history of increasing default rates on a property or program could signal the property's condition may get worse before it gets better. The exception would tend to be upper tier, Category One and Two properties that are fairly new. Most owners are just closing on the property, and there is not enough history or depreciation to actually see any decline that might be taking place. That said, default rates are a very good barometer of future events. Ideal default rates should be below 4%. This is another reason to stick with the top brands who have access to public capital because they can weather the storm and carry large portfolios through most economic cycles. It is important to note we have had a relatively robust economy over the past 10 years. Default rates will naturally rise if unemployment rises above 6% or GDP slows down toward 1% growth for extended periods of time. These macro indicators are beyond our control but should play a role in deciding on whether to extend your personal budget during tough economic times if you are considering a large time share purchase. In other words, the better the economy, the better your time share fundamentals will perform.

Deeded or not: This might seem very logical, but for those people new to time shares, it is crucial you consider how important it is to own your deed to your time share. This is the highest and most valuable form of ownership. Be careful about time shares that offer long-term leases or plans that revert back to the developer/operator after 50 years. It is not that the plan may not fit your budget but just review the 45-year rent versus buy projection in this book and you will understand that the next generation in your family will likely have to come up with a lot of cash to start the time share tradition all over again. On the other hand, time shares that expire can be a great purchase if the price is right. You will need to factor this into your purchase decision. A good rule of thumb is a payback indicator no more than 15 years on your RRC ratio the first 5 years, and then below 10 after that. Inflation will likely increase the rental rates faster than maintenance fees if your time share is with a top competitor. If the time share plan is not deeded or is on a ground lease that has rental bumps every few years, you may wish to reconsider or you should be purchasing well below what like-kind deeded weeks cost. In some programs in Mexico, this is more the rule than the exception as the market exists today.

5. **A continued increase in the rental rate/cost ratio** (the RRC ratio): We also project the gap between existing maintenance fees and market or rental rates will continue to increase and widen. For example, if your two-bedroom villa on the ocean rents for $550 a night in a prime summer month and your maintenance fee is $1,350 a year for that week, this equates to $192.85 a night the villa is costing you with your membership. If you had rented it for $500 (which should be about 65% of the rack rate), your RRC ratio is 2.85 a day, or stated another way, you receive almost three times what it cost you per night. I remind you this rate is likely below the rack rate of the resort, but even this rate refers to a top-tier resort in a prime location in high season. In recent years as the industry has grown, we are seeing prime time shares RRC ratios widen in some of the higher-demand locations. In some less-desirable locations with class B- or C-buildings you could see spreads narrow, meaning your time share is

actually declining in value on purely an economic basis. This does not mean you need or should sell your time share if you enjoy it. We discuss RRC ratios in detail in Chapter 5.

6. **Why should RRC ratios widen in most cases?** Yes, your RRC ratio should widen over time because your rental rate should grow faster in absolute terms than your maintenance fee. This is the key to why time shares work in most, but not all, cases. We believe we will continue to see RRC spreads widen in the most desirable locations because the amount of prime land is becoming scarcer, and the public demand for top time share locations is still growing very well. Remember, prime land refers to locations that already have zoning, infrastructure, water, and utilities available to the site. Just buying an island and building all of the infrastructure needed like hospitals and airports simply will not pencil no matter how much land is available. Under this definition, prime land is now very scarce.

   Hence, the industry is set up for increased spreads in the top and most pristine locations, barring any significant economic downturn. The reason this is important is because lenders are wary of lending into a secondary market that cannot be supported by an appraisal. Right now, loan-to-value ratios are virtually nonexistent in the time share industry unless you are buying from the developer. This should not be the case. As the RRC ratio widens, it provides rationale economic data for banks to enter the market.

   For example, last summer, I rented 6 nights at the beach in August for $550 a night on Airbnb and got

$3,300 in my bank account, minus a small booking fee of about 5%. If the electronic market were active, the spread on this week which cost $36,400 in 2016 dollars, might sell for $25,000 to $30,000 instead of $13,475 (3.5 annual RRC ratio) or so. In this case, I netted $3,135 after marketing cost and my net purchase price of (after the value of concessions) $26,000 in 2001. After maintenance of $1,200 for 6 nights, my cash flow was $1,935 equal to 7.44% on my cash purchase price. Not bad when 5-year CD rates are running at 2.5%–3.5% as they were in late 2016.

We currently do see increases in time share values, but it is happening in 20-year cycles instead of 5-year cycles, which is closer to what housing prices have typically done. We are just beginning to see Category One, Fixed Location, Fixed Time start to move up in just the past few years. We also believe because we have been in a low interest rate and low inflationary economy, inflation has not yet priced into the time share resale market. One of the biggest hidden secrets in time shares is, what will happen if prime rental rates continue to run wild and the RRC ratio (rental rate per night divided by the maintenance fee per night) spread begins to exceed 3 to 1? In this case, the time share gap on resell values will close, and values will rise in real terms.

A primary market would be a location like Hawaii, Vail, or a location in Scottsdale, Hilton Head, or Palm Springs on a prime golf course in high season. Right now, we are seeing these spreads occur in peak markets at peak demand times. Since maintenance fees can vary between customers on a per-night basis even within the same owner (we will discuss this under maintenance fees), we still see RRC spreads as high as 3.5 to 1 as pristine time share locations continue to see their rack rates skyrocket well past our current inflation rate. (Newport Coast rental rates of $925 per night in July of 2016 for a prime 1 week, ocean view, 2+2 villa). Prime July week consisted of RRC of $925/$285 for an RRC of 3.24 to 1. This spread is necessary to provide an incentive for lenders to step into the resell market and provide liquidity. Remember, although the vast majority of villas in every location are for owners, the hotels operators, especially, have built in a few units into their inventories for rentals, either to the public or to their owners needing more time.

This creates a nice profit center for them, and in the case of unfilled villas, allows the resort to make money on empty units, again, helping to keep resort costs down. Different companies may book this revenue differently, but it is a good question to ask your time share company because it provides some clues on software priorities. Either way, it helps with buying power, branding, and helps bring new renters into the buying pool, all things that benefit all owners. As the RRC spread continues to rise, we will see time share gaps between original purchases and resell start to narrow and prime time shares will actually start to appreciate in value over 5-year cycles versus the current 20-year cycle it takes to see values double.

Let's be clear on what has happened over time with time share values. One location on the beach on the

West Coast that I own costs about $16,000 for a week in the summer that I purchased in the mid-1990s. That same week is now over $46,000, net of concessions. Since the resell market has not matured, its resell value could put it at $22,000 or so, well below the current price, but well over what I paid for it. I predict the day when some prime-time shares will actually sell at or above their quoted market prices. Certain legacy time share weeks with certain maintenance benefits in perpetuity may actually trade above developer prices because of the value of grandfathered benefits.

Other rare time shares with below-market maintenance fees and holiday week exclusivity like Christmas and July 4th are becoming small gold mines on paper. Think about it. We will soon have millions and millions of people owning time shares in the United States as the industry continues to grow. We only have 1 week a year for Christmas, New Year's, and July 4th. Less than 3% of owners have the right to use those weeks. Where can these weeks possibly go but straight up when the market solves the liquidity issues. I predict these weeks will sell for 150%–300% premiums over regular weeks in 10 years as the resell market begins to eliminate high resell fees and the secondary market fills what is now a huge void in a growing industry. The cost per loan right now, even if one were available for resale, is too high, but thanks to the Internet, this can be replaced with very low transaction, title, and closing fees as technology is developed to replace what is now an out-of-date trading system for time shares.

Why the time share of the future needs a better exit plan? One of the frustrating things about the time share industry is that it does not deserve the bad press that a few people choose to label the industry. Since time shares are the fastest type of new vacation ownership and now involves millions of people, it is clear the market has embraced the concepts of time share. It is more efficient, more affordable, and allows average families the opportunity to create a lifetime of memories. Then why the bad rap? Two of the most common complaints with time shares are: "How can I get rid of my time share?" and "I do not want to burden my kid with my time share." This seems odd at first blush. How often does a homeowner ask a neighbor or friend if they have a way "to get rid of my house"? It is as though there is some kind of curse on any real estate labeled "time share." The reality is that time share is just a form of real estate ownership that is less than 100%. It should not have a negative connotation under any circumstance, particularly since the concept itself solves so many problems. The same way with commenting on: "I do not want to burden my kids with my time share." This is like saying you own a home, and when you die, you do not want to burden your kids with inheriting that home. I would have far preferred to inherit $100,000 worth of a time share rather than $100,000 worth of equity, in my case. Selling and marketing a home is many times more involved than doing the same thing with a time share; yet, one seems to have a bad rap, and the other is just life happening.

Creation of a vibrant secondary market: We believe this is the last piece of the time share pie that is missing. We are already seeing prime fixed location, fixed weeks in top ski resorts, and time shares located on prime beaches start to really appreciate. These forms of time shares can lead the way out of the liquidity trap that now exists with the secondary market.

Currently, about one-third to one-half of a time share payment could be eliminated if developers got out of the financing business, and lenders got into the market. We, of course, mean primary lenders, not hedge funds or pension funds that look to get 12% on $100 million tranches. While this might help retirees and investors in a few cases, the vast majority of the public that invests a meaningful portion of their net worth into a time share need to have access to top credit offerings that currently exclude time shares. This would create a huge narrowing of the gap pricing that now exists. This market could then organize the title, closing, and banking process into a more formal real estate closing similar to homes. We predict that some of the top weeks will start to trade routinely for $250,000 and more, creating a better opportunity for lenders to underwrite deals that will start to compete with homes in terms of loan amounts. This process will start with fixed holiday weeks from the top operators in about 5 years, and as the industry grows, we believe will include a national data bank that can process time share transactions in minutes. When this conversion occurs, the very top time shares will increase in value, and in some cases, by 50% or more, fairly quickly. Fast liquidity in any asset class just by itself creates value.

CHAPTER **3**

Evaluation of Time Share as a Form of Real Estate Ownership

DISCUSSION OF TIME share as a form of real estate ownership: I recall one day when a lady come into my office. I guessed she was likely in her mid-80s. I figured she may not really be in the market to purchase more time shares, but I had also learned not to judge someone regardless of how little the odds seemed that they may be a likely client. She made it very clear she was not going to buy again, had lost her husband, and as if that were not enough, she had decided to construct a new home in a nearby beach town. After about 30 minutes, I realized we were both having a lot of fun talking about world travel, sunsets, Europe, and how travel makes all of us feel young. I almost forgot I was hosting a time share tour. Before long, I found out she had a wonderful fondness for her granddaughter, who she described as a super high achiever with a very promising career with one of the top defense contractors. It became clear one of her remaining bucket list items was to take her granddaughter first class to Europe. As those of us know in the time share business, I had my reason now to provide a very good vacation plan that would fit her lifestyle and future wishes.

We promptly set out and made plans for first-class travel to London, staying at a five-star hotel, and we then repeated this process with a trip to Italy, staying in four- and five-star hotels and resorts.

It was not long after this that we shook hands on a deal and began the paperwork to process the transaction. I was thrilled and could see the smile on her face as she realized she was going to travel with her granddaughter on two very special European trips. It was planned, and she was awarded our top VIP status with her increased membership. She then told me she and her husband had purchased a home about 50 years earlier, just a block from the beach for $35,000. The real estate guy in me kept asking about the house as I wondered what she could have sold it for. As we talked, she let me know she sold it for over $2.8M cash and was now purchasing a fixer-upper in a new beach town near her granddaughter for $1.6M. I began to really appreciate her zest for life. She had just made plans to travel on not one but two trips to Europe and had drawn up plans to add a whole new wing onto her fixer-upper home, and how proud she was it would include four garage spaces, plus parking on the driveway. As anyone who ever traveled to a crowded beach town in California knows, having just *one* parking space is a wonder to behold near the beach. Here she was bossing general contractors around, telling them how to construct the new wing and just loving life. I figured she would add over $1M in new equity to what was to become a five-bedroom home with seven parking spaces very close to the beach. Clearly, she believes in living life and just her example sets a lesson for all of us. The first lesson is even at 84, she has no reason to slow down because she has chosen to live life instead of having life live her. She looked like a movie star the day I met her, and I am sure she will go on to inspire others until her last day.

The point of my story is to make an observation about what happens over long periods of time with real estate. Let's digest what I said in the paragraph above. She bought a nice three-bedroom home very near the beach in the 1960s for $35,000. Now, about 50 years later, it cost around $45,000 to $55,000 to own the right to stay at the beach for a single week. Over 50 years, we have gone from being able to own a house at the beach for $35,000 to paying well over that for the right to stay at the beach for a *single week*. As a sales executive with a top brand, I saw all kinds of people from around the world never knowing until deep into the sales process who could afford to purchase versus those who could not. That said, I knew that many of my potential tours did have the money to purchase, and it was my job to see that they did, and to find a rationale that worked for them in doing so. One of my arguments in favor of a time share is the value of money over long periods of time.

This analogy is why people buy time shares. If it cost $35,000 50 years ago to buy a house at the beach in California, and now it cost $45,000–$55,000-plus for a summer time share week at the beach, what should the price of either be in 50 years from now? Let's do the math using the same numbers as a standard for the next 50-year price increase. She sold the house for $2,800,000 in 2016 and paid $35,000, so, in 50 years, it went up in value by 80 times. So, 80 times $2.8M would value the house at $224,000,000 50 years from now under the exact same rate of increase. Might be a little hard to swing the $56M down payment, but the numbers are the numbers. It seems clear one would need a high-paying job as well to qualify for a $168,000,000 mortgage. Then again, those loans are a dime a dozen today in the commercial real estate market for large office towers, shopping centers, and apartment projects near the beach.

Trouble is, it might be hard for most people to come up with $2.8M today, and then wait 50 years. Some of us are on the downside of life and may only have 15–25 years left to live. Regardless, let's look at a time share week at the beach priced at $50,000. If this was multiplied by 80, we would see a value of $4,000,000 in 50 years. Now, this seems ridiculous, about as believable as anyone thinking a $35,000 beach house in 1965 would be worth $2.8M in 2016. No one, including me, thinks that a three-bedroom home near the beach today will be worth $224,000,000 in 50 years, but the math is exactly the same. What if the home only went up by 40 times, or half the rate of increase over what just happened? Perhaps we could all live with a mere $112,000,000 for a three-bedroom house near the beach in 2066 as a more rationale projection. Food for thought. Either way, if the time share industry can solve the secondary liquidity issues, I believe this kind of time share appreciation will become commonplace among the very best operators located in the top locations, especially in prime locations like the beach.

When does time share make sense? As a sales executive for one of the top brands, I got to see all types of people from around the world every day. I saw people in their 20s purchase time shares, and even people in their 80s and 90s buy time shares. All were for many different reasons, but in some cases, older customers were helping to set up their kids or grandkids with a paid-up opportunity to vacation. I believe this is one of the greatest gifts one could give a child or grandkid. The first thing people give up when times are difficult is often the family vacation. The sad thing is, when times are tough, this is often the time when a family needs a vacation the most.

Others purchase because their travel plans seemed to align well with what the company had to offer in the form of vacation prices, locations, and benefit plans. This made a time share purchase easy because the consumer was going to spend money in any case to travel, so buying a travel plan that allowed for travel every year just makes good sense for many people. The combination of a worldwide or regional vacation plan with locations and amenities that fit your lifestyle, and the opportunity to save money over the long run, is why most people buy a time share.

There is also a myriad of reasons why many people add to their vacation plan, often to increase their benefits and/or to purchase more points or time so their plan will offer more vacation time. Whether you are a first-time buyer or looking to add to your vacation plan, it is noteworthy to review the following checklist:

Where do I want to go in the world over the next 20 years? What will those locations cost not only today but down the road? Does this fit into your future budget? Keep in mind that an African safari or trip up the glaciers may sound impressive, but it may also be likely you may only go once or twice. Look at the timeshare portfolio and make sure the locations and resorts they control are within your plans for future travel. Think of the locations offered as either adventure travel more suited for one or two trips or as a retirement or regular vacation spot, and make sure your operator has choices and locations where you could spend a month. If this is the case, the match is likely to be a much better one. Many operators have restricted locations and offer regional choices, and some offer global choices all over the world. Make sure your program fits you today *and* tomorrow.

Realistically, where am I likely to go only once or twice? Some people go to Hawaii and just know they want to go every year. As they get older, though, I hear the plane trip is getting longer, and airport is a hassle, and they just don't seem to make the trip every year any longer. Make sure you have options to trade out of your primary location so your plan can change and adapt to the way you want it to.

Do I enjoy the style of buildings and amenities that are in my package? This may seem trivial, but over time, things that may not have bothered you at 30 might start to bother you at 50. For example, if you have a washer and dryer in your villa or unit, this makes travel much easier and lighter since you can just recycle your clothes while you are there, making a 2-week stay require only one suitcase versus two suitcases. Since airlines charge a small fortune for extra luggage, and it restricts your rental car choices, make sure all the small details that may make more sense down the road are already in place or easily accessible. The more upscale properties tend to spend more on holiday decorations, making the resort quite spectacular around the holidays. This may save you from all of the hard work at the end of the year when lights and decorations make the stay all that more enjoyable. You might also just skip the whole process yourself and let others do it for you. The Category Three and Four time shares will not have nearly the same decorating budgets. Food and beverage services may also be cut or curtailed, with smaller programs. Of course, with increased services, you will get increased maintenance fees, so it is important you look at not only today's options, but also consider what benefits you want to see at some future time. A high-rise resort, for instance, will cost a lot more to operate than a low-rise resort. Does your company tend to have more of one type of resort over the other? If you are investing in a trust or some type of pooled asset-based time share, you are likely paying a weighted average that includes all of the resorts into your maintenance fee. If you just like one or two places in your time share program, and they are relatively easier and cheaper to operate, maybe a smaller footprint with more modest maintenance fees might fit your needs better over the next 20 to 30 years. You may be able to buy an older legacy week that has a lower cost maintenance fee built into the membership.

Is the plan flexible if I need to cancel my travel plans? The most competitive time share operators now allow you to cancel up to 24 hours in advance of your stay without any penalty. This is the ultimate in customer service. This also reduces the need for expensive travel insurance that can also add up to 10% of the cost of your trip. Make sure you understand the cancellation policy when you are reviewing your time share purchase. In the old day of "weeks only" time share, I often had to leave with 2 or 3 days left when a business emergency arose. The most advanced programs with state-of-the-art booking technologies really allow you to control your lifestyle right down to the day and help to maximize your time share investment.

Does the plan come with a hotel partner? If so, what are the trading options and benefits? As the industry continues toward consolidation, we are seeing some programs linked to hotel companies that also own and manage time shares. This is a huge advantage for many reasons. The first is that this allows for significant bargaining power to purchase goods and services. A company that controls 30–300 resorts is significant in its own right, but add 6,000 hotels and ask yourself, who is going to get a better deal on a bed? The vacation industry is heavy on consumables and requires a 5–7-year cycle to replace furniture, TVs, and kitchens over time. These combined entities are going to stay more competitive on maintenance fees because they have the largest purchasing power.

Moreover, having access to hundreds or thousands of hotels can help extend your vacations since many provide increased services and benefits with cross memberships in the form of room upgrades, early and late check-ins and check outs, and many offer concierge-level food and beverages that can really help drive vacation cost down over expensive restaurants. This, again, is a key element in your future travel plans and plays particularly well for those customers who want to travel the world over time.

What are my out-of-network trading options and trading values? This is becoming a big deal because your travel time share plan is only as good as your ability to book the times and places you want to go. Many travel or time share companies own pieces of reservations systems, and also own or control resorts. When programs are intermixed to allow one company to cross into another reservation system, you need to ask who is in line ahead of you for a booking. All of the large time share companies have priority software algorithms that bump their best customers to the most desired times and places, either through early booking windows or access to reserved inventory that waits just for them to book, regardless of how late they book. You need to be aware of your booking priority both within your own operator and most especially, outside of your network. Many of these systems are highly effective in booking Class B or C products but could fall short of realistically providing the inventory when you need it the most. Have your sales executive book you a few trips right in your presence for the times and places you want to go. This will give you a real snapshot of what you could be facing after you buy, and then it may be too late to cancel your purchase.

Does the brand come with a loyalty or discount program? While this may not seem important, brand loyalty programs that offer discounts can have a profound effect on your RRC ratio and your payback indicator. This may not matter to you if you enjoy your time share without any reoccurring bonuses. The programs that couple with hotels can provide real savings over the long run, and particularly those with significantly reduced booking windows or those programs that have short-term stay discounts. This is almost a must for those time share owners that want to travel internationally as most megaresorts will not pencil in most locations, and therefore, extended travel requires the use of hotels to fill in gap cities when you are on the road. Getting premium service in faraway places can make a huge difference, especially if you wish to change plans and extend or curtail your original plans.

It is very important if you are building up a lot of points in either a time share or hotel program that you understand what happens to the points if you pass away. Most hotel points just expire, and if you have millions of points in your account, the loss could be significant, even exceeding $100,000 in some instances. It is a better practice to use them at some point versus risk losing them. Most time share points must be used within a certain period of time, so the loss risk in those programs is not as bad because they expire automatically, whereas hotel points may not.

Has the operator stopped innovating, or has the plan stopped growing? You might ask why this is an important question. The reason it matters is the long-term ability to grow and maintain a time share portfolio is what will help drive up rental rates and resale values. All of this is important if you value your time share over the long term. An operator that continues to add to their existing inventory helps bring in new investment capital, helps promote new jobs, and makes it easier for them, in turn, to raise more investment capital. In other words, if the operator in not trending up in the growth curve, then by default, it will start to head the other way over the long term. Also, be wary of programs that have limited geographical supply. While there are many fine smaller time share operators that do a very good job of building in just a few markets, time share is a business that will have to compete much harder for the next-generation customer.

As long as you enjoy the limited market and their maintenance fee increases are close to inflation, there is nothing wrong with this kind of time share ownership, but over the long term, this type of program could slide down a notch from a Category Two to a Three because of limited abilities to raise growth capital. It takes years to hire and staff a large construction enterprise with the right people, and the same is true to build a real distribution channel. Once these channels are in place, the only choice is to build more product. The public's appetite suggests we will see continued strong growth for at least the next decade. We also predict we will see different types of time shares emerge, including a new long-term stay guarantee program, and specialty time shares centered around a theme like racing, hunting, or short-term retirement stays that include hobby villages, restaurants, and on premise services like movie theaters and in-house pharmacies. Lastly, we will also see the industry begin to address long term care for those retirees that will require nursing care. **Can I prepay my time share loan without a prepayment fee?** This is a standard clause in the industry, and you should make certain this is the case if you finance your time share acquisition with a developer loan. Competition for first-time buyers on new projects is forcing developers to lower rates to increase the pool of qualified buyers. The industry was quoting rates as high as 15.99% a few years ago (2010–2016), but we are now seeing rates drop to as low as 8.99% (in 2017) for certain high-credit score (above 750) borrowers. Time shares are very much tied to credit worthiness since the deed and potential tax benefits are tied to many owners using this as a second home or a vacation asset. Time shares are also the first to default when economic times are uncertain, and hence, one of the reasons for typically higher interest rates. The cost to finance a small loan is also a reason why many lenders do not want to enter the market. This trend, however, is moving favorably toward lower rates, which will help accelerate the secondary market into stabilizing resale values over the next 10 years.

What are the rental prospects if I need to rent my villa? We advise our customers to consider why they wish to own a time share. The industry was not really designed to be a form of real estate ownership intended for rentals. That said, an unintended consequence of the industry is the fact that time share itself has been a huge success, with impressive year over year numbers that continue to outpace the economy. The top seven developers all have a number of new projects on the drawing board and will likely release enough new product over the next 12 years to double what we estimate to be about 4.0M-plus time share owners in the United States right now. This would mean adding another 8.5M interval weeks into the current inventory. This backdrop and the future of time shares has an effect on the value of today's timeshares. We have predicted there is a shortage of top-tier and luxury time shares, and we predict this will remain over the next 20 years. We also predict most of the rental opportunities will remain in the Category One and Two programs. If rental income is important, then we recommend you stick to top-shelf programs.

How hard is it to secure my first choice for travel? This can be a tricky test because you may not know the answer to this until after you have purchased and are going about trying to book a reservation for the first time. You can request your sales representative provide a "live test run" or just request the reservation number and make a few calls. If your representative is hesitant or resists this request, it may suggest they are not very sure about your prospects or do not feel confident. Common sense tells us that prime beachfront and ski in/ski out time shares are going to book up fast every year. Having some knowledge of your booking windows is important. Most time share companies have addressed this issue with priority booking options, and some even offer very high premium packages that all but guarantee availability if you book during your window. These packages are generally priced higher but do provide booking assurances. As with most things, finding the right balance and price point is the key to your being happier with one strategy over another.

This is why it is important to understand the overall hierarchy of your program, how many customers are in the program, and where your membership level starts and stops with booking priorities. If you can get a live demonstration, you also should realize that if you can get most of what you want, when you want it, that is probably as good as it will get after you decide to purchase. All of the time share programs have drop-dead dates, exchange deadlines, conversion windows, and priority expiration times of the year, which, by themselves, create all kinds of reservation windows that open and close. The reality is that with these variations, there are more than likely certain times of the year when inventories open back up. You need to look at the deadline calendars, and it is usually in the few days that precede or follow each deadline period where inventory windows can open and shut for dozens of new reservations, and then in a few days, revert right back to sold-out status. An owner may, for example, convert a legacy week into points, in lieu of booking their home resort just prior to their deadline, thus, opening up inventory that was on hold if only for a day or 2. The days just before this happens may trigger sold-out inventory back into the booking pool. Remember, think like a computer, not a person. People often procrastinate until the last minute. Computers do not.

When do I plan to use my time share and for what purpose: This may seem like a silly question but that is because most people view a time share as a place to vacation, and for most people, if your time share is filling that need, then it has served its purpose. However, as you consider either buying a time share for the first time or adding to your vacation portfolio, the concept of alternative uses may help you decide which program is best suited for you in the long run. Many programs now offer a vast array of exciting tours, homes, and sporting events, and these are a useful way to explore many parts of the world if you plan on a great deal of international travel. Other programs have what we call "value stays," where the price per night in points is well below the median price for your portfolio, and those places offer a useful place to stay if you are selling a house, perhaps building one, or just need a new, quiet environment to write that book or complete a long report. Some of these value stays can provide a very affordable place to spend 45–60 days and usually offer more amenities at a lower cost per night than a hotel stays. Also, consider what your retirement objectives look like and whether the footprint and amenities in your program will accommodate your downstream goals of using cruises, homes, tours, and other services, as a lot of variety will keep your program interesting and provide years and years of new opportunities. We therefore recommend thinking about what your goals are in 15–20 years when your time share has saved you more than it cost, and you want to really enjoy another 15–20 years with the same program.

What else can I do with my time share? The family vacation is the backbone of the industry and the reason the time share business has thrived. As with most growing families, the need for more space is the main reason many couples choose to move into a larger house. When a family has more than two children and they are past the age of 7, a family often runs out of choices about how to travel on vacation. In order to save money, many families stay with relatives or stay at low-budget hotels with two or even three hotel rooms. The logical alternative choice is to own a time share that can easily accommodate your family, and then every year, regardless of how tight your cash might be, you have a place to travel to and get in that family vacation. This is also why we recommend you consider a time share program that is within a day or two's drive, just in case buying multiple air fares is out of the question for a given year. This kind of flexibility will also allow for shorter stays if you can access properties that are a few hours away.

The new (short-term) business office: I remember the past 25 years where I spent my time buying, founding, and building companies. I always found a way to either rent very cheap warehouse space or houses instead of paying to rent office space for my companies. My last company that I was a cofounder of we had used homes in Colorado and California as office space for three to six people to come in and design, invent, test, and create software code. Offices in the San Francisco area commanded $3 a square foot in rental rates, so 2,000 square feet would cost $6,000 a month. When you rent office space, you also pay business rates for phone and Internet use, and then often have janitorial and other expenses to absorb as part of your rent. We were able to rent homes up in the hills of San Mateo for $1 a foot, so our 2,800 square foot house was $2,800 a month, almost one-third the price of office space 1 mile below on the main boulevard. While a single month may not have mattered, this $4,000 a month savings over office space, combined with cheaper utility services, saves us well over $500,000 over a 10-year period. This savings alone could have made the difference in the company surviving since our research and development period lasted well over 10 years to get the code into commercial-grade quality. I am not suggesting you can rent the same time share for 10 years, but many of the homes we rented were for a year or 2. Given larger vacancies in off-season properties, it is possible to rent the same or nearby units for 6–9 months in some locations. Sometimes using out of the box ideas is what is necessary to survive.

If your company needed extra space for 4–12 weeks to complete a project, a large, well located time share where you have utilities, free Internet, and a large, quiet workspace could be just the ticket. The space will likely be very affordable especially if you are able to procure a time share during off-season. As a side bar, I wrote the majority of this book in—you guessed it—a time share I rented every week for a few days a week in Palm Desert. The place was quiet, the views provided unbelievable inspiration, and I enjoyed getting out of town and into the writing mode in a very large and well-appointed one-bedroom suite on a prime golf course. If I needed a break, I had the option of heading onto the oversized balcony and looking at the ducks quacking away all day in the lake waters that surrounded my unit.

Time share—a short-term housing model? There are many times when a change of venue can produce positive results, including the ability to focus on a large project. Time shares are now available in just about every major city and can provide a good preview on what a new city is like to live in. A time share is a perfect choice to handle the front end of a job transfer where you are not sure what the drive times are like and you have not had a chance to really check out the real estate market. Hotels are a good choice, but the rooms and many suites are small, and after a few weeks, they can be expensive. Apartments usually want at least a 6-month lease, and shorter stays often cost more per month than a 2-year lease. Time shares provide an opportunity to get to know a town, get away from a problem, and provide time to think about a new move, even if that move is to another city. Just getting out of the extreme cold or heat in the middle of the season can bring new excitement into your current situation. Be sure to review your overall vacation plan very carefully if you think you might be relocating over the next several years, as vacation plans vary widely with both the cost and amount of locations that come with most plans. Some of them are better suited for either West or East Coast living, while others provide a very nice U.S. and global footprint.

The new winter (ski) and summer (lake) time share home: While this might seem odd at first, the new trend in increased luxury time share offerings with some of the top large operators is to offer luxury homes into the rental pool as a newer way to use points. When you review a number of luxury homes across the country and compare usage patterns against total annual costs , it is easy to conclude that paying for any size home for the period of time it is used in many cases is far more economical than absorbing the year-round cost of owning a multimillion-dollar vacation home. This option was not available previously in the high-end luxury market, but with the Internet and top operators working together to match renters and owners, this new luxury trend is likely here to stay as newer, more robust Internet models and established time share operators are now connecting high-quality rentals with high-quality residences that were previously off the market.

The biggest concern from large, wealthy families was how to rent their property to high-end clientele at a price point that was worth the risk and the effort. Today's top time share customers have been able to strike deals with luxury rental firms that can bring a steady supply of worthy renters into this previously somewhat skeptical market. We predict as this model continues to evolve, we will see increased functionality like private chefs, entertainment packages that include booking private bands for weddings, parties, and family reunions, limo and entertainment bus services, and private tour engagements that begin and end at the home, to become worthy additions to this higher-end time share concept. We also see a number of families over the next 10 years beginning to sell some of their vacation homes in favor of just renting large estates for the time period they typically gather, like over Christmas and for midsummer vacations.

While these newer rental home models are now just beginning to hit the market, we have noticed that rental rates are not tied to real estate values, meaning there is little comprehensive analysis on how and why large estates are priced often at 2 to 3 to 1 spreads over each other. What this means for the smart time share customer is you can now find large homes for a bargain if you put some time into your search. A few are willing to rent out for a week at or near what a nice two-bedroom villa costs for the same week.

This pricing inconsistency is also a huge find for the discriminating renter looking to book a luxury home below what the more traditional real estate brokerage firms charge for the same rental. Patience and persistence can result in finding a bargain rental at well below the dollar for rent model the new points-based system now offers in this upscale category.

The next family reunion: There are many reasons why the time share industry and the family reunion are ideally suited to pair well with each other. First of all, families change and often evolve with new brides, kids, and relatives that move closer back to home, thus, making the family reunion more important at certain times in a family cycle. The needs and size of a family reunion in 2017 will likely be very different 10 years from now in 2027, when the family could be much larger, or smaller. Also, as economic trends and successes or failures impact a family, the need to gather in one place for a few days can start to become more valuable over time. Longtime family reunions also demand change with better amenities, locations, and preferences all playing a role on where to gather for the next reunion. Best of all, the time share industry does not conform to the one-size-fits-all, so having choices to book homes, villas, lakefront, beachfront, domestic or island properties provides a vast array for that perfect setting. Time share properties lend themselves to renting by the slice, or choosing a location that can sleep 45 or 50 guests in one house. These choices are more affordable than ever today, as there as more options than ever before available to very large families where a couple of villas is just not going to work.

We believe the time share options will continue to see more families taking advantage of using time shares in the future. We also predict that many companies will consider certain locations, like in the mountains, to be an ideal location for corporate retreats because time shares will generally deliver the same benefits to retreats as upscale hotels, but can do so at a lower cost and provide significant flexibility as to levels of luxury for many budget-conscious businesses looking to host a sales conference.

When does time share not make sense?

It takes almost a day in the air to get there, tickets are expensive, and you are not likely to visit the location more than once or twice.

You have a large family, so airline tickets to your favorite location that require many airline tickets can push prices to travel way up for long trips if gas prices are high.

You do not enjoy the building, area, or city outside of the time share.

Rentals for your time share are only slightly higher than your maintenance fee.

The country you prefer to visit is or could someday be in economic or political turmoil.

The unit size does not work for your family.

You are using your time share just because you own it and would rather be somewhere else.

CHAPTER 4

Why the Global Economy Will Help Fuel the U.S. Time Share Market

SOME OF THE baby boomers reading this book may remember when golfing prices in Japan were so high it was cheaper to travel to the United States and play golf because the total travel costs, including green fees, were less in the United States than paying for a round of golf in a major Japanese city. In the late 1980s, many Japanese real estate experts suggested that certain blocks of office buildings in Japan had a combined net worth surpassing all of the value of the commercial real estate market in the United States—combined. This was certainly a silly concept when thinking about the size of Japan versus the United States. If someone feels that one square block is worth over $65 trillion, the real question is, when did it sell and who bought it? It was not long after this when the Japanese economy, in the late 1980s, suffered what was to be a 20-plus-year decline on what was clearly unsustainable real estate valuations.

The advantage to foreign investment in the United States in any business model is that it usually represents a point of view that is not widely accepted at the moment in our country. This can often signal a turning point that might not be recognizable by just understanding our local and national economy. One recent example was when Hong Kong reverted back in 1999 to the Chinese government. One of the most spectacular cities in the world, Vancouver, British Columbia, saw real estate values skyrocket after money exiting Hong Kong needed to be reinvested into real estate. After years of depressed pricing given the intrinsic value of high-rise apartments, condominiums went from $300,000 to over $1,500,000 in a few short years, and billions of dollars got redeployed into this Canadian form of real estate ownership. Many thousands of new businesses were also started because of friendly visa laws allowing foreigners the opportunity to hold Canadian citizenship if they bought or started a Canadian company, employing its citizens, and invested at least $500,000 into the business.

This brings up the question of how any of this relates to the time share business and its effect on the United States time share ownership. For one, we only need to look at a globe to predict what is easy to spot. If you take a look at Hawaii, it is easy to see it is about halfway to many of the world's most emerging economies; i.e., Hong Kong, Singapore, Vietnam, China, Taiwan, Thailand, and parts of the Philippines and certain surrounding island economies. The one thing that all of these economies share with the United States is the need to trade for goods and services. That trade has created a number of new foreign millionaires from China, and to a lesser extent, the other Asian economies who are eager to diversify their assets into the relative calm of the United States. But where and what can they easily invest in?

Why millennials and foreigners will understand part-time ownership faster than most of the U.S. population: While we believe there are other macro factors in the United States that will play a larger role in creating more demand for U.S. time shares, foreign ownership into this asset class will continue to rise at a faster rate than its U.S. counterpart in some niche markets like Hawaii. Factors like the Hawaiian Beachfront Index combined with a shortage of available and zoned land will continue to see prime time share prices rise for new projects, in part, fueled by foreign investment which now stands over 10.6% of all island closings with foreigners. This excludes foreign purchases that are already domiciled here in the United States.

Another cause-and-effect trend that will spur nontraditional growth will come from the 92M millennials representing the largest 30–45-year-old age category over the next 20 years. Poll after poll shows almost 30% are not interested in traditional home ownership in the coming years, shunning or delaying owning a home in favor of "sharing" cars and homes. We now have the largest uptick in rental demand in the United States, with over 9M people preferring to rent versus own. This is in part because millennials are pushing off marriage, have taken on a larger portion of student debt versus their income, and continue to prefer organic and whole food shopping over trying to own a home. This trend will spur new time share projects addressing these themes of part-time or shared housing, ironically, the very thesis of time shares.

Another major trend that will continue is the outflow of money from just the Chinese, Canadian, and Japanese millionaire's eager to pull their money out of their own countries and invest it into U.S. real estate. Because most Chinese are restricted now to just $50,000 a year leaving their country, this lends itself to analyzing the value of a time share where visas can now extend to 90 days for Koreans and longer for Chinese. Investing this money granted them U.S. citizenship, shaving years off the traditional path to become a U.S. citizen. Incentive programs created by the EB-5 programs allowing for the purchase of any U.S. business for $500,000 that employs 10 people will continue to fuel many West Coast U.S. cities, and the Hawaiian markets, in particular. These markets typically post lower unemployment numbers, and some of the lowest vacancy and foreclosure rates in the country.

These factors make Hawaii a long-term favorite for the Chinese market, but also for Koreans, Canadians, and the Japanese, who continue to out purchase properties in the United States over their European and South American counterparts. In Hawaii, where closing from the Japanese and Canadian markets are almost half of all foreign deals in recent years, we predict an even stronger trend emerging as more of this population begins to evaluate retirement options added to more leisure travel. Many people from Japan prefer the ease and cost of time shares in Hawaii due to the associated golf, retirement, and leisure options now prevalent on the island. The family dynamic from Asian investors also believes in creating family assets that can be passed down through the generations, something most of the deeded time share programs now offer. A recent survey showed that over 85% of the new wealth created in China in the form of hundreds of thousands of new millionaires now want to either retire in the U.S. or send their kids to school in this country. The Hawaiian Islands and the Western United States, in particular, will help drive and support the time share market for the next 30 years. The concept is simple: if I cannot afford an entire year, I would like to own a month or more in Hawaii. Moreover, nearly one in eight vacationers who visit Hawaii each day are staying in time shares according to a recent report by the State of

Hawaii's Department of Business, Economic, Development, and Tourism office.

Many Hawaiian Islands have traditionally supported high-rise construction: While the Hawaiian Islands have no shortage of coastlines and offer some of the best beaches in the world, they do have a shortage of prime oceanfront land that is well served with highways and infrastructure in place to handle new construction for thousands of people. One solution to this problem is to allow for high-rise development, which is why Hawaii tends to be more high-rise friendly than many other parts of the Western United States. The islands have a long history of approving large buildings for residential and office use. This type of density is only seen in San Francisco and San Diego (California) in the Western United States. We are not suggesting that Oregon and Washington do not support high-rises in some places, but they tend to have less desirable weather than the sun-drenched California beaches. The Northern states have colder climates and more rain, so they have been less desirable for vacation lovers seeking sun while they are at the beach.

The location of Hawaii near both U.S. and foreign markets makes the islands ideal for importing buyers from multiple countries. We expect that zoning and approvals will still be difficult, but new projects have a much-stronger chance of emerging in this chain of islands versus the Western United States. The East Coast also faces a lot of the coastal and environmental challenges like California, but the net migration into weather-friendly states like Florida, and the states aligned along the Gulf Coast should also help fuel future beachfront demand. We expect these latter choices in the Southeast to continue to add new projects over the next 10 years.

Why the time share market will soon split into micro markets: The industry will need to get more of these projects approved and built to keep up with the current demand for affordable beachfront time shares. It is likely that the beachfront time share will fill some of the future time share needs; however, the emerging trends for millennials and retirees does not lend itself into these high-rise locations or beach locations where density and pricing are at a premium. Their models are much more closely aligned to inland locations like the desert. The land cost is cheaper, and the developer can support the urban retail, leisure, and affordable housing needs of this emerging market more interested in 6- to 9-month stays with lower maintenance fees. These driving trend lines, we believe, will continue the net inflow of foreign and domestic dollars into time share projects, both here and around the globe. This will also help fuel demand for more offshore time shares that will grant permanent ownership rights, have favorable property right laws, and provide safe and sound governmental support for foreign visitors. Time share prices for the remaining few locations on U.S. soil are going to start to force more construction out of the country to satisfy global demand for beachfront and prime time shares where buyers are demanding vacation villas set around lakes, waterfalls, oceans, and mountains.

Why Hawaiian fixed weeks are likely to skyrocket in value over the next 10 years: Hawaii is very unique in the world because of its location to many other markets. It draws from a huge Asian influence and also benefits as our 50th state. It is also located in one of the world's nicest beaches with nearly every island offering special oceanfront views and landscapes. Moreover, its marketing is well established with strong real estate laws and reasonably favorable development laws that allow for developers to construct larger projects, a key element to keep their economy growing. We predict, however, that zoning and density issues will make some island locations more difficult to pencil, and yet the growth and demand for the islands will start to outstrip the supply. This means that prices on some time share assets will start to sell at a premium over existing pricing models. As supply is constrained and demand keeps growing, something has to give. The basic housing index in Hawaii with the median home price now over $675,000 and the average condo over $350,000, is continuing to drive beachfront property out of reach for most retirees and even local residents of the state. The state is projecting growth of between 64,700 and 66,000 between 2015 and 2020, making Hawaii the 13th in the nation for population growth. These metrics make Hawaii relatively attractive for the value of the last great real estate derivative, longer-term time shares. Many people already know they cannot live year-round in Hawaii, or do not wish to. However, the demand for owning some time in Hawaii will soon outstrip the available supply, forcing the market to reprice Category One and Two time shares owned and operated by the top developers. There is a, relatively speaking, finite supply of developable land combined with a steady increase in population growth of 1.78% per year. This may not seem like much, but adding 14,000 people a year to an island community and hosting more visitors each year is a lot of growth to manage. The island already is in need of more housing to serve the growing tourist market, now at 220,000 visitors a day, up from 70,000 visitors a day since 1980, according to the state's office on business and economic growth. This bodes well for any new time share projects now supporting over 12% of the entire hospitality market, with 25% residential, 50% hotel, and nearly 12.5% in what is defined as condo/hotel in the state's statistics. We also caution that as gas prices and inflation increase, traveling demand to Hawaii can fall, causing temporary declines in the housing spectrum. While the islands have always recovered to be even stronger, a protracted downturn can slow the economy for several years.

Why the United States, Mexico, and Canada will lead time share demand: We have now entered the age of "Big Data," where we have the ability to model predictions based on hundreds of micro- and macro variables. One might logically ask, how can anything that defined be able to predict anything? Well, a combination of social, economic, unemployment, millennial projections, workforce changes, and overall work habits are now being combined into very large-scale number crunching to compute future trends. The one thing that keeps coming up near the top is demand for U.S. stability, security, and property rights laws that can provide for a peaceful retirement. Countries next to the United States can offer a large portion of these benefits at lower costs, making population shifts inevitable as retirees are forced into finding medicine, food, and housing at lower costs. The combination of more flexibility, warm weather, and a stable real estate environment will continue to drive the North American market the fastest, with the warmth of Mexico driving their tourist market for time shares, and the relatively low populations of Canada making time shares very competitive in order to draw traffic into the northern portion of North America. This trend is more closely tied to longer term North American factors like retirement and short term stays likely meaning more time per visit than with the continued spike in demand to visit Europe, the difference being future demand models will see North American time shares use more time overall.

Why European travel matters-still the world's top travel market According to the United Nations World Tourism Organization (UNWTO), Europe, as of 2015, still far outranks their number two and three counterparts, Asia and the Pacific Rim, as the number one tourism destination. The latest figures show over 608M annual visitors to the European market. While demands seems to know no end, the political landscape, foreign labor laws, and environmental hurdles make prime locations in Europe nearly impossible to host large, mega scale projects where local communities have hovered for hundreds of years with slow-growth initiatives more the rule than the exception. We predict the top global operators will consider more island approvals, where governmental protection is available in exchange for labor at work. Many of these islands need a way to pay for much-needed infrastructure development to make new resort projects financially feasible.

The European markets still retain over 608M annual visitors, over twice as many as any other market in the world. The long and inspired traditions of Europe combined with their unique customs and traditions make returning to Europe over and over necessary just to take in the vast array of cultures and sights. That said, it can be expensive and time-consuming to acquire land and permits for large-scale projects looking for prime beach or winter locations. We predict we will see more inland developments adjacent to large cities and located near multiple attractions as a compromise to build and sell into the time share markets in Europe.

CHAPTER 5

The RRC Ratio and Payback Indicator-How to Calculate Your Time Share Value.

THE GOLD STANDARD of time share calculations - The RRC ratio: This is done by calculating the realistic cost per night to rent or occupy your villa, and then dividing it by your actual out-of-pocket cost per night which should include the daily maintenance fee and the daily taxes. In simple math terms, the goal of any payback model is to determine a relative value, using fair and rational logic, to calculate how long it will take you to get your money back on your investment, in this case, your time share investment.

In order to calculate any kind of payback model, it is necessary to figure out what is the daily or nightly benefit of owning a time share. There is really only one reason to consider looking at payback models, and that is to see, via a comparison, at what point you could just have rented a comparable time share product and otherwise saved or reinvested the time share purchase money somewhere else. Again, we stress that for many, just having to go through the thought process every year to book and go on a vacation could, in some ways, be all the payback you need. In other words, automatic vacations force you (short of just not going) to use your week or weeks and spend quality time with friends and family. If you were like me when I bought my first time share, I should just thank the timeshare company for introducing me to an unbelievable lifestyle and forget the return on investment idea.

However, many of us also want to justify our purchase, and therefore, we shall look at the different methods for running an ROI or payback model. The first thing to do is to ascertain your rental value if you were to rent the villa you use your timeshare to stay in for vacations. If there is light demand or none at all, then ask your operator what they will rent your villa for during the same stay. If you cannot find a solid answer, then use a similar property next door or down the street. Once you have arrived at this number, you will now multiply it by the nights you typically stay, so the $450 a night you would expect to pay for that one-bedroom suite in Hawaii gets you a gross rental of $3,150 for 7 nights, or $6,300 for 2 weeks.

Next, you need to figure out what your time share costs you per night. In most cases, this should be fairly easy if you own just a week or 2. Many programs now offer discounts or Premium Points depending on how you book, whether you take advantage of some special offers, and what kind of value you can exchange your locked-off unit for if you own one, which all play a role in determining your average nightly cost. Some other programs will allow you to use points to convert into hotels versus villas or vice versa, and some offer a point premium, thereby extending your stay with the extra points gained based on how you booked your vacation. Be careful here on counting nights you bought with the hotel or other points versus your ability to obtain discounts year in and year out.

The second example occurs because of special rules your time share membership may offer on short-term stays or seasonal discounts. This is not the same thing as spending currency in the form of hotel reward points. It is important to compare apples to apples here, so the only nights that count are the ones you can easily book using your regular time share weeks or points on a consistent basis. You can add in the extra nights you may qualify for if they are part of your membership agreement on the number of nights per year you actually earned, which then will be divided over the total cost per year to arrive at your annual RRC ratio. In some cases, you may need to figure out your RRC by the day, add all of them up, and then divide by the total number of nights over total maintenance cost per day, and then average all of the RRC ratios for each day.

Once you have these figures, you can divide your daily rental over your cost per day and you will arrive at your RRC ratio. In a simple example, if you could either rent your villa for $400 per day and your maintenance fee per day is $200, you then have a RRC ratio of $400/$200 or 2 to 1 for that day. If the rate changes for a weekend or season, then compute each day, and then average to get the most accurate RRC ratio.

Calculating the rental return ratio (RRC ratio) on extended night stays: It is the real amount of annual nights you get year after year that we are after here. If one year you got 14 nights, and the next year you got 18 nights on the same plan, then just use 16 nights as an average. You may be able to add in extra nights every year into your annual membership if your program allows you to rent more time under special circumstances and you consistently use that rental pattern. Remember, you may need to adjust your rent downward in this case, if, for example, you prefer to travel during the off-season. In any event, you should be able to come up with a

daily figure for both revenue per night and your cost per night by doing a little research.
Let's assume you pay $1,300 per week for maintenance, and have 2 weeks per year, to keep it simple. This will mean your average daily cost is $186 a night. Now, divide your average daily rent per year by your average daily cost per year to get to the rental rate over cost ratio (the RRC ratio). Let's review the calculation below:

Calculating the RRC ratio and the payback indicator based on a normal stay

Assume you paid $35,700 for your timeshare net of all incentives.

- 14 nights in a one-bedroom suite in Hawaii on the ocean in a top-tier program = $450 night
- 14 X $450 = $6,300 for a 2-week stay, or $450 for the daily rate$450 - $186 = $264 net per night = to a 2.41 **RRC ratio**
  Or $3,696 net rental per year
- $35,700 divided by $3,696 is equal to a **payback indicator** of 9.65 years

Remember, you do not have to rent your villa to run these numbers; just understand what you could have rented it for. In the above example, if you paid $42,000 gross for your time share, but you got 2 weeks of "Bonus Vacations" for making the purchase, you need to net down how much money really went to buy the timeshare versus the value of real vacations you could take within the next year.

In this case, we assumed a gross price of $42,000 minus $6,300 in incentives to arrive at a $35,700 purchase cost. I have seen perks as high as 35% of the gross time share purchase price and even higher when overseas airfares are thrown into the calculation. If you have a way to convert bonus points into vacations with airfares, you can usually end up with a higher value conversion in the form of a paid vacation as a gift for buying your timeshare. I knew one couple who spent $40,000 on a timeshare with me just to get first-class airline tickets from the United States to South America and felt the $18,000 in airfare value plus a 5-night stay in a top hotel was worth the price to purchase the time share. They planned on selling their time share in 2 years at near a 40%–50% discount. Remember, their real cost is $40,000 minus $18,000 (travel bonus to buy the TS), equal to $22,000, so selling their $40,000 timeshare in 2 years for $20,000 is very close to a breakeven either way, plus, they get to use the timeshare while they own it. They did it because they were committed to the South American trip and loved the airline and hotel package that came with it. It is not that they could have just bought the trip outside the membership that mattered, it was the perk package that meant more to them than the timeshare. Their numbers were pretty reasonable on all sides. They essentially bought the timeshare for the perk package. I have done the same when airline/fuel prices showed arbitrage in the perk package and brought the payback model below 4 to 1; i.e., I got my money back in less than 4 years. This is more prevalent in times where gas prices are running high and air fares eventually must rise to offset the higher fuel costs. The miles on awards, though, tend to stay the same regardless of fuel costs increasing the value of airline perks.

These details vary a lot from developer to developer, so be sure to ask detailed questions regarding any incentive packages that might be available if you make a timeshare purchase. Don't assume they will be offered to you in every case. Some compensation plans could be changing, so knowing when a developer may add or subtract bonus incentives is a worthwhile discovery.

Recalculating your RRC ratio and payback indicator based on extended stays: In the example below, we assume you can book your same time share under an incentive clause with your time share company and earn extra free days. Notice if we use 17 days instead of 14 days how the calculation changes.

We still have our annual maintenance fee of $2,600, but this time, we found a way to book 17 days using the rules of our membership dropping our average daily cost from $186 a day to $153 a day. In other words, the free nights do not have any maintenance fees, so your average daily cost is going to head down. It may not matter that you saved $33 a day in this case. The important thing to remember is the principle of averaging down your maintenance fee. If it can be done for 3 days, given enough time share ownership, it can be done for 3 weeks or even 3 months, given enough time share ownership. It is possible with enough rental income to live in a time share year-round for little to no cost once you can engineer your average daily rate to zero cost per day. This is not for the faint of heart and requires about 30 days of rental per year to cover maintenance fees.

Regardless of how many nights we are able to lower the average daily cost, we can see that by just extending our stays by 3 days, we have a reduced **payback indicator** as depicted below:

17 nights at $450 = $7,650 or $450 a night, the same as before, but notice the maintenance fee drops to $153 a night.

- $450/$153 is now a $294 daily net income times 17 nights or $4,998 per year
- RRC is $450/$153 for an **RRC ratio of 2.94**
- $35,700 divided by $4,998 is now down to a **7.14 year payback indicator**

You can see under some programs with certain time share products that might include a locked-off option, premium bumps, or positive conversion features, it is possible for the same owners buying the same time share from the same operator and paying the same price, could end up with different RRC ratios and therefore, different pay-back results. It is all dependent on how many nights per year you are able to book without any additional cost or very little incremental cost. This is one of the keys to extracting more value out of your time share. The best example would be an owner that owns a 1-week unit with three bedrooms but because the third room has a separate entrance, usually referred to as a "lock-off" and more common in many large-scale resorts, now they can exchange their 1 week for 2 weeks without a penalty and book at least a one- or two-bedroom suite for 2 weeks, or book two 1-week vacations, and in the process, gain an extra week. In some cases, an owner can get two benefits, gain an extra week, and pick up a second bedroom, and in many cases, this can be done for 2 weeks.

This extra week could then be rented or occupied, but in either case, you would be driving your average daily cost down and increasing you RRC ratio and reducing the payback indicator because the extra week is maintenance free. Some programs do not have booking discounts, or you may not own a lock-off legacy week, in which case you would end up with the same RRC ratio in the above example. Other programs allow you to earn premium points or gain extra days under certain circumstances. Knowing these rules can lower your costs. This again is a feature you should look for if having more control over your payback model is important to you. The "lock-off" unit can be a hidden secret in the time share world because the maintenance fee is based on the purchase price, not necessarily the value of controlling "two units," and although time share lock-offs tend to sell for more, they can carry a lower price per square foot charge for maintenance in many cases, allowing you to convert your 1 week into 2 weeks but only pay 1 week of maintenance fees. Imagine owning 1 month of a lock-off time share and paying 1 month of maintenance fees. Now, with a quick booking flip, you have 2 months of vacation time.

In the above example, stretching our nights from 14 to 17, we took our net purchase price of $35,700 and divide it by our $4,998 in net rental, and we got down to a reduced payback of 7.14 years from the original 9.65 years. This is another example of reducing your payback indicator because of just getting 3 extra nights per year. Please understand you could have run this calculation at a different time of year and/or at a different resort within your own operator/developer, and it is likely you would have ended up with a different number. You should run the calculation at where you most like to stay, when you like to travel, and make sure you are quoting like views, villa size, and time and day of year, as these things all effect rental rates. If you live in an area where a special event is happening, i.e., like a PGA golf event, you could see rental rates skyrocket just for those days. These types of events make very good rental windows because they reduce your RRC ratio if your time share is used as a rental during this high-premium window. If you use your time share in Vail to ski, run the numbers for rentals in the winter, but if Vail is hosting the X games, as an example, rental rates could double from the year before for the exact same week in certain high-profile resorts that are hosting a popular event. Know thy neighborhood and recognize that world-class locations like Vail, Newport Beach, Hilton Head, New York, and prime desert locations like Scottsdale or Palm Desert often host events that temporarily drive up rental costs but only for a few precious days.

It is normal to get different payback model results from year to year, but in general, if you have a top-tier timeshare, your payback ratios should be coming in below 11 years (very important you are assuming inflation equal to the past 10 years; i.e., about 3% per year), including maintenance fees and a payback indicator of below 8 with just the purchase price of the time share used in the calculation. In essence, your time share starts to really pay for itself after the first 10 tears when inflation and maintenance fees are factored in. This is important because failing to account for maintenance fees is a false calculation and provides no real value. I have seen paybacks as low as 1.5 to 1 on the resale and foreclosure markets and well over 25 to 1 for marginal midpriced timeshares sold usually to first-time buyers with average accommodation profiles. I am not picking on first-time buyers, but they tend to be less knowledgeable than multiple time share owners who have purchased four–five times or more. Experienced owners tend to buy time shares that have lower payback indicators and higher RRC ratios.

Again, what have we learned is not all time shares have the same trading value, and the more exclusive the location and amenity package, the more likely you will be in the top tier of rental rates. Remember, only about 20%–25% of all time shares fit into this category. Many more moderately priced time shares may save you $15,000 to $30,000 up front, but they could carry a payback indicator over 15 or even 20 years. You might have saved $20,000 buying a time share over the top competitor pricing models, but it may take you 20 years to get paid back instead of the 10 years. The more expensive $50,000 time share may likely command a better RRC ratio because it rents for a higher multiple over its average daily costs. This means the higher-priced $50,000 time share could have more economic value than its lower-priced

$25,000 time share. Would you rather pay $50,000 and have it all back in 10 years or pay $25,000 and recapture all of it in 20 years? That is the purpose of running the payback indicator model.

Regardless of the payback indicator, most programs now allow you to will your time share interest to your children or other heirs. This puts less importance on how many years it takes your RRC ratio or payback indicator to pay for itself. It is the next 50–100 years covering two or three generations that will more than cover the few extra years it takes for your payback to begin if you are happy with the plan you are invested in.

> Remember it is not the price of the time share that is of most concern under a payback model but rather the RRC ratio attached to it. The higher the RRC ratio, the more expensive the likely rental rate is because rental rates can sell at a premium to the normal rental market (a PGA event in town, for example), resulting in rental demand far outstripping short-term rental supply. There is nothing wrong with lower RRC ratios that extend your payback indicator if your timeshare fits your lifestyle and budget.

> Please note our payback indicator does not attempt to calculate any financing in the picture. It assumes you paid cash for your time share. While there could be some tax benefits to a time share mortgage that are favorable, they are usually offset by a higher interest rate between 10% and 15% per year, but competition and favorable industry trends are making these rates more competitive. A leveraged time share properly rented could actually increase your RRC ratio and payback, but this concept is beyond the scope and purpose of this book.

A multiple week's owner—how to calculate your portfolio RRC ratio: The most accurate way to calculate your portfolio RRC ratio requires that you take all of the nights in a single year you either stayed in, rented out, or gave away, and be sure to include all of your stretch points, coupons, or exchange upgrades or certificates, as well as their cost added to your maintenance fee. We are after the total amount of money you spent to stay in your villa, which represents the total number of nights you controlled for the year.

Again, it makes no difference if you actually rented your villa out or just checked in and occupied all of your nights, as long as each night is accounted for. The important thing is you use an accurate rental rate reflecting the rate you would have to pay in the event you gave the villa away or occupied the villa. If you got a coupon or other discount or points off for a nonpeak stay, you must make sure the rental rate for that night reflects the real rate you might have paid for that night. I.e., a Saturday night stay can often be more than twice the next night (Sunday) in many resorts.

Let's look at an example of an owner who got 32 days of time share out of their membership for a given year in both one and two bedrooms for the year. We assumed the median Internet rate for a rental on the same night.

Month	Nights	Location	Type	Per Night	Total	Notes
February	5	Phoenix, Ariz.	2 beds	$650	$3,300	Phoenix Open
April	7	Hawaii	2 beds	$700	$4,900	20% below rack
June	6	St. Thomas	1 Bed	$725	$4,350	Ritz
September	3	New York	1 Bed	$725	$2,175	Mid-Town

November	5	Palm Springs	2 Bed	$500	$2,500	Thanksgiving
December	6	Vail, Col.	2 Bed	$800	$4,800	Prime ski in/ ski out

Assumes about 4 weeks of time share using a combination of stretched and discount points to get to 32 days.

$22,025 Rental Value

$8,314 (A) Maintenance Fees

Portfolio RRC: 2.64

The portfolio RRC return—conclusion: The above example is very within the range of possibilities with many of the large operators and does not assume any unusual discounts to either book these locations or achieve the stated rentals. In this case, an owner that might own either 4 weeks or owns enough points to vacation for 4 weeks would take the rental rates they might have paid for these locations at the same time of year, and then divide all of the stays by the annual maintenance fees. In essence, their resort bill was equal to the maintenance fee of $8,314 for the year versus the $22,025 they would have paid without their membership and just paid the discounted Internet rate for the same stays. In essence, if they paid $74,500 for their time shares, they saved $13,741 this year on travel, equal to a 2017 payback indicator of 5.42 years on their time share portfolio. After the 5.42 years is up, they will be traveling in first-class locations for 67%-plus off, since the discount will go up over time due to rental rates rising faster than the maintenance costs.

What does it mean if your RRC ratio is trending up? This means that rental rates are rising faster and higher than your maintenance fees, creating a wider margin between market rates and your cost of ownership. It could also mean you are being more economical in your vacation choices using your points to stay in off-seasons or looking for ways to earn discount points. It may also be a combination of the two. What matters is if you have the same travel pattern every year and your ratio is heading up or down, and then you can determine if your time share is adding or losing economic value. Remember, the RRC ratio is a financial report card on how you spend your money on lodging in most cases. There is nothing wrong with staying in either high- or low-priced per night venues as long as you know its impact on your overall cost.

In summary, if your ratio is trending up over the years, this means your time share is gaining in economic value because the RRC spread is widening in your favor. This also means your payback indicator is going down; i.e., it takes fewer years to recoup your investment. This tends to happen more often in luxury and Category One timeshares at peak seasons and can also occur when rental demand far outweighs market supply for rentals. These rental windows can be very short, in some cases, just a weekend. A prime beach, mountain, or desert villa, in high season, with great snow, sun, or expected weather forecast, can bring renters into the villa rental pool very quickly. I spent 28 years in Denver and was always amazed how fast the ski resorts started selling out reservations when it was snowing in Denver and the Broncos were playing on national television. Rental rates soon skyrocketed the following weekend as remaining time share inventory became scare, almost always selling out on news of a major storm.

As an extreme example, I was able to purchase a foreclosure week from a top brand for $4,900 for a summer week at the beach (every other year), and the first year I owned it, I got $550 a night for 6 of the 7 nights. I calculated my maintenance costs were about $100 a night at the time, leaving me $450 X 6 or $2,700 minus my $600 cost for a $2,100 net profit for that year. Clearly, about a 2-year payback on the purchase price.

This produced an RRC of 4.5 to 1, well above the industry average of just over 2 to 1 with a payback indicator of $4,900/$2,100 equal to 2.3 years versus a more normal 8 to 9 years. In other extreme cases, I have seen payback indicators coming down below 2 to 1, meaning your money is off the table in 2 years as your net investment drops to zero. RRCs that are trending up year after year will start to appreciate first when the industry converts to an electronic trading platform. I predict this will take place in about 10 years, and then prime luxury timeshares will trade only slightly below newer retail prices in real terms. This means they could start to appreciate at a faster rate over time. This is already true today when I review my own purchases. My prime beach weeks cost me between $16,000 and $24,000 a week over the years I bought them, and those same weeks now cost about $38,000 for the same week. If I apply a discount of 50%, that would net about $19,000, netting a small profit on my oldest weeks purchased for around $16,000. This is the power of owning prime timeshares over 20 years. I can actually sell them at a 50% discount to the current market, but since my payback indicator was under 10 years, the time share weeks are now worth more than I paid for them.

The future, of course, is subject to several economic trends remaining positive and is not a reason to speculate in time shares by any means. However, if you are looking at entry prices now starting to exceed $125,000 to $150,000, or more, in some cases, for 2 prime beach weeks, knowing your RRC ratio and payback indicator could provide some peace of mind. If, for no other reason, this information will let you know how many years it will take to zero out your investment. As a benchmark, any RRC ratio at or above 3 is quite outstanding and means you are earning three times what it cost you to rent your villa per night, and you have a net margin of at least 67% on your rental income. Don't expect this to be the case the first year you purchase your time share. It may take 5–10 years for your RRC share to rise from about 2.0 to 3.0 to 1. Remember that if your RRC ratio is a top-tier time share, it should see the RRC ratio widen over 10 years. In some cases, as you stretch your stays, your RRC ratio could get as high as 7 to 1 or more, but this generally means you own over 4 months of time share and are recouping some of your maintenance fees by renting out 10–20 days a year. This is as good as it gets in the real estate industry. Whether you chose to rent out your villa or stay there for 15 cents on the dollar, either way, you are on your way to a very nice lifestyle at reduced price points.

What does it mean if your RRC ratio is trending down? If your RRC ratio is trending down, it means the economic value of your time share could be losing value, but then again, you must be careful to make sure your ratios are measured exactly the same way year after year. For example, a prime beach week on either coastline might command $600–$1,000 per night for a top ocean view, two bedrooms in July.

Let's assume your cost is $175 a night in maintenance fees. Assuming there was sufficient market demand to rent the unit in February, for example, you might only get $300 a night. In this example, we get $300/$175 for an RRC ratio of 1.71, whereas in July, you have $600/$175 to arrive at a RRC of 3.42. I prefer to use the highest rental season possible when I rent my villa so I can get a much-higher return. I also prefer to rent my villa during these times because they offer the highest payback, and the rental could be tax free if you stay under 14 days a year. In order to calculate your trend year after year, it is very important you compare like-kind times of year, same views and size, and that the event calendar is the same. As a benchmark, any RRC ratio at or below 1.5 is barely covering your maintenance cost and is likely pushing your payback indicator past 20 years.

If this is the case and your RRC is trending down, it means market demand is seeking other rental choices over your unit, creating either flat or declining demand, or your maintenance fees are rising faster than market demand to rent your unit, or both things are happening at the same time. Keep in mind it is possible you could have 1 year go up and the next year go down, and then repeat this trend as current national economic and employment data play a big role in vacation demand. It is often the first item to fall out of a family budget and the last to come back during tough economic times. If, after careful analysis, you see your RRC ratio dropping year after year, you may need to follow some other strategies in this book if you are not using your time share. This means your unit is losing economic value over time relative to other time shares with rising RRCs.

Again, as we have repeated in many places in this book, if you are enjoying your unit and creating valuable memories, you do not need to worry about the economics here as over many years, your family memories will far outweigh your RRC ratio. If, on the other hand, you are frustrated with both using it, renting it, or not being able to rent it, we will cover some tips, tricks, and solutions for you in Chapter 19, "How do I Sell my Timeshare" .

Understanding RRC opportunity cost model: This is a very complex subject, but we are going to cover it for all of the economists, accountants, and other financial wizards who like to bring up this subject. The discussion starts with "time shares are really not a very good investment." This is then followed by "I would be better off just renting a villa and investing the money in an alternative investment." First, let's set the table for what argument on opportunity cost really means and why it is tricky to create an accurate payback model that actually fits the real world. This calculation is a bit of a nonstarter because we all have very different opinions about what we might earn on our money. I have made 100 to 1 on a few deals in my career. Should I just suggest to others that if I spend $40,000 on a time share, I am giving up $4,000,000? We all know that if one is lucky enough to earn that kind of money, how much did they lose looking for the 100 to 1? The answer could be they lost $5,000,000 on other deals and would have been better off putting their money into bonds over a 10- or 20-year period. No, that was not me!

Regardless of these two extremes, I have heard some time share pundits argue that they could do better by investing their money and just pay the current rental price for a unit. Under certain conditions I could build a model that proves this. I could also just as easily build a model that disproves this and therefore suggest that a time share over the long run is a better value.

The key in any rent versus buy scenario is one must compare apples to apples. Telling us you could go to San Francisco and find a hotel for $89 a night is probably likely with today's fast-moving Internet platforms looking to dump unrented hotel rooms. What does that have to do with a 1,350 square foot villa, on a top floor with a kitchen and two bathrooms that is lavishly appointed? What if you could have a villa in San Francisco that rents for $1,300 a night for the same $89; i.e., about the price of a maintenance fee? In this case, two people both spend $89 for the night in San Francisco, but one is in a 225 square foot hotel room and the other is in a 2+2 villa, with 1,350 square feet in a suite that rents for $1,300 a night. Is either person wasting money? No, but one of them is wasting intelligence on how the world works if you travel or like to travel.

So, finding inferior hotel space in the same town means absolutely nothing. Therefore, we need to establish some ground rules. Let's assume if you invest in a time share, you do your homework, pay a little more, and find a top-shelf program that matches your needs and the needs of your family. Let's assume you travel with at least your spouse or a significant other and, in addition, from time to time, may want another suite for either guests, your kids, or other family members. Let's assume you prefer top locations with easy access to whatever the town's main events and locations offer. Now we have apples to apples.

Next, the calculation is also made more difficult by the fact that not all timeshares are priced the same, and under special booking rules using stretched points, make it is easier to build in a large RRC ratio (above 5 to 1), which will then outperform in favor of the buy versus rent argument without much trouble. Therefore, we have chosen to use a few simple rules to really analyze this question.

The first is that while one could argue about a risk-free rate of return, we will use basic alternative investments, open to the general public, designed to safely pay interest. We will use the following assumptions as both conservative and within what most economists would accept as valid assumptions. We will then run a 15-year comparison on what "renting versus buying" a prime 2-week, ocean-facing 2+2 villa timeshare really looks like.

1. We will assume all money is invested in tax-free bonds yielding 3.5% a year for 15 years.
2. We will use a 15-year period from 2017–2032, but we run the model out for 45 years.

3. We will assume a time share purchase price of $75,420 based on current market prices in January of 2017 for the buy comparison. This timeshare example is for July every year for 2 weeks with a major developer (excludes July 4th week).
4. A rental rate of $788 a day starting for 2017 for the rental assumption, 16% below rack rate.
5. Rental rate increases of 5% per year. (Past 5 year increases have been 5%–12%.)
6. Maintenance fees of $4,743 from the developer with 3.0% increases every year. This is in line with the historical averages where RRC ratios have widened because rental prices outpaced maintenance fees as demand for high-season time shares continues to rise faster than supply for prime West Coast beachfront villas.
7. The buyer, in this case, pays cash and owns the time share on Jan. 1, 2017.
8. 3% per year appreciation is assumed on the value of the time share.
9. The difference between what the villa might rent for and what it costs per day (RRC ratio) is credited to the buyer.
10. The "renter," in lieu of purchasing the time share, must rent the unit for a 16% discount to "rack rate" and gets 3.5% per year in interest on his or her $75,420 investment into A-rated tax-free bonds.

Now, looking at the spreadsheet, we note that the renter earned $126,355 in interest over the 15-year term. The renter also paid rent in the amount of $237,904 over 15 years.

The buyer paid $75,460 for the time share but saved over $149,689 in rent after paying his or her maintenance fees.

	Years 1 through 15		**OPPORTUNITY COST OF INVESTING $75,420 AT 3.5% VERSUS BUYING TWO WEEKS OF TIMESHARE**														
			ASSUMPTION ASSUMES RENTAL IS A 2+2 VILLA WITH A PRIME OCEAN VIEW-TOP TIER DEVELOPER														
			RACK RATE FOR THE PER DAY RENTAL WAS $935 BASED ON 2016 ACTUAL, DISCOUNT WAS 16.00%														
		2017	**2018**	**2019**	**2020**	**2021**	**2022**	**2023**	**2024**	**2025**	**2026**	**2027**	**2028**	**2029**	**2030**	**2031**	
Inflation	**Cost of Time Share**	Year 1	Year 2	Year 3	Year 4	Year 5	Year 6	Year 7	Year 8	Year 9	Year 10	Year 11	Year 12	Year 13	Year 14	Year 15	**Value of**
																	Time Share
3.50%	**$75,420**	$78,060	$80,792	$83,620	$86,546	$89,575	$92,710	$95,955	$99,314	$102,790	$106,387	$110,111	$113,965	$117,954	$122,082	$126,355	**$126,355**
Return	**Assumes Tax Free Bond**																**Value of Cash**
3.50%	**$75,420**	**$78,060**	**$80,792**	**$83,620**	**$86,546**	**$89,575**	**$92,710**	**$95,955**	**$99,314**	**$102,790**	**$106,387**	**$110,111**	**$113,965**	**$117,954**	**$122,082**	**$126,355**	**aftertax**
	Interest Earned	**$2,640**	**$2,732**	**$2,828**	**$2,927**	**$3,029**	**$3,135**	**$3,245**	**$3,358**	**$3,476**	**$3,598**	**$3,724**	**$3,854**	**$3,989**	**$4,128**	**$4,273**	**$50,935**
																	$126,355
	2016-Rent per Day																
5.00%	$750	$788	$827	$868	$912	$957	$1,005	$1,055	$1,108	$1,163	$1,222	$1,283	$1,347	$1,414	$1,485	$1,559	**Total Rent**
	Days Per year	14	14	14	14	14	14	14	14	14	14	14	14	14	14	14	
	Total Cost to Rent Villa	$11,025	$11,576	$12,155	$12,763	$13,401	$14,071	$14,775	$15,513	$16,289	$17,103	$17,959	$18,856	$19,799	$20,789	$21,829	**$237,904**
															Renter Cash for Rent		**$237,904**
	Savings from Owning																
	2016-Rent Per Day																
5.00%	$750	$788	$827	$869	$912	$958	$1,006	$1,056	$1,109	$1,164	$1,222	$1,284	$1,348	$1,415	$1,486	$1,560	
	Days Per Year-Vacation	14	14	14	14	14	14	14	14	14	14	14	14	14	14	14	
	Cost if Rented	$11,025	$11,576	$12,155	$12,763	$13,401	$14,071	$14,775	$15,513	$16,289	$17,103	$17,959	$18,856	$19,799	$20,789	$21,829	**$237,904**
3.00%	Maintenance Fee	$4,743	$4,885	$5,032	$5,183	$5,338	$5,498	$5,663	$5,833	$6,008	$6,189	$6,374	$6,565	$6,762	$6,965	$7,174	**$88,215**
	Rental-Rate Ratio-RRC	2.32	2.37	2.42	2.46	2.51	2.56	2.61	2.66	2.71	2.76	2.82	2.87	2.93	2.98	3.04	**Rent Saved**
	Net Savings from Owning	**$6,282**	**$6,691**	**$7,123**	**$7,580**	**$8,063**	**$8,573**	**$9,111**	**$9,680**	**$10,281**	**$10,915**	**$11,584**	**$12,291**	**$13,037**	**$13,824**	**$14,655**	**$149,689**
											RESULT AFTER FIRST 15 YEARS						
2031	**Buyer Owns Time Share worth:**		$126,355		Owner Cash Out of Pocket through 15 years				$88,215		**Winner is Owner**		**$149,689**				
2031	**Renter Sitting on Tax Free Cash of :**		$126,355		Renter Cash Out of Pocket through 15 years				$237,904								

Conclusion: The buyer owns the time share free and clear and has an asset equal to the renter's tax-free bond portfolio worth $126,355, same as the time share. One is a cash asset, and the other is a time share asset. The buyer could collect $14,655 a year in net rent if he/she chose to rent the villa versus occupy it. This is equal to a 19.43% return on investment in year 15.

The renter is out of pocket a net $186,969 after getting $50,935 in interest on the tax-free bonds.

The bottom line is the 15-year rent versus buy only assumes a 5% increase in the annual rental rate, well below the last 10-year average. If inflation or the historical trend line for rent increases holds, this gap will widen in favor of the buyer. On the other hand, the renter does own its asset in cash, and the buyer would have to sell his/her time share to generate the same $126,355 in cash. We do think, given the future metrics on beachfront villas, this will be less of a problem, but there is no guarantee a liquid market will be in place. It could also be higher than we are projecting.

Neither one is necessarily vastly superior to the other. However, under another 30-plus years of modeling, the gap widens considerably in favor of owning a prime asset versus renting one. If you love the beach, the mountains, or love to look at and play on that favorite course, the decision to own combined with one of the true remaining tax shelters makes the ownership model a better choice for most of us. We have run the model out for 45 years just to reflect what happens over a very long period of time. You can review these numbers in Chapter 23 where we ran the numbers on a Rent versus Own Analysis using a 45-year shoot-out comparing renting a villa versus owning one and investing the cash in tax-free bonds.

What is my time share worth? A good place to start with how to value a time share is with common sense. We know there is not a liquid market for time shares and won't be until the industry creates an electronic marketplace. It is also true that a 1-week time share in Hawaii with two bedrooms and two bathrooms could sell for below $10,000 or for $50,000 or more on the resale market, depending on the company, location, time of year, the size of the unit, whether it is a desirable fixed week of floating, if it has a lock-off, and if the deed is forever. More importantly, a buyer looking to pay retail may view a resale at 25% off the retail price from the developer a bargain, whereas, a desperate seller needing a quick sale on the Internet is forced to settle for 75% off. Same resort, same villa, same season. Time share is not always fair, and neither is the time share resale market. There could be other factors involved like financing and maintenance fees that affect value.

The one thing that is universal is the concept of return on investment. While this is not a reason to buy a timeshare, it is a darn good reason to defend its potential value. In other words, money is invested all over the world every day. If there were a consistent way for anyone to earn a higher-than-normal return on investment, all things being equal, that investment will attract an investor ahead of other inferior, higher-risk investments.

This is why we developed the RRC ratio because it is the same formula for all timeshares. It does not matter whether it is a Category One or Two or Three time share (although the higher the category the more likely the RRC will be higher), as a return on the dollar is a uniform measure of value. Therefore, if one could pay for an entire investment in a few years, say 4 to 6 years, it is likely one could sell a time share based on economic theory rather than just using plain utility value. The capital markets will migrate to where money is treated the best. This is simple economic theory. This involves aligning the risk and level of effort required to create and maintain a return on your time share investment. Our formula is simple.

First of all, you must be able to prove your RRC ratio is accurate. The numbers below assume you own either a Category One or Two time share. In some cases, you may need to show rental receipts from your renter or document what the cost of renting your unit would be if you were to rent your villa in the same unit every year. This has not been the way traditional time shares have been sold. Let's say in the example earlier in this chapter, your annual net income (whether you rented it or rented it out) is $4,988 a year, and you paid $35,700 net of concessions. What does the current Internet resale market value your time share at for a fast sale? Your time share is worth this number multiplied by 2.0 on the low side and multiplied by 4 on the high side for a prime summer or winter month equal to:

1. **Low value is $4,988 times a 2.0 multiplier for a low value of $9,976**
2. **High value is $4,988 times a 4.0 multiplier for a high value of $19,952**

Please be advised there are a number of factors that could cause these numbers to vary, like economic conditions within the U.S. and foreign economies, your ability to market your own time share, and the buyer's ability to obtain financing through sources other than banks, a drawback that continues to drag down the resale market for time shares. Most important is also where interest rates are since many people can buy a time share on a credit card, using promotional rates for a year or so if they need time to pay off the acquisition. If you own a prime holiday week like July 4th, Christmas, or New Year's, then you will likely be in the 4.0 to 6.0 area on value. You could see multipliers of between 5 and 6 on exceptional holiday weeks that are fixed for Christmas week and/or the 4th of July and have lock-off capability with three bedrooms. If you list your time share with a broker, they will need to sell it for 20%–30% less than depicted here to cover marketing, sales, and transaction costs and earn a brokerage fee.

Recall the original purchase price we used above was $35,700 net of concessions. This means you could recoup between 35% to 55% of your money back for a Category One or Two timeshare if the property is marketed properly, you've own it for at least 10 years, and you can prove your RRC ratio is at or above 3.0 through rental receipts. Category Three and Four time shares will trade down at .5 to 1 up to 1.5 to 1 for the high and low values, assuming there is legitimate rental demand in the season you own. These numbers reflect time share owners who have not held their time share past their payback indicator. In an ideal situation, you should own your time share for at least as long as your payback indicator, and preferably twice that long. For example, if you have a payback indicator of 9.6 years and you held it for 18 years, these numbers will prove very accurate because inflation will price your unit back up to 50% or so of what the then current market prices for your same time share and may well net you a small profit.

As an example, I bought a prime 2+2 villa facing the ocean in Newport Coast, California, from a well-known operator in 1998 for around $16,000. That same week is now about $56,400 equal to $46,400 after concessions and purchase perks. If I were to sell my time share under the formula above, it would look like the following:

$750 per night, so $5,250 for the week. (July 2016 rack rate was $925.)

5% Internet rental fee: $262.50.

Net rental: $4,988 after marketing fee.

$4,988 times 3.5 equal to $17,458.

Net cash flow after maintenance fee of $1,425 is $3,563.

Payback indicator in 2016 is **4.49** on my **1998** purchase price.

Payback indicator in 2016 is **13.02** based on the adjusted **2017** purchase price.

RRC ratio in 2017 is $750/$203 a night for **3.69.**

Purchase price was $16,000 around 1998.

Percentage of return on 20 years: 1.09% or 9% over cost, about one-half of a percent per year.

PS: My rental assumption was about 80% of what the resort charged per night in July of 2016.

Personal value of the memories: Cannot put a price on it, but to me, they are priceless.

These numbers can vary widely, however, if there is a lot of inventory for sale or you are using a broker and they have to absorb marketing fees. Remember, many of these time shares will fall short of these numbers, and it is likely you may only recoup 10% to 30% (or less if your time share is a Category Three or Four) of your initial investment if there is marginal demand for your villa and you elect to sell well before your payback indicator has expired. If your payback is under 10 years and you sell your time share for 25% to 33% of its original cost a few years after you got it, then you did not do near as well if you had kept it over 10 years and preferably at least twice your pay back indicator. Remember, the cheapest years to own your time share are after your pay back indicator has passed and you are playing with the house money.

> If your payback indicator is 9.6 years, the next 10 years or so (years 11–20) will save you the most amount of money because your investment basis is at zero, and with even modest inflation, your rental savings will likely be substantial during this time to replace the same vacation. Time shares do not necessarily offer quick paybacks, but the top brands in top locations really shine after the payback indicator has been reached.
>
> In the example above, the reason I would receive 9% back on my investment if I wanted to sell this time share week is because I have owned it for over 20 years and have already got my payback twice over. In rental terms, during years 11 to 20, I was staying there at less than three times what it cost to rent it. Over a 20-year period, that is a lot of cash saved.
>
> So, we end up with two ways to look at my original $16,000 investment.
>
> 1. The first is after 20 years of ownership, I might get 109% of what I paid if I wanted to sell it.
> 2. The second is I would get a small profit by selling for $17,458, but that is 38% of what the same week currently cost at $46,400.
>
> The key to remember here is I have saved over $250 a night (average for 20 years in rental savings without assuming I

stretched my points), so I did not spend $35,000 on additional rent I would have had to pay over my maintenance fee. It is the rental savings that make the numbers work since the savings were over twice what I paid for it. It really would not matter to me if I sold the time share for $1 since it has already paid for itself twice over. Over the next 20 years, it will have paid me back over five times under regular inflation assumptions; i.e., 3%–4% per year, again making its resale value somewhat irrelevant in the grand scheme of things. In essence, one does not buy a time share to make money but rather to save money. Most of us would not pay $925 a night to stay in a prime 2+2 oceanfront villa, so the way around that is to use the time share as an inflation hedge and therefore, just pay the $203 maintenance fee per night versus $925 rental fee. I want to point out here, this particular time share is one of the more expensive in the United States and well above the price point of 75% of most time shares. Oddly, that is why I like it so much, because I can stay there for well under even the $203 maintenance fee because of how I manage my time share. This is the maintenance fee on owning just a week. My real maintenance fee is around $40 per night and falling every year because of how I manage my time shares.

Why do time shares seem to be discounted on the secondary market? The discounts in time shares exist because of the reasons we cited earlier about the lack of a secondary market, the need to help make a same-day decision, and because large operators can offer occupancy incentives at typically much-lower costs than the value of the vacation. These discounts are now rooted in the industry and will likely remain until a strong secondary electronic platform to lower transaction costs can develop and help lower the bid/ask spreads now prevalent in the industry.

In addition, the concept of common sense will begin to enter the picture when the Beachfront Index continues to widen, which is more than likely over the next 10 years. This index is the cost of buying a beachfront home on the water in any given beachfront town, and then comparing it to buying the exact same thing in a time share. Right now, the spread is over 2 to 1 for a condo and about 4.5 to 1 for a comparable home. As this pricing index continues to rise toward 5 to 1 for a beachfront home versus the cost for a year to live at a beachfront time share, prime time shares will start to appreciate faster than beach homes until a more reasonable index just below 2 to 1 has been restored.

In order to prove our theory, we ran the numbers in Chapter 21 and arrived at a Beachfront Index ranging from over 2 to 1 for a like-kind condo and over 4.5 to 1 comparing a year at the beach in a time share versus a year at the beach in a purchased home. The home cost $317,498 a year to own, and the time share was $83,860 in operating cost for a year. The condo was almost the same in annual operating cost.

The Beachfront Index is so wide it means that many people could realize their dream of living at the beach if they just switched from the concept of owning a home to owning the right to stay at the beach for a year. The demand for this type of living will force developers to look for more beachfront properties in other parts of the country where land may be a little more reasonable. We predict demand will continue to rise for top luxury time shares that offer warmer weather and an ocean view. Eventually, these assets will start to rise in value in real terms as the Beachfront Index widens past 5 to 1 and real estate brokers are directed to investigate what it would take to buy a year at the beach through a time share. The day is coming.

This logic is no different than a CEO moving his company to Mexico to produce a product for 30% to 40% less than the United States counterpart. Eventually throughout history, money has always moved to where it is best treated for like-kind goods and services.

CHAPTER 6

Should Businesses Own Time Shares?

SHOULD A COMPANY or business buy a time share? While not perfect for a lot of companies, we predict with the continued rising cost of hotel stays, it won't be long before some small, well established companies start to look at time shares as a hotel alternative. When I had my villa, I would often host senior executives from some of the largest tech companies in the Fortune 500. It was not at all unusual for some of these companies to have the CEO impose a "travel freeze" at the end of some quarters to paint up the quarter-end numbers. There is nothing illegal here just by imposing this practice alone. It had an impact on the bottom line. Missing a quarter by even a penny can devastate a stock price. You can imagine the travel bill from a Fortune 500 company if 1,000 people travel for a week. Some, of course, have tens of thousands of people who travel every month. The cost of travel can be so high, sometimes it is more effective to shut down sales travel for 2 weeks and freeze expenses in order to increase the quarter-end earnings report.

I have a strong emotional connection about this concept because I was able to stay in a large two-bedroom villa with my membership at a per day cost for my own companies at well below what a comparable hotel cost for over 20 years. I constantly remarked every now and then about why other businesses don't do this. I believe that in many cases they just have not examined the math enough.

The question that any business has to address is, what does the payback model look like since any business success must consider how to deploy cash, and will it be accretive to shareholders? We believe the question is easily answered for any large, private financial companies, law firms, accounting firms, or any partnership-level company dependent on a highly skilled group of men and women. The up-front cost of buying a time share is what, of course, would keep most businesses from making this type of investment, and clearly, it is not appropriate for business start-ups. On the other hand, any business that throws off over a million a year in profits might want to look at this option because, in the long run, it is not just the money that can be saved on three-, four-, and five-star hotel and villa stays, it is also one heck of a perk for overworked executives living in a diminished world of disappearing perks. I most liked the fact that as a former CEO, chairman of the board, and as a writer, I could be more relaxed in a luxury setting and did not have to feel guilty I was charging my shareholders four- and five-star rates. They paid the regular three-star hotel rate, while I got a five-star villa, often nicer than any hotel room.

The math side of the decision: We have presented many cases in this book that show under certain circumstances a luxury time share portfolio can be purchased from almost any amount of initial capital contribution. Once the real terms of many top programs are compared, it may be possible to earn a payback in 5 years or less, if certain discount and off-season rates apply. Business happens 24/7 these days and really does not care about off-seasons. There is no off-season for business, and there is no off-season for hotels. Can you imagine checking into New York and having the desk clerk mention you are getting 35% off because it is off-season and another 25% off because you made the reservation within 60 days? While hotels do regularly offer some combination of weekend rates of even off-season reductions, they do not compare with time share discounts. The two operate as different real estate models, one earning income from hotel management and the other earning income from real estate development. That provides different income windows where the time share model, although capital intensive, can afford to offer a more opportune discount model because the development return is captured on the front end with the sale of each time share. More important, the time share discount model does not change with the wind like the hotel model does. The discounts apply 365 days a year, year after year. The only requirement being subject to off-season dates and booking and discount windows.

The villa versus hotel room shoot out-which cost more? : I often like to use a city like San Francisco where I challenge a potential time share buyer to look at the cost of the cheapest hotel room in the city. It could, of course, be Los Angeles or New York as well. Once the Internet is searched and the fake ads are thrown out (the kind that advertise a rate that is sold out routinely) and the only request is just a clean room, the best choice is usually a Motel 6 or a Super 8-type of hotel. Clean, well located, and affordable. Depending on the city, this room can easily cost $150 plus taxes, and may have an assortment of small fees or may not, depending on the hotel and operator. In any case, prices on the lowest end can range from $99 to $199 for most peak periods assuming you can even find these rates.Ironically, that is about what it costs to stay in a time share suite that rents for about $900 to $1,200 a night, right down the street from the hotel you might be in under the economy model. So, in essence, they both cost the same, but for, of course, the membership fee. While this is just not affordable for most businesses, I would rather my law firms absorb the cost of the membership on its own, and then bill me, the client, $175 a night versus the $600 a night they will pay to stay in a four- or five-star hotel. In the long run, I would also much rather be a partner in any firm that offered this travel perk if the compensation packages were equal.

The hotel versus time share ROI (return on investment) analysis: Most profitable businesses making over $1M a year likely use or have access to a number of Web sites they use to book business trips. Most executive assistants are very good at making plans and have a lot of experience booking small trips, often packing in a long weekend for the CEO or other senior executive if there is something fun in town to do. We decided to take a middle-of-the-road approach to seeing what type of ROI a small firm can expect to achieve if they were to use a time share for some or all of their travel needs. The challenge that arises is that even small, profitable firms are somewhat price sensitive, and most partners in a law firm or small investment banking firm would rather bank more cash per year in partner distributions than unleash a new travel policy that involves staying in $1,000-a-night suites. The challenge here in trying to run a comparison is the fact that many luxury time shares often involve upscale villas encompassing over twice the square footage versus even a large hotel suite. So, the question arises, what is the comparison? There are two schools of thought here.

Do you assume a best hotel suite in the hotel for comparison? In this case, the number we use of $565 a night for a small suite or executive hotel room is inaccurate as many junior suites up to a Presidential Suite can run up to $5,000 a night, well beyond what even highly profitable firms would approve. Presidential Suites tend to rent to entrepreneurs, top athletes, movie stars, rock stars, or the world's top CEOs, in some cases. So, if we eliminate this type of room in favor of a more practical room like an executive hotel room or minisuite in the 400 to 650 square foot range, we are then comparing some time shares that run up to 2,000 square feet for expansive three bedrooms or 1,450 square feet for two bedrooms. We also now have to address the fact that with a large two-bedroom suite, each with separate bathrooms, do we need to offset that with two hotel rentals if two partners fly to town and each rent a different $565 room for the night? Under these scenarios, we can create almost any outcome favoring one over the other. Lastly, if a company can book a 2+2 villa, there are some trips where two people may likely agree to stay in the same villa because it affords a high degree of privacy, if needed, and can save a lot of money over two separate hotel suites. We, therefore, assumed that out of the 30 nights, a firm would use 10 of those nights to double up. Therefore, the hotel equivalent would have to be 40 nights to make up for the same amount of room stays as in a 2+2 villa that could accommodate two people very comfortably.

The other option is to assume that the time share will just be bigger than the comparable $565 hotel room, and that is a compelling reason to consider a time share for business travel. We also recognize this analysis can be done and create almost any outcome desired, depending on the input assumptions. The goal, however, was to take a conservative view and see what the numbers said. In our spreadsheet, we assumed

40 hotel nights at $565, plus tax, versus the cost of a 2+2 villa, where the cost to acquire the annual rights for 30 days is around $105,000. We also assumed a combination of resale and original purchases with a medium total of $105,000. We did not assume short-term stay discounts or major off-season discounts.

We can see that the business investment of $105,000 yields about a $17,495 savings over providing hotels for 30 days in a villa and 40 days in a hotel. We assumed in the case of a time share stay a 2-bedroom villa could be used reflecting 10 days that are doubled up in a 2+2 villa, whereas the one-suite hotel room option requires a business to book two hotel rooms if two people are traveling together. A 2 bedroom villa while it may not be ideal, still grants plenty of privacy even if the two people do not prefer to stay in the same villa.

This represents a 16.66% ROI. This ROI could easily be cut in half or doubled if different rates are assumed, if we bump up to a true 5-star hotel, or if we pay retail for the whole time share portfolio. The point was to show under a median example, that some businesses may be better off using time shares to solve a portion of their travel budget. Regardless of the debate, it is clear that most Category One time shares are at least as nice, if not superior, to many standard hotel suites, and are often twice as large, and provide a much more relaxed environment.

It is also possible there could be a savings on meals, as most time shares have a full kitchen, and it is not inconceivable any partner in a firm may not prefer to watch the big game on TV and throw a nice steak on the grill just outside their door. I did this many times and felt the associated relaxation in blue jeans was a nice way to keep an already 10-hour day from becoming a 15-hour day because of a long business dinner. Many times, my client was sharing my suite at my invitation for a day or two, often resulting in our conducting business. We acknowledge this arrangement is not likely to fit most companies, but for a select few, this alternative could be a huge executive or partner perk, and in the end, after the membership is paid for, result in larger profits to the firm because of reduced travel costs.

It is possible it may require some small business adjustments to get to the right time share location, or your city just does not provide a good time share solution. Sometimes, client meetings can be in any one of a few cities that might be convenient for both parties or a short Uber or limo ride away. Either way, a bit of research in this area can really provide a leg up for those firms that want to hire the best and the brightest and treat them well. Given the vast array of perks now associated with the top time share operators, a firm can also procure top VIP tickets to sporting events and use them for either top clients or partners who got that big deal closed. The owner of the firm could also elect to just take the points with him or her when retirement time has arrived. There are many options with these programs that could help make the dreaded business trip much more productive while actually cutting costs in the long run.

What are the time share benefits to a firm? These benefits can be worthwhile on both the tax and morale side of your business. There are different tax strategies involved since using your time share to conduct business may or may not allow you to deduct the value of the villa stay. In most cases, if your villa is priced at or below the cost of a hotel stay, it should qualify as a legitimate business expense. In any case, the villa stays at or below the same hotel stay provides a much more relaxed environment and a better place to unwind and be productive.

In other cases, it could make sense for your business to purchase the time share although the tax deductions are best advised by your tax advisor. The other intangible is the value of having an employee use the time share after they closed that big deal. Nothing says "thank you" more than a warm beach or nice ski vacation. Perhaps the biggest value is when you sell your business company, and you can take the time share with you, thus, converting a necessary business tool into a great retirement perk. I was able to add to my portfolio by using many weeks of time shares for business and now enjoy those weeks in my preretirement years.

Cost of Business Travel in major US city
for a small hotel suite in 4.5 star hotel-2017

# of Nights	Nightly Rate	Tax 7.500%	Total day	Total 30
30	$565	$42.38	$607	$18,221
10	$565	$42.38	$607	$6,074

Cost of buying 30 days of time share using a
50/50 purchase from org developer and resell market

Low Price	High Price	Average	12 months Main Fee
$85,000	$125,000	$105,000	$6,800

Hotel Bill	Maintenance Fee	Savings from Hotel	Cost of TS	**ROI**
$24,295	$6,800	$17,495	$105,000	16.66%

1) Assumes 30 days of Hotel Use in a Mini Suite 4.5 Star Hotel
2) Major US city like LA, New York, Dallas, San Francisco
3) Assumes that for 10 days, 2 partners share a 2+2 Villa, hence the hotel model reflects the need for 40 nights in a single room.
4) Does not assume using streched or discount points.
5) Time Share alternative may be quite a bit larger and may include 2 bedrroms, 2 baths, and a kitchen, living and dining room.

CHAPTER 7

How Gen X, Boomers, and Millennials Will Change Time Share

THE TIME SHARE appraisal dilemma: In a normal real estate environment in most neighborhoods throughout America, it is a fairly orderly and disciplined process to evaluate what a home should be worth. Most appraisers start with a land value built into the price of the home, and at some point, the cost of the home minus depreciation enters the appraisal process. Many like-kind homes built at the same time with five or six models often trade within a few thousand dollars of each other, even when they sell for over $1M. As consumers, we buy a home to live in and provide a safe and nurturing environment for our kids. We then, over time, may trade up into a nicer home that is usually bigger with larger rooms. This can mean more landscaping, more maintenance, and the eventual remodel, followed by the inevitable refinance to help pay for the remodel to bring the home up to what brand-new homes offer in the same neighborhood. After all, we look at the last one or two real estate cycles and convince ourselves the market will certainly reward us for a bigger kitchen, an extra bathroom, and we also know buyers will have to pay up for the house once they see that media room we gloriously assembled to watch the Super Bowl.

This appreciation pattern, despite occasional setbacks, has worked well for many decades since World War I, all the way through the year 1995. It seemed normal in the United States to just expect that new and remodeled homes, in particular, always go up in value until the mid-1990s, when the next 10 years saw some price declines as high as 50%, even in some top markets. Interest rates had risen, the economy had slowed, and housing started to come to a crawl as Wall Street had overfunded the housing market. Most baby boomers saw, for the first time, what always had gone straight up in the form of home appreciation had finally gone down, and it was not until late 2008 when markets hit the bottom. It would take years to slowly recover. The big short was on. Too much debt, too much lending, and too much fake income. The bubble had to burst, and when it hit on a national level as it did in 2008–2009, it meant the recovery would likely take years to heal, unwind, and reprice.

The prior trading patterns for home appreciation from 1970 to early 2008, despite their own cyclical downturns, were supported by the bottom of the pyramid always being bigger than the top. This prior housing upswings of the past decades have always been solidified by tens of millions of baby boomers who have been in line to trade up, pay more, and take out the family above them so they could retire, and then downsize. Millions and millions of homes have now entered the $1M price tag, with nearly any home with three or four bedrooms near an ocean now priced well over $1M. Those that are not far off from the beach trade happily for three-quarters of that amount, and so forth. I remember growing up in Los Angeles and attending a high school near downtown Los Angeles.

I was also a real estate broker in Los Angles at 20 years old and remember the prices of homes 25 miles inland in tough neighborhoods were selling for $45,000. These homes today routinely sell for nearly $200,000 or more. Many of these homes are not as big as a large three-car garage. This across-the-board repricing had to occur as the slightly higher neighborhood 1 or 2 miles away went up. It was a natural real estate occurrence to see each pricing market readjust to reflect the new prices paid just above and below comparable properties that were close by.

We are facing an interesting real estate forecast unlike anything in the past 50 years. Let's start with what the current U.S. population pyramid is facing: According to a recent study by Goldman Sachs Investment Research, we had the following estimates for millennials, Gen X, and baby boomers:

United States aging statistics and the relationship to future housing as of 2015

Millennials	Gen X	Baby Boomers
92M	61M	77M
Ages 15–36	Ages 37–50	Ages 51–70

In a normal real estate bell curve, this might pose an exciting picture. We see that millennials will exceed the population of baby boomers, meaning that as they enter into the prime life cycle to purchase homes, they will have a bigger base and more income. One would think this would bode well for continued price increases for housing on top of U.S. net migration. Baby boomers will actually start to decline as more boomers begin to die off than migrate into the population. The problem with the millennial population is that they are holding off getting married, with the average age moving from 23 in the 1970s to just over 30 years old in 2010. Even worse, married couples living in their own home has now dropped from 56% in 1968 to 23% in 2012. Under any scenario, almost 33M people moving into their prime income years are not buying a starter home and/or will not need one for at least 7 years later from what used to be the majority of people in their late 20s or 30s. This delayed trend does not count the number of millennials who have no desire to ever purchase a home or do not have the income to purchase.

According to Jeremy Rifkin, a noted author and economist, in 25 years, one-quarter of millennials will not own a car; instead, will rely on Uber or use a "shared car" plan. If almost one-quarter of the auto market in the millennial age does not wish to own a car, and with nearly 75% of baby boomers retiring without enough money, where do we think auto sales are going to go in the United States, and what does this trend suggest for the housing markets?

The new millennial time share model—the perfect fit for shared housing: Now this brings us back to the time share concept of "shared housing." The millennial generation is filled with statistics on Internet shopping with over 57% routinely checking prices on their iPhone, even for everyday purchases. Most millennials in study after study want more activity, more exercise, healthier food, and do not want to be constrained with even a car payment. This does not seem like a good market for a jumbo mortgage. Millennials do not want the same debt as was typical with baby boomers, nor do they want to be tied down to a mortgage. They want shared cars and, increasingly, we believe they are going to demand shared housing that feels like home ownership. The challenge for developers is how to anticipate this trend. According to *USA Today,* on March 21st, a survey by Fidelity revealed that over 60% of current-day millennials between the ages of 18–35 are living with either friends, roommates, or their parents. This is the highest level of non-apartment or home living in 115 years. This is a serious trend line. Not since the horse-and-buggy days has our early adult population been so far removed from traditional forms of housing. How are expensive move-up homes going to be purchased if the driving economic engine of the past 3 decades is not even starting with housing until after age 35?

This will, for the first time, create a need to adjust the current time share model to fit the needs of first-time buyers seeking a time share rather than a home. This should include a small urban component because millennials have grown up with coffee and juice bars as part of their routine. They also have a stronger commitment to exercise, so walking and hiking trails in nature environments will need to be included. They also will need workout and gym space that is more spread out, includes TVs while working out, and likely some yoga and other classes geared toward a more relaxing lifestyle and state of mind. Having a shared car lot for that occasional car need and being on the axis point for public transportation will be critical. Millennials understand the last mile connection issue with both the physical world and the Internet world. Of course, free Internet on-site will be assumed. On the plus side, some design elements like partial lofts with a pullout or permanent bed, nearby storage, and any access to the physical world like coffee shops, the local tavern or drugstore, will complete the top wish lists for millennials. They do not require access to information like libraries and universities. They grew up learning on the Internet. We predict that developers will soon offer 3-, 6-, 9-, and 12-month time share stays which will be the perfect fit for the mobile lifestyle this age group embraces.

While this new "portable mortgage concept" has yet to emerge fully, its roots are already in place, thanks to the time share industry. The millennials who now shun a $250,000 home mortgage for a permanent home are more likely to embrace a mortgage that allows them the freedom to move to a new place as their mood and lifestyle change. The idea of just packing up and moving to the next place is exactly the selling point they want to maintain, an open and free-flowing lifestyle. This will require developers to hone in on design elements, initially designing this concept into a larger, more traditional time share while using a portion of the land to specifically address this market. We predict this concept will be a reality within the next 7 years.

We predict these newer, longer time share stays will add some luxuries, like upgraded sheets and bed covers, custom dishes, and a dining room option complete with china, crystal, and upgraded silverware. Artwork niches will also allow these new buyers a chance to display their artwork, and combined with high-tech photo walls, this shared home will now have all of the individual features that are aligned with home ownership. Of course, one building will have to include pet owners with dog runs.

CHAPTER **8**

What Does the Ideal Time Share Portfolio Look Like?

EXPLORING THE TIME share allocation model: The new time share world has changed immensely over the past decade, with more products and pricing plans than ever before. I often get asked, what is the best way to purchase a time share? The answer is that it depends on what you want out of your time share. The first thing to do is ascertain over the next 20 to 30 years, what you think your vacation and retirement plans will look like. This is very important because it will help you set a strategy to acquire the right time shares at the right prices over time. For example, do you prefer maximum flexibility with a large global footprint, or do you want to go to Hawaii every year at the same time and stay in the same place? These would utilize different approaches to purchasing different types of time shares.

If you wish to travel 2 to 3 months after you retire every year but only need about 4 weeks of time a year before you retire, then this would require you planning on buying about a month of time now, with a well conceived plan to add certain time shares to your portfolio as you near retirement. There can be a great reward for those who know what they want and are willing to exercise caution and patience to assemble a world-class time share portfolio. Understanding what the expectations are, what type of budget you can work with over time, and how active you want to manage your time share all play a vital role in putting together the right mix of brands and time shares. Some people will be better off using just one brand and getting a high-level membership in one company, while others will do better buying two or three brands because a combination of different time share operators will better fit their profile.

Other consumers may want a more balanced "retirement portfolio," designed to get them more time for their money. Another buyer may want a high-luxury portfolio with a large percentage of fixed weeks in ground-zero locations. This will cost much more money but could provide millions in savings over many years if acquired across different platforms looking for top-shelf Category One properties. Whatever time share requirements you may have, taking the time to learn about how the products differ can help provide decades of enjoyment right from the start. The enclosed type of timeshares can create dozens of possibilities, to provide a blend of different products that should help you pinpoint your time share objectives.

Basic types of time share weeks:

Get a workhorse week or two: We call a workhorse week an old legacy week that has high trading value and comes with a lower-than-normal maintenance fee. A workhorse week could also be a time share that is perhaps less popular than a prime time beach or ski location, but it offers excellent value for a long shoulder season. A good example might be a desert week for the months of January or February, where you could stay for 3 of 4 weeks for what a week in ski season costs. In the former case, this might be a time share that was sold over 10 years ago and had a maintenance fee formula for a fixed location but provides significant up trade options every year. While the maintenance fee has likely risen over time, its 1 week equivalent likely sells for more money and has a higher maintenance fee. In the second case, the location is not quite warm enough to entice prime season, but still has weather in the 70s most of the time and offers exceptional occupancy value, providing the opportunity to double or triple stretch your out-of-pocket cost to stay there.

These legacy weeks allow you to stay in the same resort or find a superior trade without much trouble. These are hard-to-find time share weeks, but they do exist. You must understand the trading value of this type of week. Generally, it will be a lock-off unit offering up to three bedrooms and could be a holiday week or very likely it is in prime season, either in Hawaii or in ski season. It is likely in a ground-zero location that may be even better than some of the newer properties. The value of the week is that you can convert it into points and routinely get 2 to 4 weeks use at other properties, year in and year out, with little effort. You also end up saving up to 10% to 15% on maintenance fees because it uses an older formula that vested with the week well before the new points-based system became more commonplace.

Buy a foreclosure week: A foreclosure week is likely a week that the developer took back for lack of payments or acquired via a short sale. While these weeks can also be difficult to find, most developers want to return these weeks back to consumers so they can collect the maintenance fees. They often sell for 75% less than conventional weeks or points. Many developers will let their top customers or employees buy these weeks. They may also, at times, allow an open sale to the public but may usually require you also buy an equivalent week of equal or greater value and pay full price for the second week. These can be very good deals if the total package fits your future travel needs. If one or both of these weeks can provide a good portion of your portfolio needs, this is a great way to average down your total acquisition costs.

Purchasing a secondary market time share: The secondary market can provide huge savings in the short run, but depending on your overall strategy, could also actually cost you money in the long run. You need to understand how the membership rules effect your future benefits, like short-term booking discounts, as an example. While the secondary market purchase makes more sense for a fixed week, fixed location because it only has one purpose, the trading value of such a week could be compromised if you purchased the week on the secondary market. These details are important relative to your overall objectives, so make sure you get the facts from the developer on how a secondary purchase will impact your booking and trading rights. Secondary week purchases can make good sense or work against you, depending on the circumstances. As a general rule, if you like the week and intend to occupy most of the time, the waived developer rights will not matter. However, if you needed the developer to add your week to your membership level and the week does not count, then its purchase would not suit the reason you bought the week. Also, you need to understand how the time share you bought can be traded and whether it brings any real trade value, both in and out of network. Understanding what the week adds to your portfolio in terms of trading and booking rights will help address this question.

A fixed week and fixed location-the Rolls Royce of time shares. : A fixed week, fixed location is the "Rolls-Royce" of time shares if you are on the beach or have a ski in/ski out villa and the week is a prime holiday week. This type of purchase is the closest thing to actual ownership because you have the right to occupy the same villa, at the same time, every year. One of the elements of time share is uncertainty of time and location. By removing these concerns, a fixed week and location begin to represent actual home ownership, especially in those situations where the owner has 6 or 8 weeks. If you own just a week, this is a great asset, and we believe owners of this type of time share will see real appreciation over the next decade. Holiday weeks in these types of time shares are even more valuable and will far outpace every other kind of time share. In an ideal portfolio, everyone that can afford a holiday week should at least look into the cost, as these weeks have a very high trading and renting capability, and demand is always very high. Even if you never planned to use the week, just owning one or more holiday weeks is a real asset to the family. Although these weeks are usually more expensive, they also more than make up for the premium because of their trade and rental demand.

The lock-off week: Lock-off owners know all too well the power of buying one villa, and then trading it for 2 or 3 weeks. These types of time share ownerships are strong workhorses for just adding time to your portfolio. They are the engines of retirement planning since they can deliver, pound for pound, lower maintenance cost per night and more nights per year, thus, providing plenty of ways to season your maintenance fees and increase your RRC ratio through longer stays. They also can make great rentals, particularly in ski locations where an extra bedroom is always in demand. Lock-off weeks are now hard to find and usually just available through the secondary market or through the developer resale list where the developer took back the unit from the original owners.

These have a lower default rate because owners have learned how to maximize their value, often renting out one side of the lock-off and staying for free every year on the other side.

Own a prime holiday week: We remain very bullish about prime holiday weeks that are well located and managed by the top operators. We believe they are currently undervalued by 50% to 100% and could see very good appreciation over the next decade. The fact is, there is just a very limited supply of these weeks, and there are more and more owners realizing that owning a prime holiday week is just as valuable as owning a home in Vail or Hawaii, since the main reason for owning is to gather families over the holidays. While this transition will take time to unfold, we believe the combination of an electronic network aligned with higher resale prices will start to spur banks to enter this market since the very top 2-week holiday time shares in the best locations could easily start to trade north of $500,000, making the price points closer aligned to the housing market in many parts of the country on a pure dollar basis. This liquidity will spur more speculation into this product since owners and families will feel better investing larger sums into this product as the possibility for exit and resale becomes more efficient. We see this trend already underway in year over year resales in 2017 and some of the best increases in many years.

Buy a maintenance fee week or 2: If you dig hard enough on the resale market, you can find some older legacy weeks that operate under maintenance fees that are based on the cost of a particular property versus a weighted average of a regional, national, or even international formula. If you are allowed to trade this week into points, and the week has a, relatively speaking, high trade value, you now own the "trading currency" at a discount to the market. Over many years, this will have a very positive effect on your RRC ratio, as well as help reduce your payback indicator, ultimately providing more high-quality vacation time at a lower cost. To determine this first, find out how much it takes to buy a fixed some of points for the program you are looking at buying. Then you can find out if you can buy a legacy week that converts into roughly the same amount of points. After squaring the price per point, you can then compare the maintenance fee for each one and see which one has the lowest maintenance fee per point. While this spread may not be much in many cases, we have seen spreads as high as 30%, meaning, in one simple transaction, you can forever reduce your fees by 30%, just by acquiring the right legacy week.

Time share opposites attract—Portfolio Conclusion. I have often been asked does it make sense to buy different kinds of weeks or even buy time shares from more than one company. The answer is, that depends on what your goals are with your time shares. Many types of time shares products are complementary, like, for example, a holiday Christmas week is a very nice way to tuck away a 1-month ski vacation or Hawaiian holiday because you can book around your holiday week with other kinds of time shares, thus, assuring yourself of entry into the busiest time of year. Fixed holiday weeks can also pay for over a month of regular weeks on the maintenance side, so often, you can set up your portfolio to provide all kinds of financial or vacation time at the price point that works best for you. We recommend once you determine what your long-term time share and retirement goals are, you take a look at assembling some complementary time share products that will best fit your future needs. We have these forms available on the Web site which can guide you through the process and help determine how best to acquire a dream portfolio that will provide for a very comfortable vacation and retirement future.

CHAPTER 9

Fourteen Clues Your Time Share Company Will Be Around in 20 Years

THE FOLLOWING LIST is something you should pay attention to when looking at a time share company that will survive the test of time over the next 20 years:

1. **Land acquisitions —history and process**: It may seem odd at first blush, but the biggest challenge for large private or public time share companies is finding land that can be zoned at an affordable price to build a new resort. In addition, multiple jurisdictions like the local zoning bodies, FAA in some cases, environmental boards, coastal commissions, and city ordinances can, combined, make zoning for a large resort almost impossible. In extreme cases like in parts of California, it could take up to 20 years just to complete zoning for a large-scale oceanfront project. The entire coastline of California at the time this book went to print, likely does not have even three or four properties that

could be developed into a large ocean-facing project. Every single timeshare company would likely start construction tomorrow on such a project if it were available. Land is so scare in some parts of the world it can take up to 35% of an entire budget to acquire, build, and construct a large-scale time share project, easily now topping several hundred million to build just one large resort.

While you do not need to drill into great detail on how and where your time share company intends to build, just look at their current footprint, number of projects, etc., and ask them what have they opened recently, and what is the next project they plan to open. If they have not opened any new projects in the past 5 years and do not have any under construction at the time you purchase, just be aware this could be the case for years to come, or worse, they may not have the personnel, budget, and talent in place to pursue a growth plan. Planning to build even small but well located projects takes time, large resources, and many talented teams to get through the zoning and construction process, and this is why "What have they done lately?" is an important clue to their potential downstream plans. For some, this may not matter if you like your time share company's current portfolio, and their current inventory is all you are looking for. However, a company that is opening new resorts is a good sign the company will lead with new products and locations rather than just hold on with little or no growth.

2. **Mastering the entitlement process**: For those of you not familiar with what "entitlement process" means,

in a nutshell, it means having all your permit and approval ducks in a clean, neat row. In order to build, you need an overall plan and very detailed plans that specify how big a project will be, unit sizes, building footprints, building heights, architectural and structural plans, amenity packages like golf courses and/or tennis courts, as well as details for parking, sewers, drainage, electrical, etc. Obtaining these approvals can be costly and expensive. This is why it is better to align with a time share company that has been developing their own properties, and preferably for many years. This gives them proven teams of people in place to help add and redevelop properties that existing owners can enjoy. Also, the pace of building new properties is important, so all customers have plenty of choices in which to book vacations and the amount of online and coming online inventory is always high enough to service the amount of vacation customers with high satisfaction numbers. Some of the top time share brands have satisfaction numbers in excess of 90% for overall satisfaction, and even for first-time booking choices. This requires a huge effort to achieve year in and year out.

3. **Real estate development**: Since we know land can be very expensive, we also can assume the actual construction process is a large part of the budget. Time share companies that have long project track records both here and abroad will likely play a major role in time share over the next 20 years. In particular, managing projects in multiple countries requires a large legal and accounting staff to keep projects on time and on budget. Since many of the larger time share

companies are public, it is easy to keep abreast of their project plans by reading their press releases and their annual reports, 10-Qs, or audited financials. These provide important clues about projects underway, setbacks, lawsuits, and many regulatory issues. They also provide guidance on how well your time share company is growing. While most consumers will likely never read these documents, having a handle on how time share companies are managing their current and downstream projects is another clue on how well the company will likely be doing in 5 years. New projects tend to be located in high-demand or wait list areas. This helps create new sales for those customers who may have the hottest new locations in their future vacation plan.

4. **Hospitality alliances**: It is not a surprise that some hotel companies chose to enter the time share business. Who is more capable of understanding how to maintain a hotel suite, keep cost low, and more important, create and develop a hotel brand with customer loyalty? The large hotel chains that are in the time share business. How much more at stake than nonhotel-vested companies. A bad customer experience in a hotel or villa could cause serious customer ill will in the other. It is vitally important to build consumer loyalty that these companies maintain the highest degree of customer satisfaction rates.

   The top hotel companies also benefit from huge supply chain discounts, have the budgets to invest in technology, and can offer cross vacation experiences in both hotels and time share properties. This helps create a more flexible global footprint that really makes international travel seamless. I would highly recommend considering using a hotel operator as your time share company of choice if you plan on visiting smaller locations around the world where large-scale resorts meet demand profiles to warrant construction.

The large international time share operators with hotels also have deep experience in overseas management, and most of all, are set up to provide for a lower maintenance fee because they can create a much-larger footprint at a lower cost per night given their buying power on the hotel side. Remember, villas require furniture, flat screens, bathtubs, and even full kitchens, something the hotel companies have been building for many decades. They understand how to reduce costs. They also understand the traveling customer better, having decades of studies under their belt.

5. **Marketing and sales**: In addition to absorbing the high cost of land and construction, the next biggest cost for selling time shares is marketing and sales. The time share industry now employs over 600,000 people, all of whom support and execute the marketing and sales process. It is vital in order to grow, that large-scale time share companies be able to move inventory as it comes online. The time share business can be fickle and can experience challenges in tough economies. The industry, however, requires successful sales in good times and in bad in order to support billions of dollars in acquisitions to help fuel newer projects. This makes the sales process

very dependent on top sales executives. Large global or North American companies that have invested in technology and sales have the infrastructure in place to handle this task. Interestingly, they will also play a vital role in helping to solve the secondary market process as information and technology improvements will allow them to lead this effort. It is important to understand if your time share company is experiencing year-over-year growth, particularly when the economy is fairly stable, as it is a sign they have the resources to weather an economic downturn, again, all of which may affect your membership many years down the road.

6. **Food and beverage**: This may seem silly but think about your favorite locations and ask how the food and beverage service is. You should call your favorite resort directly to get the best information. In some cases, there is none, and if this is not a big deal as an amenity, it may not matter to you. I have been to some really great resorts, out at the pool with dozens of people, only to discover the food and beverage service is either closed or nonexistent. I would just sit there and count how much money is being lost, only to become frustrated that such a simple service is not being offered. When cutbacks or seasonal demand falls, sometimes F&B gets cut, and our vacation experience is then compromised.

   As consumers spending money on vacation in prime locations and in any season, most of us would like some type of food and beverage service. This helps drive revenue and profits to help operate the resort but also adds a convenience factor to the vacation experience. While not critical in three-star locations, it is a must for most travelers today looking for a total vacation experience. Plans and restaurants can vary a lot, even between the same companies. It is not a question that comes up often, but if lying around the pool and not having to get up and drive to lunch or make lunch is a nice benefit, check and see if these services come with your locations. They are generally included in the larger resort operators, especially those who operate on the hotel side as they are used to investing in this type of offering anyway. If a time share company can support an F&B program, it is likely they also have more staff for security, maintenance, and the grounds will be better maintained. F&B is just a clue as to how complete the commitment is to make sure your stay is top notch. All of these items can, and do, vary a lot. If you drive through a large pothole in the parking lot to get to your unit, chances are, something is not going to work in your unit.

7. **Computer infrastructure and networking**: Large-scale data centers and multi-hundred million to billion dollar-plus computer networks are now the norm in the Fortune 500 and are a necessity to keep up with rising regulatory requirements and to service large-scale customer service demands quickly and efficiently. The world is becoming more complex with the largest Fortune 500 companies now having as many as 8,000 critical and noncritical applications and data banks to run worldwide applications. We now have dozens of software programs just to run and check on the thousands of programs running. In other words, the world now uses software to run, manage, maintain, operate, and fix . . . you guessed it, the software it monitors.

A simple 1-week time share reservation—what that means for a global network: Let's look at what software of today and what software a few years from now will have to do in the time share industry for you to just make a simple reservation. You start by entering a Web site that has to check one or more data banks to see if that December week in Hawaii is available. It will then also check to make sure your account is in good standing and that you have the currency to pay for the vacation. Once you decide you want the week, it may ask details about your vacation, and then query special requests on beds, high chairs, special needs, or things like views and size of units. In other words, what may look like seconds to you is actually a computer sourcing several pieces of information to get you your answers. Now then, what if this resort was adding another building to accommodate more guests? The first tower is sold out, and the second is nearing completion. It is now February, but the tower expects to open 100 of their 200 units in November. The computer now needs to check a construction calendar and make sure certain approvals are in place, proving the project will remain on schedule. More databases, more searches. It concludes the three bedrooms are sold out, but an increased query reveals the system does have a two-bedroom available. You agree and the reservation gets booked. You might think this is the end of computer involvement. Many downstream statistics will remain in motion. For example, the three-resort restaurants need to order food so F&B needs to understand with the new tower opening, it will need more pineapples, so your stay now may now be the one that triggers another pineapple order.

Supply chain management continues to monitor the new tower filling up, now triggering a need for more security guards. Human resources now can start interviewing in a few months, so it sends an advisement request to, you guessed it, another computer. It knows to activate an interview request in April based on analysis from a research firm that checked data banks and concluded the resort will need 4 months to fill the position. Once again, one computer talking to another one. You ordered extra pillows, and housekeeping just got a notice their order has been delayed by 3 months due to a strike. Now a pillow disaster is unfolding quietly as your reservation nears. This will, of course, require actual human intervention. Will an actual human-to-human meeting help solve this doomed event? With a bit of luck, your pillow will show up and you will be spared the inconvenience. Thank God computers were able to communicate this emergency in plenty of time.

The wind surfing instructor will need more equipment because the recreation data bank gets notified to expect 100 more rooms filled for December. Better order more surfboards. Once unit 54 got booked, another computer figured out based on the first 54 reservations what day the resort will likely hit 100 rooms sold with a 98% degree of probability. This is the power of predictive software helping you out on your vacation. The marketing department now has to activate its marketing plan due to the increased wave of traffic to, of course, do its job of selling more memberships. More computers need to talk to more computers. Certain blind data may be sold to certain island computer data banks that pay money, not to have your name and phone number, but just to know how many guests are expected on the island. The emergency number 911 likes to know this as an example. They can predict heart attacks with this information which, of course, might trigger the computers suggesting another ambulance is needed to keep up with the predictive demand.

Naturally, the resort bars now know for every 20 guests that book, they need 1.6 cases of beer for the week; hence, the need to convey your reservation into the F&B ordering pool and the process is once again repeated. What happened if you called in your reservation and wanted your travel advisor to handle this reservation, including the airfare? Now we have to start all over again with not just the above, but we need to check 15 airlines to see if they can help fly you back and forth. One airline now needs to see if the new plane order will arrive as projected because current traffic capacity is sold out. They will need to check some computers for this answer. When your reservation is finally complete, it will then be logged into a safety and weather advisory data bank so if that type 4 category hurricane that was not supposed to be there at that time of year, suddenly developed, you can be contacted in route if necessary to warn of an emergency evacuation. We could go on with more examples, but suffice it to say virtually any large-scale global business is now dependent on investing in large-scale networks for their business to remain competitive. Communicating in real time is no longer a wish list item. This ability must be present throughout the network to minimize the loss of customer goodwill when things go wrong and to maximize economic returns when crowds are at a peak and supplies are needed before guests arrive. Most of all, the time share company of tomorrow will need this network more than ever to deliver on emerging trends in the industry. It is this level of commitment that is and will continue to be necessary to make your stay more enjoyable, and for that matter, to help you sleep at night with that extra foam pillow you ordered.

8. **Human resources**: The time share business requires expertise in many industries. In fact, the skills are so varied and so wide, it requires a full-time staff to help, organize, hire, train, and manage so many disciplines ranging from land acquisitions and construction management through hotel and resort management, and then marketing, sales, and just as important, the thousands of employees needed to manage it all. Human resources, in the long run, helps hire better people, reduce turnover, and maintain compliance. While not a direct issue on looking at your time share, a large international and national footprint helps reduce employee turnover and lawsuits, all something that eventually will show up in the time share maintenance fees. The large international time share operators who invest in managing people will have lower maintenance fees in the long run because they can optimize the hiring of people at a lower cost by using technologies and by having better hiring processes necessary to reduce lawsuits and employee turnover.

9. **Supply chain management**: Again, while not something you may think about firsthand but keeping cost down is a huge part of why firms need a supply chain process to maintain competitive pricing. Since the time share business requires so many raw materials to source, build, and maintain large-scale real estate projects, it is essential to be able to source goods and services all over the world. Even small adjustments, if unexpected, have a profound effect on sales, and therefore, require a constant monitoring ability to keep prices as low as possible. The larger time share companies have long established supply chain teams and computers in place to help manage this challenge. Finding and closing on great land parcels and knowing how to purchase 5,000 beds at the lowest cost for the quality you need is important in keeping operating and product costs as low as possible.

   You may again ask, what does supply chain management have to do with my time share? It has a lot to do with it if you care about your maintenance fees. Our evaluation of owning a time share must consider the costs, and as owners, we must absorb the cost to build, maintain, and grow with the company or companies we have chosen to invest in owning as a time share. Supply chain management in simple terms is just the process for procuring, ordering, and renewing everything from raw materials, food, equipment, renewables, and even personnel. Large international companies spend lots of money on just software to help them find the lowest cost producer that has the highest quality products for the price level they are shooting for. Saving in fractions of pennies on worldwide supply needs can help get your fee from going up 2% from 1.5%. While that may not seem like much, the problem is that savings on products or finding materials at below what the competitive landscape pays for them, all provide valuable savings to the customer, who ultimately pays the bill.

As we all know, our time share, well managed, regardless of how you chose to value it, is worth more if the time share company is up to date with the latest in supply chain management technology and execution. You know your time share company is doing a great job if your fees have risen at or around the rate of inflation year after year. Conversely, if your fees went up 6% in a year when inflation was 3%, your time share company is executing at well above the overall inflation rate. That said, it is very possible your fees could rise slightly above annual rates of inflation under a well managed program because all time share companies need to operate in several different businesses and tend to require a great deal of human capital in order to grow. If medical costs and premiums are running at 20% year after year increases in a critical area like health care, then time share companies must absorb this into their budgets. The industry has a self-vested interest in keeping fees as low as possible because these fees affect their ability to sell their product. If your bill runs slightly higher than the rate of inflation, understand that tens of millions are needed to pay for medical plans across many subindustries like real estate development, marketing, and sales, on top of resort maintenance and operations.

It is also possible for many time share companies with smaller footprints to struggle to keep up with this formula. The important thing is to back test your time share company and research the past 10 years and analyze past fee increases. The past 10-year track record will reveal a very good clue on what the next 10 years is likely to look like in the way of fee increases, assuming similar interest rates and inflationary cycles for the next 10 years.

10. **Web-Site development and technology management**: As a cofounding and former chairman of the board of a software company for over 15 years, I can tell you that the future of time shares is in many things, and of utmost importance is creating and maintaining large global networks with state-of-the-art software. With new generations of customers managing nearly all of their purchases on laptops and cell phones, next-gen sales to baby boomers and millennials put even more pressure on the industry to keep reinventing the marketing, sales, and reservation process. This takes enormous capital to design and develop, and often can take 7–10 years to fully implement. The challenge is at the end of that life cycle, how much of your prior systems will be outdated and what type of design changes are needed to keep up with next-generation demand cycles.

11. **Ability to innovate and lead**: The times share company of the future will require even more complex Web interfaces, real-time recovery solutions, more point of sale opportunities, state-of-the-art mobile applications, larger and more complex databases, and most

of all, a network design that allows hundreds or even thousands of mission critical applications to work in a seamless fashion 24 hours a day, 365 days a year. The company that can provide that private, over-the-water suite in Bora Bora, with a virtual tour before you book inside and out will continue to grab the market share. In addition, information like real-time water temperature, live streaming video showing the fish swimming below your floor in real time, taking your grocery and wine list order for predelivery to your hut while delivering a confirmed reservation with your airfare, shuttle, and special ticket events, all in a few keystrokes on your cell phone, will lead the time share industry of the future.

12. **Public access to the capital markets**: It is hard to imagine a business that needs more capital than the time share business. Customers continually want to see more locations and choices with increasing flexibility. Just finding one gold mine in a remote location, getting the land properly zoned, and then beginning and completing the construction process can take years and require hundreds of millions of dollars for just one project. Raising equity on Wall Street is dilutive to shareholders and requires the time share company be able to prove new and more expensive projects will add more shareholder value than it will take to create a new project. This can often be a debate among the analysts who follow public companies. If your time share company was missing a key location in Hawaii, and the studies confirmed it will be very expensive to construct, will take extra time and money to get through zoning, and due to completing economic

projects, may not allow for large rental or time share price increases, do you build the project? The answer may come down to what is your cost of capital? Time share companies that cannot access the public markets easily cannot grow as fast as those that can. If you can obtain capital from Wall Street, you need a strong track record in place to continue to raise hundreds of millions. Either way, the process is a balancing act, and with one large mistake, companies could need years to recover. Pay attention to your time share's company's track record. Where are recent openings in high demand a year later? Did the project sell out in high season? If not, that is not a good sign. Many time share companies will plan to build two or three towers, and then wait to confirm the first one fills up over and over before constructing the second tower. This is smart and means they are protecting your investment in your time share.

13. **A large and existing hotel/resort footprint**: In the time share business, you cannot get bigger unless you grow by either acquisition or build more resorts. It is easier to grow a larger footprint with thousands of people in place than to start from scratch. It is hard to get bigger unless you are already big, and you cannot get really big without being bigger in the first place. In other words, size matters because things like your cost of capital and supply chains are far more competitive when doing billions of dollars a year in business versus hundreds of millions per year. This does not mean smaller regional time share companies cannot thrive, but their margin of error is very small, and keeping too much debt off their balance sheet is critical to staying

competitive so they may have to grow very slowly by completing one project before starting another one. Today's larger companies can have $500M-plus under construction and still have the gunpowder to tie up downstream properties and close on them, if only to hold the land for a few years.

14. **Maintenance fee management**: Maintenance fee management is usually the most important element of your membership. You have control over how much time share or "points" you wish to purchase, but you do not have control over your maintenance fee and/or the future rate of increases and/or assessment. The time share companies that will produce the most consistent RRC ratios of 2.5 or higher to 1 or are trending up are examples of time shares that are managing their maintenance programs efficiently. This also means they have pay back ratios below 10 years, factoring in all of the maintenance fees as well. Remember, it is very difficult to compare maintenance fees by the price per foot or price per time share purchase unless you are sure you are comparing apples to apples. Many of the large-scale programs have significant amenity packages with multiple pools, golf courses, restaurants, and many on-site activities.

    These programs cost money to maintain, so you need to carefully examine what is important to you when evaluating fees from one company to another. Be sure to ask whether your fee is based on just your home property or is it a weighted average among some regional choices. Some of the largest time share companies now have global portfolios where fees are pooled among many dozens, or even hundreds of properties. Therefore, local maintenance fees would not apply. The best way to look at maintenance fees is to ask for a printout of the past 10 years and see if the rate of increases has exceeded the rate of inflation. The past 10 years we have been in a relatively low inflationary environment, meaning maintenance fees should be fairly mild, in the 2% to 3% range per year. If your company is much higher than that, then it means their costs are running higher than the rate of inflation, and you need to understand why.

CHAPTER **10**

The Time Share Maintenance Fee Debate

WHY TIME SHARE cost(s) are lower than you think: Where and how are maintenance fees subject to increase? Perhaps one of the biggest issues surrounding time shares is the purchaser who is concerned about the maintenance fee that is associated with time shares. The irony is, most people do not know what their own maintenance fee is for the house they live in, and if they did figure it out, many people would be shocked! Owning a home or even renting an apartment costs a lot of money beyond just the mortgage or rent, taxes, and insurance payments. Many homes and even small apartments routinely get utility bills in peak heating and air-conditioning months that run up to $1,000 a month. In some luxury neighborhoods around the country where water is scare and the home involves a large yard, water bills can run over $3,500 a month in the summer. Most of all, every home requires maintenance that, in the end, always comes down to a cost per day. In many older homes, things like roofs, septic tanks, older electrical systems, pools, Jacuzzis, and deck remodels can easily take up to $50,000 to upgrade or replace. Somewhere in the math, when a home gets bought, that number needs to be understood. Factoring in all of these costs plus a mortgage, it is not unusual to see a couple living in a modest home that really cost them $150, $300, and even $400 a day . . . or more when all of the costs are considered. We provide a detailed example of this in Chapter 21, "The Time Share Beachfront Index," where we compared a 1,550 square foot time share on the beach with a 1,550 square foot home on the beach.

Time shares can, at first blush, look like they have a high cost per day in expenses until you understand all of the rules in your program. When you factor in seasonal discounts, membership status discounts, a few days of rental a year you could receive, all of a sudden, that $175 or $200 a day when you first bought can be managed down to under $50 a day under certain situations. Unlike homes, the time share company does not have the option of delaying repairs, not fixing the fountains, or maintaining the landscaping in top condition. Many time share owners have come to expect their time share villa to be in much better shape than their own house. Every villa I have stayed in over 25 years has had a TV or flat screen no older than 5 years or so, and all of the furniture, mattresses, and bedding is always in new condition. Ironically, we all have furniture older than 4 or 5 years old. I am not debating here the value of antiques, just everyday dining rooms and coffee tables. We also support and keep TVs that are out of date, and many of us are guilty of owning our beds for well beyond the 7 or 8 years most experts recommend replacing them. In reality, we have a double standard. Our time share must be perfect in all respects, but the house we live in can just bump along until the wheels fall off and it is obvious a repair is needed.

This is precisely why we advocate a large multinational company can do a better job of running the physical aspect of a building, along with managing the interior, utilities, appliance repairs, and replacements that we can do at home. They can also do it at a lower cost per unit, per bed, per TV, per refrigerator, etc., such that this number is actually lower than what we routinely pay at home. We also get air-conditioning, heating, a gym, spa, tennis courts in many cases, multiple pools, and Jacuzzis, and never ever need to worry about repairing or replacing them. It is like owning a home but someone else has to pay to maintain it. While we end up paying for this cost through our maintenance fees, the cost is lower than what we pay for similar work at our home. Is this not a better way to own and pay for housing?

The trick to a better retirement is not to argue with reality but rather figure out how to lower your cost per day of living. Rather than add a vacation home or time share on top of your current cost per day from your primary home, subtract these costs by selling your home and buying a far cheaper one in a smaller city or less expensive neighborhood. Then pay cash for your smaller home and purchase 3 to 4 months of time shares. Now that $250 a day can get down to under $50 a day and you have $200 more a day to live life. The math is the math, and each of us are in control on how to manage the math. Most of all, by default, you will lower your stress level just knowing your life in many ways is paid for on the housing side.

When time share maintenance fees are NOT the same: We have tried to suggest in this book it is important to change your thought process when it comes to thinking about getting what you want out of life. In our case with this book, we mean getting a higher quality of life at a lower cost per day. As all time share owners know, that Christmas week or

July 4th reservation can cause months of stress just thinking about making that 6:00 a.m. phone call on Monday morning and hoping the line is not busy. The same type of stress endures when we get our maintenance fee bill and we have to pony up thousands of dollars in one check. Of course, in most cases, we are just prepaying our expenses, so in reality, if we paid all of the bills separately during the year but paid them monthly, we would have 10 or so very small bills every month just to cover 1 or 2 weeks of a time share stay. We cannot change the annual maintenance fee bill we receive from the operator, but we can change the maintenance fee per night as discussed in this book in the RRC chapter and how to rent your villa. We can also be smarter about how we buy time shares by understanding how the time share relates to the maintenance fee. While in today's point-based systems or regional share systems where you have priority rights to a certain group of properties, you can add to your portfolio by searching out those old maintenance formulas that have very powerful up trade capability, thus reducing your actual maintenance fees per night. In other words, you pay a YMCA maintenance fee to stay at the Ritz Carlton.

You recall we have reviewed in this book how and why reservation systems work and why sold out for some people may or may not mean sold out for someone else looking to book the same week. They are just coming into the system through a tunnel you did not use or were unaware they even existed. Well, fortunately for the savvy time share owner, maintenance fees also run through a complex maze of formulas that also may include grandfathered rights. You also may have one type of product with a maintenance fee of X, and be able to easily trade into Y every year that has a much-higher maintenance fee. Some older legacy weeks that predate the newer points-based models may have attached formulas that provide up trade power but yet only come with 1 week of maintenance fees, but because of their seasonal value and points rating, can buy you 2 weeks instead of 1 by doing exactly the opposite—trading into points that convert 1 week into 2. Some of these old-time shares sit on the market like an old dog waiting to be adopted, and yet, they have within them real economic power and can reduce your overall maintenance fee within your time share portfolio.

They are the work engines of how to get free vacation time. It takes work and persistence to find them. They are like foreclosures. There may be a lot of them out there, but only a small percentage of all the time share inventory will ever hit the maintenance fee jackpot. Pay attention to old-time shares that have exclusive occupancy rights for Christmas week or July 4th, or prime time shares that are located on a famous beach or at the bottom of a world-class ski mountain. See if they have three or four bedrooms, also quite rare. Some time shares may also vest with an older maintenance formula, but can usually trade into shoulder seasons just before or after the prime seasons end, in some cases, granting you double or triple the time to occupy. If you have any combination of these attributes, you likely have a time share that could be worth more than a new one. This would indeed be a rare find, but just because there are not a lot of white tigers does not mean they don't exist. Some people get lucky with oil wells or a gold mine. Some of us find artwork at a garage sale worth 100 times more than it sold for. A few of us find time share gold if we know what to look for.

How to reverse engineer your maintenance fee: We have stated in this book that the exciting thing about a time share is that it is not a perfect science, any more than any other business. There are going to be times and places where you can get something in one place and trade it for something else in another place. This is precisely the formula for international trade, hands-down the largest business in the world. Every day, millions of goods and services are made in one place, and then shipped halfway around the world for someone else to purchase and use. In theory, it is cheaper to buy the product from halfway around the world than to manufacture the same product down the street. In other instances, the expertise to produce the product is not available in the local market.

One of the by-products of time shares is that the business is now approaching 50-plus years old, and when the time share business started to explode in the 1980s and 1990s, many of the old rules on maintenance fees were first adopted. Allocation models were derived and the industry had to figure out what is the fairest way to allocate maintenance fees. Should we do it by the size of the unit or the number of bedrooms, the time of year, or charge a premium for the best units? When you think about this, all kinds of arguments can be made about how much water and utilities might be used. Maybe we should do it by the number of people the unit is designed for, perhaps we should allocate expenses on the actual number of people who stay in the room . . .

Now what happens if someone trades a small unit for a large one the next year? Should their maintenance fee for that year be higher? What if the taxes, utilities, and operating costs in Hawaii are higher because of its island status? Should those people pay more than the rest if all they do is mostly go to Hawaii? You can see how difficult it could get to decide what is fair. What is fair to one person might be punitive to another. The time share industry has managed to evolve, and with that evolution it needed better models to allocate expenses.

We believe with most of the large public time share operators now offering a pool of properties held in a trust or other entity, that the ideal of spreading all of the cost among all of the members is very fair since each one can stay at any property. The older model, while having some pricing advantages in a very small number of cases, has been replaced with a much more even model that spreads the highs and lows of each property into a smoother bell curve. The individual properties each have their own independent board of directors which include elected owners and overall, we have found their expertise and level of commitment to be very professional and effective. The developers also maintain both a presence on these boards as well as have individual monitoring of each property. Since most of them have significant hotel experience, they are very adept at spotting most any kind of pricing inconsistency, and because of their size, can afford to finance a number of preventive maintenance practices that, in the long run, will keep expenses at a minimum.

The conclusion here is that, with enough research, can you find trading windows where the originating side of the trade has an attached maintenance fee that is lower than the trade up fee for that same week? This generally occurs only on an up trade; hence, after the trade, you have earned more economic value from your time share because you likely have not used all of the points or trading power from the trade you gave up. An example might be a lock-off that routinely trades 1 week for 2 via splitting the unit. There can be other hidden gems like valuable ski weeks or beach weeks that trade for a huge premium over other weeks. Some time shares have double value, like a three-bedroom during Christmas week. In extreme cases, this type of time share can obtain 4 weeks of time share for an off-season two-bedroom as an example. When you are reviewing a purchase, be sure to look at the power of holiday weeks in the same resort because Christmas week, July 4th, or older legacy weeks may have either significantly more point power or may have a smaller maintenance fee under a very old formula. Any combination of these unique time share clauses can result in pound for pound your netting a reduced maintenance fee equal to 50% or less of what the trade value brings. This is like trading a lock-off 1 week for 2, although in most models, that maintenance fee is higher because it is a lock-off unit. Regardless, there are old legacy weeks that have gold hidden in the maintenance fee when the up trade value is considered. This is what we mean by reverse engineering your maintenance fee. You still pay the developer the same fee you got billed, but by making an up trade, you gain extra days with lower per day maintenance fees. These prime weeks can perform like champs every year. This is why paying more for a holiday week might make you a lot of money over 20 years of vacations. I have seen a single holiday week trade for a month or more of beach time within the same operator.

Time share is heavily regulated: Many time share owners may not realize that the time share business is heavily regulated. The vacation business is very competitive and requires a high degree of skill to balance growth and attract more customers. Time share developers not only have to endure all of the ramifications of being public and comply with hundreds of SEC rules, they must also comply with a significant amount of zoning, building, and construction laws. Once federal and state laws are followed, these developers must deal with local subdivision laws. Every county then has to adopt rules and regulations to keep up with next-generation designs and will remain busy adopting new laws specifically designed to monitor time share projects. Most large-scale projects routinely run into a number of laws requiring environmental studies, toxicity reports, coastal commission issues and restrictions, height and variance issues, and even, in some cases, challenges with the FAA. Then there are the Army Corps of Engineer requirements on drainage and grading. Developers also face a myriad of sewer, electrical, gas, and water regulations. The industry then has to comply with the cost to maintain handicapped rooms, access, and now, even pool and Jacuzzi access. No wonder the cost of land and regulatory fees can absorb up to 35% of the cost of a time share, and this is *before* construction begins.

The time share operators also monitor each other and are well aware of what the prices and maintenance fees are within the industry. In order to maintain large marketing staffs and attract continuing capital from Wall Street, they must constantly find new opportunities to sell more time shares. It is not like they can just keep selling without being accountable for each sale. They must prove every sale has a bed to sleep in for every year equal to the number of nights they have sold. They must also maintain a forward supply of unsold inventory sufficient to meet the needs of their marketing department, often forecasted 6 to 12 months in advance. While they hold this inventory, they must pay the maintenance fees for every deed until it can be replaced with a new customer. They have little advantage in raising fees beyond what is necessary to do a first-class job of maintaining and running the properties.

I have been asked if the large operators make a profit on the maintenance fees. The short answer is yes, they are able to book either some form of general and administration allocation for the buildings, staff, and human personnel needed to manage this side of the business, along with a small management or some type of operations fee. It is a small profit center, but remember, the G&A fees are really a reimbursement more than any kind of profit. This is very normal and is done in almost every business throughout the world. This is not something unique to the time share business. The fee in this area is generally a very small percentage of the overall cost, and although it can vary or be broken up into different fees, most management fees run between 3% and 5% for most large operators. There may be other fees involved but given the competitive nature of the business, most of these fees are within a very competitive range.

The bigger picture, selling time shares and booking the real estate profit is where the time share operators make more money. They also can earn marketing and management fees running the properties after they are built, thus providing a steady source of revenue to pay for their corporate overhead and provide working capital for new initiatives and acquisitions. It is very important these operators maintain some ability to move fast if an exceptional deal comes along. The industry is thirsty for large tracts of land that are suitable for a successful time share deal. The companies that can move faster when the opportunity arises will have a leg up on earnings in the following years.

The time share maintenance fee-the rules are the rules: As we have noted throughout the book, we cannot change what the maintenance fees are since they apply equally to every owner. We can, however, examine the possibilities on how to buy time shares and how to manage the time share in a manner that reduces the average daily cost of your maintenance fee. We stress again that we do not recommend buying a time share, and then look only at every off-season and short-term discounted option because you may be overmanaging your time share on the math side, and then fail to enjoy it for the reason you bought it. The main reason you should buy is to create valuable memories for yourself and your family.

If that means you pay more for the summer months, so be it. You won't have that many when your kids are young, and paying the highest points for the high season is important because you get to enjoy the best of the best . . . the best time share, best time of year, and perhaps with that, the best memories ever. Ironically, you may have a higher RRC ratio when you pay the most because the villa is also worth the most. We have run numbers on off-season RRCs and high season RRCs, and the results can be very close because off-season gets you more days for fewer points per day, but your rent per day is much higher in high season, making your stay more valuable if you had to pay the nightly rate or you rented it out. It comes down to a longer stay versus a shorter stay at a higher cost benefit per night on the rental side.

A balanced approach to managing your maintenance fee: We discuss in this book the importance of understanding your actual RRC ratio, both at the time you purchase a time share and as you use your time share over the years. Your RRC ratio will either go up or down, but in most cases, it should increase slightly every year over time. We have provided a 45-year look at RRC ratios, assuming a modest inflation of 3% per year. We used a 5% per year inflation rate on rentals in prime beach and ski seasons. We did this because the rental rate of $125 a night in 2006 for a prime West Coast beachfront in California went to over $925 a night in 2016 for a July evening. If we assumed increases along what a 15% increase in the rental rate for this project is, the rent should have gone from $125 a night all the way up to $506 a night. It would be $774 a night had the rent gone up just 20% a year. If the demand pushed rental rates in the United States for this resort up 25% for just the period 2007 through 2017, the rental rate would need to climb to $1,048 a night, pretty close to the July 2017 expected rate of $968 a night.

The rent has climbed to well above $900 for prime summer nights in July. The actual increase over this period was therefore about 23% per year. This was again the rack rate charged at the front desk, not necessarily what the secondary markets were getting. I can confirm this rate because I got $625 a night in July of 2016. This fits right into the 67% limit (off of what the resort charges) for self-renting if you desire a faster and stickier reservation.

We therefore decided in order to keep the rental rate significantly more conservative for a prime U.S. beachfront rental, to use an inflation rate of 5%, realizing that actual inflation for expenses should rise about 3% per year in line or slightly above the past 10 years as of 2017. You can see under this scenario the RRC ratio started out at 2.32 in 2017 and increased to 2.76 through year ending 2026.

This ratio is what helps determine if your time share investment is treating you well. If your RRC continues upward, you are saving more money every year, which, in turn, is working toward reducing your pay back indicator to under 10 years. We, of course, use 67% of rack rate in our assumptions on the rental side.

It is still possible to reduce your actual cost per night if you elect to rent out a portion of your time every year or every other year. This greatly reduces your cost per night for the remaining stays. You can also scrutinize the resale market both directly and indirectly and see if you can find an old legacy week that has a lower maintenance fee or has a high trade value that, pound for pound, grants you more vacation time for the same maintenance fee. These weeks, like a Christmas week, typically trade well above normal weeks because the owners know they are sitting on a real diamond, an extremely valuable week which, as a bonus, trades into 2 or more weeks but contains only a 1-week maintenance fee. These weeks are still underpriced for their value, and when the industry gets an electronic marketplace, we expect these exceptional weeks to trade for over twice new regular weeks trade for today. These weeks represent the top 1% of time shares. Acquiring one of these weeks is like buying your family a 100-year gas well that pays out every year. They are truly rare white elephants and should be coveted and ideally never sold. They are also a good way to cut your maintenance fees in half for life by using them as prime rentals.

CHAPTER 11

Time Share and Retirement

YOUR VACATION PLAN—CAN my time share really act as a 401 (V): A 401 (V) refers to a vacation plan and is not intended to mean there is an IRS provision for vacation savings. It is just a reference we use in this book and is NOT intended to reflect any IRS provision on a 401 (V). There are a number of issues to review in connection with how your downstream travel plans and your retirement plan could dovetail with a time share purchase. Let's review them in concept, and then we will review some of the concerns if you are considering using a retirement plan to acquire a time share.

First of all, we have two separate ideas here. The first is, can the IRS help you purchase your time share on a tax-incentivized basis? Second, can one use funds in an IRA/Roth or other plan to purchase a time share? The final issue revolves around retirement planning and has to do with how much, if any, time share benefits make sense as a part of your retirement. We will address these three different concepts independently.

Can the IRS help pay for my time share? As with all advice related to tax matters, we strongly advise you seek guidance from your accountant or other tax advisor before proceeding with any investment into a time share if you have any tax concerns. Please also note the advice given here is based on existing tax laws under very specific conditions and may or may not apply to your individual situation. If any one of these conditions is not followed properly, any tax benefits could be compromised or even disallowed, and/or these rules could be challenged as with any IRS ruling as tax and time share deductions are constantly evaluated by the service. As with many tax questions, the best place to ask a question about tax benefits is often with the IRS itself. Under **Publication 936**, the IRS could allow the deduction of interest used to purchase a time share under very strict conditions. Included in these conditions are the following:

1. It must have at least one bathroom, a kitchen, and sleeping facilities, preferably a bedroom and/or very clear sleeping facilities like a built-in bed, for example.
2. You must either occupy the unit for longer than 2 weeks or at least 10% of the time you rent your time-share to others.

The IRS further requires compliance with **Publication 527**, which goes on to require:

1. The only time that counts is the actual amount of time you control. I.e., if you own 2 weeks, the rules apply to 2 weeks out of the year, not 52 weeks. This ruling will need to likely be modified given the new points-based systems in place where it is not clear how many weeks you control since locations, even among the same operators, can vary widely, depending on time of year and where you choose to stay.

2. You do not violate any mortgage interest limits currently at no more than $1M for mortgage debt on your primary home.
3. If you have a nonprimary deduction like for an existing vacation home, then your mortgage interest on a time share will not likely meet the test and, therefore, is not deductible.
4. Your time share company sends you form 1098 at the end of the year for mortgage interest.
5. You may qualify to deduct as a certain expense like home owner's insurance, and upgrades to energy-efficient HVAC systems may be allowed but could be hard to pinpoint under your maintenance fee.
6. If you rent your time share for less than 14 days, time-share owners do not have to report the income on their taxes, but remember, under this rule, you cannot claim rental expenses.
7. You could be eligible to deduct the mortgage interest if you use your timeshare as strictly a vacation home on Schedule A, Form 1040. Pound for pound, time-shares retain some great tax advantages and can help reduce your after-tax cost of ownership.
8. You may also be eligible to deduct the property taxes on your time share on Schedule A, but be sure to get proof as many developers now have the tax bill buried inside the maintenance fee.

To summarize this point, you only own one home, and that is your primary residence. You deduct interest from a mortgage on your primary home that is less than $1M. You also own a time share that has been financed on a loan from the developer, and you stay there at least 2 weeks a year or least 10% of the time it is rented.

Under these conditions, you may be allowed to deduct the interest against your income as "mortgage interest" and are likely in compliance with current tax laws. Under all circumstances, check with your tax advisor and make sure he or she is in agreement. We have provided a copy of both publications at the end of this chapter that you can show your advisor.

Can I use a retirement plan to purchase or pay off a time share?

The Investment Retirement Account and time share. : In general, the idea of mixing a time share investment or purchase into a retirement account does not make a lot of sense for most people. The primary reason is you have to decide why you are buying the time share. If the answer is to use it, then many rules governing time share investments (we use this term loosely) will conflict with the investment rules which require the asset be held for investment and not personal use. The rules change on usage and can be interpreted slightly differently, so we will use caution here and advise you to check on this rule with your investment and tax advisor if you are considering such a purchase within any type of retirement account. In general, the purpose of a time share and the investment rules are not very aligned, whereas in an after-tax world, getting up to 14 days (again, check current rules) to collect rent, and being able to take a 1098 mortgage interest deduction under certain circumstances would seem to favor purchasing a time share outside your retirement account.

That said, we like to always keep an open mind and have come up with one possibility that could make some sense. If you are 15–20 years outside of retirement and perhaps already own a time share, it could make sense to purchase a time share inside your retirement account if you are not going to use it in the foreseeable future. The answer might be yes under very limited circumstances. We know as a general rule only the top 10% of time shares are highly rentable all of the time. If you are pondering trying to buy a Christmas week or prime July beach week and the time share also has a three-bedroom, it will likely always be rentable with little effort. If you see yourself wanting to pay cash or just purchase with retirement dollars, you could set up the purchase as a rental every year. This would avoid the personal use as long as you do not work on the time share which is unlikely since your operator has that obligation under the maintenance fee program. Under this scenario, this could make sense. You could then use it after you retire and begin taking distributions. The key is to make sure all of the inflows and outflows come from the trustee, not yourself, and confirm with your tax advisor as to the timing of how you can transition use from business to personal after you retire. In some cases, prime beach or holiday weeks could produce payback indicators of 20% or more per year, making these previously undeserved investment ideas star performers against other alternative types of investments currently allowed in IRA and 401(k) programs.

The Roth account and retirement. This is a very tricky plan and generally will not work for a Roth account if you intend to use your time share. We advise you to seek counsel from your tax advisor, and if you can set up your purchase as an investment purchase and follow the very strict guidelines for nonusage, you may be able to craft a plan that can work for you. In general, this is not a typical Roth investment.

The 401(k) and time share. : Most people would not use a 401(k) to purchase a time share product since most time shares are not intended as investment vehicles where the goal is to achieve a return on investment every year. Once again, we advise you to consult your tax advisor about the rules of investment. A highly rentable time share, like a prime Christmas week, could provide rental income, but the rules can be tricky, and you will not likely be able to use the time share for personal use.

Time share as a part of retirement planning: In concept, most of us agree that at or around retirement we will look to save money and reduce unneeded expenditures as much as possible in order to protect the money that is supposed to last us another 15 or 20 years or more. One of the difficulties we face today in 2017 is that it is very hard to predict where our country is headed, what the future tax laws will be like, and to a large extent, when we will see inflation rise again, putting even more pressure on fixed income or low return retirement plans.

As a tool itself, the first issue in discussing a time share as a form of retirement planning really should be looked at as something you can and will use, and does your vacation plan provide for some assurance you can comfortably retire and handle the maintenance fees under a worst-case scenario.

In theory, this makes sense, you pay for the right to book vacations or stays around the world now, and then, if the maintenance fees do not overly strain your retirement budget, a well crafted plan can insulate you from the ever-increasing cost of renting beachfront or prime mountain locations. It is important you feel comfortable that your maintenance fees do not consume a large percentage of your retirement income (less than 5% of your retirement income) so that other higher priority needs can be met. Second, you must consider that none of us can control the future price of gasoline or plane fares so look at your plan and make sure if these costs sky-rocket out of control, your favorite resort in Tahiti or Hawaii could then start to look very expensive. You may have to re-place your favorite spot with one that you can drive to with one or two tanks of gas. In other words, the more choices you have to avoid airports, depend on rental cars, long transportation cycles involving a lot of meals, the more defensive value your time share will retain in tough times while your ability to use it remains viable.

When we think about retirement, this is supposed to be a time when your life gets better. You have time to visit family and grandkids, write that book, or finally get that gourmet cooking degree. This time should be busy with things like productive volunteer work, pursuing hobbies, and playing golf or engaging in your favorite pastime. Retirement for many should also include as much travel as possible while you can get around and really digest those parts of the world you have always wanted to see. Passing on and leaving your kids tons of money in the bank is not living for you or them. Taking some time to travel today and leaving them the gift of travel is, in many ways, worth more than money.

Many of today's point-based programs can be passed onto them and therefore, they end up benefiting from a lifetime of memories, meaning their life was more enjoyable and richer in a cultural and family sense than just making the mortgage and using the word *someday* every year. *Someday* is not a day of the week. In the end, traveling with family and friends is something we will wish we had done more of during our last days.

Understanding amortization math—why a few extra upfront payments changes everything: In most cases, people chose to finance a time share as a matter of convenience, knowing that within 1–2 years, they will likely be in a better position to pay off the time share mortgage. This works great for most people; however, those that have to rely on paying off a high interest rate ranging from 10% to 15%, this method can prove very costly. Sometimes, share companies provide additional benefits to consumers if they start with the developer financing. One idea is to see how much you can put down and still receive any financing awards. They are usually in the form of additional points either on the hotel side or the vacation side of the operator. Sometimes, you may get a choice of one or the other.

In any event, see if you can put down 20%–40% and still qualify for any financing bonuses. This will help reduce your interest cost and lower your payment. Second of all, see if you make double payments early on in the financing window and make sure the extra amount paid can go to reduce the principal. Even a few extra payments in the first 120 days will go a long way to reduce your interest paid over 10 years, and it will also mean a larger percentage of your monthly payment will then go to the principal, further reducing the time it will take to pay off your note. This method can turn your 10-year loan into an 8.4-year loan with just two up-front payments. Imagine what an extra payment every 6 months could do. (See table below.)

For example, if you have a $20,000 time share loan at 12.99% interest, amortized over 10 years, you would end up with a payment of $380.50 a month for 10 years. Your first month requires $216.50 just to pay the interest, and then leaves $164 for reducing the loan from $20,000 to $19,836. Let's say that you made a double payment for just the first 2 months to start the loan off instead of just one payment and requested the extra $380.50 go to reduce the principal. Let's look at what happens to the rest of the loan.

1. **Under scenario one** we have a balance of $19,836 after one payment, which will require $214.72 to pay the interest in month two, leaving $165.78 to reduce the loan balance. Note that you get an extra $1.78

going to reduce the loan balance over the first month and an extra $1.78 plus additional principal reduction every month from there. So your new balance is now $19,670.22 after the first 2 months.

2. **Under scenario two** we had a loan balance of $19,455.50 after the first month because we sent in an extra $380.50 that all went to reduce the principal. Now the loan will require $210.60 to pay the interest in month 2, leaving $169.90 to reduce the loan balance. We also sent in another $380.50, so the total principal reduction is $550.40 for the second month, equal to a new balance of $18,905.10. Notice now that two things have happened. The first is you owe about $765 less on the loan which, at 12.99%, will save you $8.28 every month for the remaining life of the loan, but let's see what happens from here.

Now, let's repeat the process just one more time, and then plan to never again make an extra payment and we'll see how much faster the loan will pay off after just two double payments.

1. **So, in scenario one,** it still takes the remaining 118 payments to complete the 10-year loan at $380.50 a month because your debt is using the full 10 years to pay off the loan.
2. Now, **in scenario two,** the loan gets paid off in just the next 100 payments, or 8 years and 4 months. In other words, you save **<u>a year and one-half</u> and thereby save the last 18 monthly payments by just paying 2 extra months up front!** This is $6,842.70 you do not need to pay on your loan and with a very high interest rate of 12.99%, you end up paying a total of $38,760 versus $45,660. Of course, most of us prefer not to use

> this financing, but if you do get stuck with it, just a few up-front principal reduction payments will make your life much easier a few years down the road. This is the power of compounding interest in reverse, where the math can work in your favor with just a small up-front commitment over and above the loan terms. Avoiding 10 or 20 years of interest on any amount of money will just go to reduce your loan balance much faster. The trick is, you must do it as early as possible in the loan cycle so the interest saved can work for you for the longest period of time. One early extra payment in month one or two is significantly more valuable to you than an extra payment made three years into the loan.

Lastly, under a more aggressive approach, you could make double payments on a 10-year loan and in about 3 years, the loan would be paid off, saving you nearly seven (7) years of interest. The point here is that even if your time share debt is at a high interest rate, it does not take much to really start reducing your balance, especially if you start on the front end of the loan. Time shares are way more enjoyable if they are owned free and clear, so plan to get your time share debt paid off if you have a loan earlier than the loan provides. The extra savings will increase your disposable income and give you more cash flow for your vacations. If you forgo just one vacation for a week and, instead, rent out your villa and use the proceeds to pay down your loan, you will end up with a paid up time share years ahead of schedule.

The 401 (K) and Time Share-Under normal circumstances a 401 (K) is typically used to leverage your retirement savings by coupling a contribution with your employer, allowing

the beneficiary to benefit by earning a return tax free and combining it with a tax free contribution from the employer. This combination really helps build a nest egg quickly with little risk if the funds are directed into a conservative account. By most definitions this would not include any type of time share investments. In addition the IRS has strict rules in place about how alternative investments can be made and in particular with time shares, any personal use or even management of the asset must be monitored and managed by an independent third party. That said, I have had a number of investors make speculative investments into my start up company's where if successful, might result in a 10X or even 50X plus return, then having this asset held in a tax deferred account makes a lot of sense. The first thing is to find a third-party custodian that will agree to manage the paperwork. This takes some effort but can be done. In the case of a time share the only real play that comes to mind would be if you intend to purchase the very top of this asset class, a Category One, fixed week or weeks product like from December 15th through January 14th, every year in a top shelf location like a Vail, Colorado, where you occupy the same unit year after year. As of this writing I am aware of some resales in a three bedroom where the asking prices are now well over $750,000, not too far from what small homes in Vail could be purchased for. Remember these are the top 1% of time shares, in the best locations, ski in/ski out with full amenity packages. The other main condition is you likely could not occupy the unit until after your retire but could command top rentals for ten or fifteen years to offset the maintenance and purchase costs. This is a perfect storm for a very small percentage of the population but if you feel this might fit your criteria, then be sure and confirm with your tax advisor on additional requirements so you can defend your asset purchase in the event of an audit. This type of top time share could command up to $3,000 a night on a 30-day rental so the payback here could well be worth your time and trouble. Regardless of asset class or even return on investment, the fastest way to accumulate wealth is through tax free or deferred plans so even a sleepy time share purchase can be acquired at much lower after-tax cost if all of rules are complied with under the IRS code.

CHAPTER 12

Understanding the Tax Benefits of Time Shares

A Summary of Tax Advantages

PLEASE, AS WITH all tax strategies, be sure and consult your tax advisor before trying to utilize any tax advantage for a time share as IRS rules and guidance are subject to change yearly.

Pretax Time Share Rentals Generally favorable for up to 14 days of rental tax-free subject to the IRS restrictions. Also, as of this publication date, Mortgage 1098 Interest could allow for a mortgage interest deduction if you qualify

After-tax—Time share mortgage rates, although high at 9%–15%, can provide a deduction resulting in a significant after-tax savings

Time share property tax deduction—generally allowed

Time share mortgage interest—subject to $1M mortgage limitation and other qualifying information

Time share rental expenses—reasonable and customary can be allowed against income from rentals, but check with your advisor

Tax deductions on time share gifts made as donations

As a general rule, the IRS can be difficult when reviewing a time share "gift" to a church or other worthy charity. The theory is that the time share itself has little or no economic value (although this is not true in high season in prime locations) and is composed of a vague intrinsic value (in IRS speak, this means not a valid deduction). One of the reasons for this is that they can reason the time share likely may have stayed empty or the value of the deduction may be overstated, causing an audit of your return. This is a valid point in many cases.

One potential way to help fortify a time share deduction is to rent it to a worthy charity or even a church as long as you can prove the time share had real economic value at the time of the donation. We mention this because you will need to work with your church to abide by all of the rules. Under the tax law, you are allowed to claim up to 14 days of rental income tax free. You can either donate the rental money to your church or, in turn, the time, and they, in turn, can rent your time share to a worthy family and you have a bona fide deduction. Another variant if you are close to the charity or your church is to ascertain how much you currently donate per year to your favorite church or charity. Let's say it is $100 per month. Instead of $100 per month, write them a check in December of any year for $3,200 as a charitable contribution for that year and waive your $100 per month for the following year.

Have them rent your time share during the next year at 75% of market value, whatever that is for your time share, say $2,800 value, rented at $2,000. Our example assumes a Category One or Two time share in high season. You pick up the income tax free for that year as long as you do not collect more than 14 days rent. Be sure your rental income is not the same as your donation and the timing is not real close to avoid any issue on a wash-sale rule where it looks like you are just exchanging money. This type of transaction is rightfully discouraged if each portion of the transaction is out of line with market conditions. The amounts should be different, and both must be arm's-length transactions independent from each other.

The church or charity can then sell or auction off the week at the church auction or give it to a volunteer or gift it to a worthy church member or needy family. They also get $1,200 up front versus all year long. You get a $3,200 charitable deduction made payable to the church. Now your $1,200 per year donated to the church is paid for by the taxes you saved and you got another $2,000 from renting your time share to the church which should be tax free to you under the 14-day rule. Your church could then donate the rental to a needy family. Please check with your tax advisor to make sure they will support your deduction in this matter and make sure there are not any IRS rulings that may negatively affect this type of deduction. The IRS can and does change and modify their positions on charitable deductions, and we want to make sure any deduction in this area is within all of the IRS guidelines.

Time Shares-A strong tax advantaged asset

Time Share(s)-A strong tax advantaged asset. There are few asset classes that contain the combination of tax advantages that a well-designed time share plan can do. In a more typical American family environment, a time share can be purchased with ten percent down and the balance financed as low as 9% from a developer and much lower with a HLOC. The interest is deductible and the asset can bring up to 14 days of tax free income under current law. This income can more than cover the annual maintenance fees if the right time share is acquired at the right price, something that is not difficult to do. In other words it is possible to earn up to 10 percent per year, after the maintenance fees are covered if the right plan is followed. In ten years the time share will be paid off and the owner will have the use of 14 to 20 days per year forever. This is one of the best combinations of use and benefit left in the tax code, yet few of us really use the time share laws as they relate to legal deductions to the fullest ability. As Congress likely looks to reduce future tax benefits to finance our deficits, it will be interesting to see of the time share industry can lobby to maintain what is by comparison a favored asset under the current IRS code. Should these provisions survive, future time shares will continue to shine as a brilliant way to increase family wealth, save money, and travel at the lowest possible cost per square foot as compared to any hotel, AirBnB, or any other known lodging options.

CHAPTER 13

Analysis and Review of the Top Global Time Share Companies

ANALYSIS OF SOME of the larger time share companies, size of global markets, North America, United States (2017-2018): The North American vacation time share market is primarily controlled by seven well-known and highly branded hotel and time share developers who operate and are domiciled in the United States. These brands include:

Parent	Headquartered	Ticker
1. Diamond Resorts	Las Vegas, Nevada	N/A
2. Disney Resorts	Orlando, Florida	DIS
3. Hilton Vacation Clubs	McLean,Virginia	HLT
January of 2017 HLT was spun into two public companies		PK HGV
4. Interval Internationalday Inn Vacations	Kissimmee, Florida	

5. Holiday Inn Vacation Clubs	Apollo, New York	
6. Marriot Vacation Club	Orlando, Florida	VAC
7. Wyndham Holdings	Orlando, Florida	WYN

All of the top global brands have some type of overseas operations that includes both time share and hotel alliances, providing extended services for travelers seeking international travel with access to hotels, villas, and increasingly now, private homes. We are also seeing continued mergers and spin-offs with many chains now taking their vacation clubs and putting them into separate public companies, noting the recent Hilton Hotel chain now spinning their 45 vacation properties under the newly created HGV ticker representing the Hilton Grand Vacations Club. We believe this continued trend of isolating the vacation Profit and Loss Statement from hotel operations will help smooth out some of the development cycles inherent in the development business and allow the hotel and time divisions to focus on just their franchise and hotel management models. Vacation clubs require large sums of debt and equity to grow, and at times, these business models can drag down the relatively stable earnings that come from hotel operations, particularly during economic growth cycles where increasing occupancy rates fall right to the bottom line for hotels.

We believe this trend could also lead to a few more consolidations as the public vacation clubs will be able to use their stock prices to obtain smaller regional time share operators who are not public. The recent consolidation trend could result in combinations of the top seven brands being reduced to four or five brands over the next 10 years. The key to maintaining growth in this highly competitive field is obtaining growth capital at the lowest possible cost through the public markets. Unlocking the hotel side gives each division the opportunity to plan for capital independent of each other's performance or balance sheet issues. This puts pressure on the top vacation club brands to continue to report upward earnings so they can issue new stock on a less dilutive basis to finance large capital expenditures like new projects and technology upgrades.

These operators will also need to provide an increasing value proposition to the end customer beyond today's offerings, like luxury rental homes, long-term stay resorts, car rentals, food and beverage services, and premium hotel perks to attract new customers. The need to separate from the competition puts pressure on these firms to acquire more premium brands and infill locations and highly sought after resort locations that can be entitled. In addition, new products like upgraded food and beverage choices, long-term stay time shares, retirement time shares along with sporting, limo, and VIP events will also likely find their way into the mainstream time share models. These dynamics all point toward more mergers and acquisitions that can shave years off the traditional path of just constructing and marketing new projects from the ground up.

Another recent example is the large established brands like Marriott International and Interval International sharing their 31 branded hotels on the hospitality side as a result of the Marriott acquisition of the Starwood Hotel brands in 2016. However, these two giants still maintain very different and separate vacation programs under established brand names like Weston, Sheraton, and Hyatt vacation clubs now under Interval International control. The hotel portfolio from Starwood that included the Sheraton, Westin, St. Regis, and the W brands, along with another eight brands, is now controlled on the hotel side by Marriott International.

The hotel count for Marriott and Interval now exceeds 5,700 properties as a result of the Starwood merger rounding them up to an impressive 31 brands of hotels around the world. Each company now provides certain preferential hotel and villa rights available to their respective vacation customers.

Interval International now markets the Four Seasons, Hyatt, under their respective brand name, while the Westin and Sheraton vacation programs are marketed through their Vistana vacation club division. Although these brands are under one umbrella, you have to be very careful and not just assume they are all in one giant rental pool. Many of the vacation brands still operate under their own very separate rules and booking priorities, so be careful and ask a lot of questions about what is included in your vacation membership and what, if any, hotel benefits are included. Also, cross bookings across both vacation and hotel brands can be subject to different rules when talking about reservation priorities.

Time share industry trends for growth: In a recent and extensive report done by Ernst & Young in 2014, they reported the United States as having 1,540 time share projects at year end 2013. They also reported we have over 192,420 units dedicated to time share as of 2014, and the industry has seen over 8.5M interval periods sold. This does not mean we have 8.5M owners, as many owners now own 4–8 weeks or more of time shares. We suspect, based on our investigations, we now have as many as 3.5M-plus owners in the United States who own at least one time share. Based on the U.S. Census prediction of 325,000,000 people in the United States as of 2017, this means that time shares have a penetration rate of just over 1%, a surprisingly small statistic given the relatively high growth of the industry, growing at between 4%–6% over the past 5 years, well ahead of GNP for the country as a whole. The time share industry is very good for the economy, creating over 411,000 jobs directly tied to the industry and over 1.1M worldwide jobs per year. Time share sales are now estimated to exceed $8B per year. Some of the top global operators are now forecasting growth into double digits of over 10% for 2017, an incredible achievement given the backdrop of the real estate industry as a whole.

We expect that 2017–2018 will again prove to be a banner year for the industry as each of the top seven operators continues the expansion binge with several top projects now coming online. This list is not intended to be all inclusive, and new projects well into the entitlement process could be sold or delayed and therefore, may not be represented here. Below is just an example of some of the new projects:

Top seven global time share developers—2017 summary digest

Diamond Resorts International

Diamond International owns a portfolio of 379 national and international locations with a strong global presence focused in the United States, Europe, and the Asian coastlines. They were purchased in June of 2016 by Apollo Global Management, and we predict they will be on the acquisition trail over the next 5 years as part of their growth strategy. They are based in Las Vegas, Nevada, and have a strong brand name with a vast array of price points. They also feature a unique concert series tied into promotions and targeted resort locations.

Disney

Four theme parks, two water parks, and 33 resort properties. Disney offers a number of Disney-related travel packages, including over 33 Adventure by Disney travel options located around the globe in Europe, Africa, Asia, South America, and Australia. The Disney Vacation Club Web site reflects over 2,607 possible combinations of hotels, resorts, Disney cruises, and Disney clubs. One of the strongest entertainment brands in the world packaged with the magic of Disney that allows owners to escape to five continents around the world. They have a custom Concierge Collection that is aligned with some of the top hotel brands in the world offering luxury choices within their brand. This is certainly a strong contender for those looking for the magic of Disney. They are also aligned with RCI, expanding into a number of out of Disney network locations.

Hilton Vacation Club

Forty-four vacation clubs with access to over 4,400 hotels in over 100 countries. Hilton has recently spun off their hotel division in late 2016, and now the hotel and vacation club trade under separate company names, in line with an industry trend to split hospitality verticals from vacation divisions. Hilton is also aligned with RCI and provides over 4,000 affiliated resorts in more than 100 countries. The Hilton Grand Vacation Clubs boast a strong domestic lineup due to multiple projects in many of their target markets which include South Carolina, Florida, Oahu, Hawaii, New York, Nevada, and California. They have three ocean locations in Southern California in Carlsbad, including one that sports three bedrooms. Hilton is also strong in Las Vegas with five distinct projects to choose from. They also provide a unique Motor

Home option for those looking to hit the road in a motor home. Hilton is a good choice if you require larger accommodations and like their U.S. footprint. These locations provide for multiple choices in their target markets and include several projects that support three bedrooms. They also have the Hilton Hotel name to help augment and extend your vacation options along with the RCI worldwide network.

Holiday Inn Vacation Club

This vacation group reports over 340,000 customers according to a public statement issued by Wyndham in December of 2016. Holiday Inn recently entered into an agreement in Q4 of 2016 to allow their customers access to RCI's 4,300 international locations. RCI is a controlled vacation reservation and vacation club owned by Wyndham Holdings. Holiday Inn Vacation Club is now controlled by Orange Lake Resorts and offers 24 resorts located primarily in the Southeast with a few projects in Las Vegas and Scottsdale. The also host eight signature resorts, and together, these projects are well located for those looking for a strong regional brand located in the Southeastern United States.

Interval International Group of Brands

Four Seasons, seven exclusive residence clubs

Hyatt Vacation Club, 14 residence clubs, 637 hotels under Hyatt hotels

Marketed by Vistana, an Interval International Company

Sheraton Vacation Club, 20 clubs

Westin Vacation Club, 20 clubs with four new projects opening

Marriot Vacation Club, International

Marriot Vacation Clubs now host over 60-plus United States and international resorts, five luxury Ritz Carlton Clubs, over 2,800 partner affiliations, plus over 5,700 hotels under 31 brands encompassing 110 countries. Marriott Vacation Club also sports an impressive array of homes, VIP trips, cruises, and staycation hotels (known as the Pulse Collection) in the Marriott Vacation Club lineup. The Marriott Vacation Club is rolling out their Pulse Collection of hotels designed primarily for their vacation club owners. They have a demonstrated track record of finding ground-zero locations as indicated by their top locations in New York, Boston, Washington, D.C., South Beach, and now, San Diego. These are bargains in the hotel world and each of these projects offers prime views or ocean locations and are well appointed and are a great way for vacation club members to enjoy stays in the larger, high-demand downtowns across the country. We expect MVC to announce a few locations a year for the next 5 years for this division.

Wyndham Holdings

Wyndham has over 221 home and subsidiary resorts plus 8,000 affiliated hotels. It is the largest time share operator as measured by locations through all of their subsidiaries, including their seven-time share divisions that each operate as separate entities. They do allow customers to cross trade in and out of all of the divisions under their membership rules. Wyndham now owns and controls:

1. Club Wyndham, World Mark, Shell Vacation Club, Margaritaville Vacations, Club Wyndham-Asia, and Club Wyndham-Brazil, as well as World Mark-South Pacific. Wyndham was the first large time share

operator to roll out a points-based model in 1991 and now boasts over 900,000 customers, making it the largest time share operator in the world. They also have a very large global footprint for home and villa rentals (even including houseboats) encompassing over 121,000 properties in over 110 countries that they market through their Destination Network. The combined Wyndham network has an impressive array of vacation choices in the United States, Canada, Mexico, the Caribbean, and the South Pacific, with growing divisions in Brazil and Asia.

The time share global growth model

Our sources further predict that time share will continue its upward momentum, with several, large megaresorts and infill locations moving through the entitlement process in both the United States and abroad in Europe, Asia, South America, and Mexico. This bodes well for continued growth, at least through 2020.

We have chosen to focus on primarily the large international developers in this book but do wish to acknowledge there are several smaller, local time share operators like Lawrence Welk in the Southwest and Blue Green in the Southeast that have been very successful over the years. The time share principles, formulas, opinions, and recommendations in this book will apply in most cases to them as well. Our goal is to share a wealth of knowledge garnered from examining the trends and rules of today's time share while providing the tools to help you make the right vacation choices. If a smaller local resort footprint suits your needs and includes some of your favorite locations, a smaller regional operator could well be the right choice for you.

Which time share company is best? Given the complexities of today's time share models and the multitude of pricing plans that exist, it is difficult to compare price points and maintenance fees because the actual cost of ownership can and does vary even within the same company. This is why we have developed formulas in this book to help convert all of the plans into an apple-to-apple comparison. Our goal is to teach you how to fish rather than recommending you buy a certain fish. The prices and programs will change over and over as these companies sell off, merge, or acquire new locations.

The methodologies we recommend will not change. We have examined the top U.S. developers and reviewed their individual price points which offer various levels of membership. Given the various rules of the top brands and different pricing models that exist, it would be unfair and inaccurate to recommend this brand over that brand because for every recommendation of one over the other, you could make a statistical argument that under a different booking strategy you could have four or five winners out of the top seven developers, depending on the assumptions used. It is possible different developers could each rank number one or two, depending on how the numbers were crunched, and factors like membership discounts, off-season rates, incentive packages, and membership status could each effect a number of different calculation outcomes.

When you consider a time share addition, you should evaluate not only the pricing but also the availability, flexibility, and whether the company you chose will be able to accommodate your future vacation plans. For example, some of the top brands in the hotel industry also offer fairly small vacation club portfolios with some small premium brands having just six or seven locations. However, if that brand is suited to your vacation preferences and your choice is very much city and location dependent, the smaller footprint could be a better choice. You might also enjoy that favorite beach or have a need to be close to family where a time share project is located. Some people don't need or want thousands of vacation options, while many others want a large international program that will be there as their needs change over time.

We are confident if you follow the guidelines outlined in this book your choices will narrow from the top seven, down to the one or two programs that are best for you. There is nothing wrong with owning from more than one time share company, but you may sacrifice membership status for a wider variety of locations, perhaps even next to each other.

The United States time share market—the 2017–2027 growth profile: We estimate based on pipeline reports from the largest developers, the United States will have over 1,700 time shares as of 2017 with online production bringing on another 25 major projects in 2017 and 2018. We expect less than half of this amount to emerge from the smaller regional developers focused on locations within 500 miles of existing properties. Most all of the top seven operators reported they are actively looking for prime sites in high demand areas like certain beach and prime desert and ski locations.

These and other growth dynamics, like a willing supply of investment capital, are likely to provide fuel for the industry to maintain its relatively high growth rate. The industry continues to lobby and maintain favorable tax advantages on small rental incomes (under 14 days) and still provides Form 1098 mortgage interest deduction possibilities for most time share buyers with qualifying mortgage status. Newer time share models continue to provide essential peace of mind and affordability to millions of families looking to lower their future vacation cost by prepaying for downstream price increases. Programs can and do vary widely with some vacation programs providing very good value depending on how the rules are used.

Time share purchases can even be used in certain retirement accounts, although the rules here can be very tricky and can eliminate personal use of the time share. The other tax benefit like the mortgage interest deduction and 14 day untaxed rental incomes, even given the limitations, still provide for a very healthy after-tax environment for those seeking both intermediate and luxury travel, without the hassles of ownership. We continue to see and forecast additional growth of 5% to over 10% per year from most of the top-tier operators for the near term with a slowdown in traditional time share development that will be more than offset by new markets emerging. Economic uncertainty, increased interest rates, and ever-increasing zoning challenges, however, will be offset by the industry creating new products like long-term stays, assisted living time shares, and millennial and boomer retirement packages that will allow the industry to surpass 10% growth rates for the next decade. Top operators with access to public capital will lead this change.

A quick review of the Canadian and Mexican time share markets:

Canada: We believe that Canada has some of the best views, beaches, and mountains in the world, not to mention the charm of Old Town Montreal and the international appeal of Vancouver. Most of the top seven operators can book time share stays through their affiliate programs with a few firms like Wyndham having resorts in Banff and/or Whistler. Canada offers a challenge in that while it is the second-largest country in the world, it has a relatively small population base of only 35M, a few million less than the state of California.

This combined with the colder weather limits demand in most places outside the larger major cities. Of course, most top operators can book into the top ski locations, where much of Canadian time share demand is located. Some of these time shares can offer excellent value in shoulder and off-season for both purchase and rentals. Many of these locations have tremendous summer appeal and make great vacation choices offering very good value. We believe the United States will outperform Canada in growth and price increases because of the above limiting factors; however, a few weeks in any one of the larger Canadian cities is always worthwhile.

Mexico: Mexico has some of the world's most beautiful beaches and year-round warm weather, making it a top tourism destination. This has caused an explosion in both resort hotel and time share development along their coastlines, which offer a full array of time share or vacation ownership products. One of the biggest issues facing foreign owners is the restriction from owning land within 50 kilometers of the coast or within 100 kilometers of the border. There is legislation pending that may loosen this requirement, but it will likely take decades for real fee ownership to work its way through the time share market in Mexico.

For these reasons, the vast majority of time share products are deed restricted and instead, provide a right to occupy over a period of years. The building codes, labor laws, and regulatory agencies in Mexico are less restrictive than in the United States, and therefore, construction costs are lower, along with labor and some supply costs like cheaper wood from Brazil and within Mexico, that help keep building costs below similar buildings in the United States. These vacation or time share packages can start as low as $2,000 to $4,000 for entry pricing and can be very tempting. These timeshares provide a right to occupy for a fixed term, say 20–35 years, and even provide that you only pay maintenance fees when you use the property, or is some cases, have reduced fees for when you do not occupy. All of these variations provide attractive entry and closing emotions, particularly while you are enjoying the Mexican sun and elect to purchase while on-site.

Under current Mexican law, an owner has 5 days to rescind a contract after purchase, but it can be very difficult to get your deposit returned. Purchases made in Mexico are subject to Mexican law, and the state you live in cannot offer any jurisdiction benefit so the rule is very much a "buyer beware" market for purchasers.

If you do have a question, you can contact the Office of the Federal Prosecutor for the Consumer or the Procuraduría Federal del Consumidor which is there to help consumers with fraud-related questions or inquiries. If you need assistance, you can contact them at "PROFECO" by e-mail at:

extranjeros@profeco.gob.mx or mail them at the address provided on the Web site.

Their Web page is:

www.profeco.gob.mx (www.profeco.gob.mx/) for Spanish and www.profeco.gob.mx/english.htm or http://www.profeco.gob.mx/english.htm for English.

The Web sites can direct you to helpful tips on how to buy in Mexico and what scams to look out for while considering a purchase contract.

We advise you make sure you actually visit the time share you are looking at and do not rely on pictures or promises to develop. You should also try to deal with the developers that have been around for at least 20 years and have multiple projects completed. As with any scam, avoid tempting free gifts or offers of free gifts. Remember, even with a relatively smaller $4,000 time share purchase, it only costs $75 or so to buy you a dinner presentation at a local restaurant, so a free dinner should not sway your due diligence process. Also, spend some time trying to figure out the booking and confirmation process to make sure your purchase is available at the times you want to use it. Regulation of time shares is a special process and requires a great deal of effort to monitor. Memberships are limited in scope and match the available supply. Reading the fine print is even more important when purchasing a foreign time share.

That said, Mexican time shares can represent some of the best purchases and offer prime beaches at very affordable prices. Be sure to do your homework about the surrounding areas where you intend to shop and purchase goods and services. You should also verify what security precautions help protect the resort and if the project has on-site security personal. Some of the marginal projects may not provide these services, and access to your unit could involve a long list of other people, so inquire about safes and how access to the property is permitted.

You may also want to inquire about what it costs to rent the units you are looking to purchase. Make sure your RRC ratio is at least 3 to 1; otherwise, you may consider just renting as the risk profiles and limited deed ownership justify a higher RRC ratio if you are putting substantial capital into a deal. Remember, you can also own a domestic plan with a large U.S. developer and just elect to exchange your U.S. week for a Mexican vacation week and thereby avoid many legal issues inherent in Mexican ownership laws.

We believe that both RCI and Interval International support a broad array of timeshare products in Mexico and have strong established relationships in Mexico. One safe option is to use this network for your Mexico travel since most of the top operators allow for direct exchanges with these two top reservation brands. They also control a significant inventory in Mexico allowing them to offer top vacation values. Make sure you understand what is included with your trip and what level of luxury you are purchasing. Also, validate all of your travel, dining, and entertainment needs before you travel to avoid surprises.

Should I consider a foreign-owned operator? If you have home residency or live outside the United States, you may have certain tax or other benefits that make ownership from a regional time share company worthwhile. We would recommend that for most people living in the United States, they consider owning from a United States operator where property protection rights and the strength of the time share industry provide solid cover to protect your ownership rights. The United States also has enough proven time share operators to cover the globe, with some operators providing more or less service to certain parts of the world. In other words, you can have the benefit of foreign occupancy in high-quality time shares but also have the protection of the United States court system.

If you do decide to purchase from a foreign operator, you need to understand what your property rights are, and how transferable they are. Deals that seem too good to be true usually have some type of rules that can work against you over time. Be wary of deals that expire or are properties that sit on land leases. They may be perfect for 10 or 20 years and serve your needs well during that time, but if the leases expire, it could mean the end of your property rights. Lastly, investigate your operator and make sure they have a good reputation. It is very tempting to be impressed by large suites on the ocean, but how the resort is managed and by whom will matter a great deal over the long run. Also, be wary if maintenance fees seem too low. This is a red flag. While it is true foreign labor can greatly reduce maintenance costs in overseas operators, they still should be providing for adequate reserves to replace furniture and HVAC and the roof over time. Read well anything you sign. Neither foreign nor U.S. ownership is necessarily better over the other. Each provide different price points and product types. If you have done your homework and made a purchase, get out there and use it and enjoy it.

CHAPTER **14**

Time Share Checklist-What to Look for if You Are Buying a Time Share

TIME SHARE CHECKLIST: All of today's top brands have connecting hotel alliances with their time share customers although they may be controlled by different parent corporations. This is important to follow if you value a hotel and villa relationship with your time share purchase. While it is unlikely any of these alliances will end anytime soon, the possibility of future mergers and acquisitions could change the program mix you are invested into and thereby sever or alter one side of your vacation experience either on the hotel or vacation side. Below is a summary of what the hotel relationships look like for 2017.

TIME SHARE DEVELOPER	HOTEL PARTNER	2017-EST HOTEL FOOTPRINT
A. Diamond Resorts International	N/A	350 Plus Destinations
B. Disney Resorts	Disney Hotels-Partners	4 Parks, 33 Resorts
C. Interval International-Vistana	Marriott International	5,700
D. Hilton Grand Vacations Club	Hilton Hotel Brands	4,800
E. Holiday Inn Vacation	Holiday Inn Brands	4,300
F. Marriot Vacation Club	Marriott International	5,700
G. Wyndham Vacation Club	Wyndham Hotel Brands	8,000

Understanding your Cost Per Point or Per Week: Most all of the above time share developers have now migrated to a "points-based system" which uses points as a currency to book your reservation or have packages that may convert to points if you wish to trade your time share. When you purchase with most of the above time share developers, you are essentially buying a package of points that entitles you to stay at the resorts either owned or aligned with them. In other situations, you may be purchasing into a pool of properties that contain trading rights both within the developer network and likely outside the network through a pooled reservation network.

Some of the smaller premium brands like Hyatt Vacations are still in the process of considering a points-based system, but they have solutions in place to handle internal trade requests using points. While a larger resort footprint can be the most desirable for ease of booking, you need to understand the relationships between those properties that are directly owned versus those that are in various partnerships or exchange clubs. The latter could have more diluted booking rights. Ask what your deed or ownership interest is secured by and if it includes the assets of a trust or holding company. It is possible only a small portion of the total property footprint is within the deed or within your primary booking rights, so be careful that you understand the overall rights that come with your primary purchase and those that have conditional booking rights.

Confirm what form of ownership you are buying: While this may just be a technical issue to some people, it is important to know if your ownership interest is in a club with a membership interest or is it backed by the real estate. Be sure to ask if your time share purchase is secured by a deed or trust which is the strongest form of ownership. This form of ownership also provides for a more solid long-term investment. Remember, in today's complex maze of time share options, your parent company could be a different entity from the time share subsidiary you purchase from in some cases. The closer you are to the original ownership, the more senior your booking rights will be in most cases. Most developers now have three different layers of time share choices. These divisions are:

A. Home resorts the time share company either bought or developed with direct control.
B. Alliance contracts with sister companies or even third parties that have either reciprocal reservation rights or have transferred the right to occupy within your overall villa footprint.

C. Exchange companies that provide access for exchange members to occupy villas usually owned by a party outside the original developer.

Confirm your reservation priority: It is the combination of these three possibilities that provides for the overall villa footprint. The line between these distinctions can be hard to follow since alliances could involve either direct or indirect control of the realty assets. This information is not always easy to obtain, and it may or may not be easily found in the public domain. This is important to understand because some of these time share companies now control over 100 or more brands of time shares, exchange companies, and hotel brands, either through direct or indirect control. Understanding who controls what really helps if you are buying your time share for a particular location, and your primary goal is to occupy either one or just a few prime locations within your overall villa footprint. We recommend you take some time to ascertain which ones are under direct control and what the pecking order is for all guests, including those that may be external to the system.

Overall, I have interviewed all of the top time share companies and have found them to be pretty straightforward, but the fact is, your sales representative may not know the answer on how a specific property fits into the system, merely that, as a guest, you have access to the property. I have usually found the best way to get a reliable answer is to ask about four or five people in different locations with different titles the same question, and then you can start to eliminate some answers that don't seem to make sense. This can involve calling the corporate office and tracking down a vice president. I have also found myself advising them on some calls when it becomes apparent I know more than they do, so don't assume they know more than you do if you have been on the research trail.

Given the high likelihood of future mergers and acquisitions, you could see your favorite brand on either the vacation or hotel side sold or traded, which could make downstream reservations more difficult if any future merger complicates your ownership rights or priority booking rights. On a positive note, these large time share companies are compelled not to do anything against the common time share owner as they could face a class action lawsuit if a particular move was in stark contrast with the owners' prior rights that were part of their investment decision. I have found my timeshare company to be more than fair as they have grown their resort portfolio, always grandfathering past rights for owners who bought 10 or 20 years ago, and making it very clear what the new rules are for future owners. A large acquisition could also be a positive thing since the developer would likely have to add to the reservation pool more properties to lawfully allow more users into the system. This is why it is important to establish what your deed includes and how your level of membership could be affected by current and future mergers and acquisitions.

Generally speaking, if your deed or ownership title includes your favorite property or properties, you will be tied to them as long as you own your timeshare. Alliances, third-party exchange rights, and sister company relationships could change over time, or at the very least, these relationships could juggle reservation priorities. This is why some older legacy weeks have much more intrinsic value to the owners because they came with priority booking rights tied to a specific home resort. Some of the newer plans with some of the new time share models no longer offer primary home resort preferences. Instead, you will have preference rights to a group of properties. Membership hierarchy could also play a role in both past and future booking rights.

We believe the points-based systems are superior to the past weeks only system because they allow you to spend your currency more accurately by giving you the flexibility to buy only the time, space, and view you desire. Many programs now allow for stays as little as 1 night, and some provide discounts for short-term stays under 30 or 60 days. Others provide exclusive booking windows for 8 to 13 months ahead of time. Be sure to ask about ALL of the levels of membership and how the points work at each level. In general, the fastest way to recoup your investment and improve your RRC ratio and payback indicator might be to buy more timeshares from the same company that provides a discount and location package that is one or two levels up from your current level. I have found over the past several years that the vast majority of my stays worked best at the last minute, saving me many points that I used for more vacation nights. This has allowed me to dramatically lower my cost per night well below the weighted average from other members even within my VIP level. We cover this concept in detail under calculating your RRC ratio.

Now that we see that some members in a time share system could pay less than someone else for the same unit and week, it is easy to see why investing up to a bigger discount could be very worthwhile. It only takes a little practice for anyone to figure out what the cost will be and how many nights the system is likely to grant an owner year in and year out by using all of the discount rules. This can then be used to value what points are really worth under different booking strategies. It clearly does not matter if a place cost you 50 points a night or 500,000 points a night since the numbers themselves are meaningless. Don't be fooled by the size of the number. I know of one time share company that provides an outstanding value for a two-bedroom villa on the beach for

50 points a night. It may just be the best deal in time share—not because it is 50 points a night—it could be 1,000,000 points a night. It is because the maintenance fee on the unit was about $26 a night in 2016, well below any cheap hotel on the beach, and it comes in the form of a 2+2 villa.

What matters is how many nights your points program gets you at the time and place that is important to you. Once you convert your net purchase price into points and factor in the discount benefits that apply to you, and then figure out your RRC ratio, you can then take all seven time share companies and stack their RRC ratios from one to seven. This process could scramble some of them in different orders depending on how and when you vacation, so it is important that you use accurate data on the times you want to stay and what is the realistic cost to rent that same villa that same night. You can then also add in days you might get from discount windows. However, it may take you a year or 2 to figure out what discount windows are open for you and how they might vary from year to year.

This will provide an economic rating for each time share company. This does not mean the time share with the most economic value is the best one for you. If you prefer other properties and other competitive booking rights, it may be in your best interest to pay a little more and be happier with the total result. Either way, it is important to understand what the future benefits of your membership could be in order to qualify for upgraded benefits that, in the long run, may well reduce your occupancy cost.

Maintenance fees—rate of increase versus inflation that matters: Many owners complain that their maintenance fees are too high. This is a natural reaction, and since they are reoccurring, it is an expense item in your budget that should be taken seriously. While most time share companies have some type of general and administrative allocation built into the fee, they also have a vested interest in keeping the fees to a minimum while also making sure the property portfolio is adequately maintained. Chapter 9 covers the 14 things a competitive time share company must do today to be competitive. As long as your RRC ratio starts out at least measuring 2.0 to 2.5 to 1, you will recoup your investment in just under 10 years and have the peace of mind that any type of inflationary period, even at a modest rate of 3%, will not take the family vacation off the table. Family vacation memories are very important and the type of memory that will last. Your maintenance fee is the only way your property can look as good 25 years from now, and it will seem like a bargain compared to the rental rates in 25 years. I would recommend you ask for information on what the past fees were, and then calculate what the rate of increases have been over a 10-year period. Your maintenance fee increases should ideally be right around the rate of inflation for the period you are reviewing. Be wary of huge increases in maintenance fees well above the rate of inflation for the year you are examining. The larger operators tend to be fairly close to each other because they know they must remain competitive to outpace their competition in this area.

We initially planned to list each of the top brands and their respective maintenance fees for a week in Hawaii. The problem is that not all had similar properties in Hawaii, with some being brand new versus older properties, and not all brands are located in the same place, even in Hawaii. In addition, if we had used a two-bedroom as a standard and list the maintenance fee on what we found, we noted the fees are not that far apart from the median price of every company weighted together, usually up or down by no more than 30% from the top to the bottom. One time share company that might be rated the highest for maintenance fees could conceivably fall to the bottom and rank first if maximum discounts were used, thereby almost doubling the number of nights stayed with the same annual maintenance fee but with a vastly different maintenance fee per night. This is why we cover this subject many times during this book to give you many opportunities to understand the best way to monitor your actual time share costs. For these reasons, however, we did not feel it was fair to just post a certain ranking but rather to teach you how to run your own RRC ratio and see for yourself. Remember, the higher the RRC ratio, the more economic value your time share has with it. We cover the terms used in this book many times but also have them in the glossary if you are reading along and need to recheck a term used in these pages.

The raw data is, therefore, not enough to suggest that one firm over another is worth considering due solely to maintenance costs. The luxury market is priced higher, but even then, it offers a more luxurious vacation package so these maintenance fees would not constitute an apple-to-apple comparison. Lastly, one could book a vacation in Hawaii under a 60-day discount window and the RRC ratio, the only real objective way to measure true cost, would change dramatically, under, say a 30%–50% discount window, which would, again, make anything we printed inaccurate.

We therefore have chosen not to print maintenance fees because they will also quickly become outdated as fees change regularly to keep up with rising costs. The two best barometers of maintenance fees are to understand the past rate of increases and what your RRC ratio will be for the package you are considering, making sure to note that your RRC ratio will change substantially between low and high seasons. Your RRC ratio should be at least 2.2 to 1 or you are paying too much for your time share on the original market.

Your real RRC ratio is best calculated at the time of year you enjoy since that is the only real cost that applies to you. You may have one RRC ratio in the summer and another in the winter, depending on the season. In this case, you would add them together and divide by two to get to your overall weighted RRC if you, in fact, use your time share for a week in the summer and a week in the winter. This same rule works even if you have 10 weeks. You just divide the sum total by 10 in that case. Make sure you are comparing apples to apples, though, and are just using weeks; otherwise, you will need to calculate a ratio for each day, and then divide by the total number of days used or rented for the year by your actual daily cost, including any free nights earned through discounts. This would give you the most accurate RRC ratio. In other words, make sure your numbers are weeks over weeks or days over days, never a combination of the two for your rental values and maintenance fees.

The Vacation club—board of directors—makeup and tenure: This may seem like it does not matter, but frankly, good management always matters. In some cases, it could mean the difference between out of control costs and very predictable maintenance fee increases that are quite fair. In nearly every time share operation, each property is represented by either a local board made up of members that own or stay at that property and representatives from the developer. This generally provides a good balance between the parties that have a vested stake in a particular property. This even applies to the newer points-based systems as owners still have their favorite vacation spots and some owners feel compelled to give back to a property that has provided so many great memories over so many years. The vacation club may also have oversight boards from the development company that reports up to the parent company or entity that controls or monitors all of the operating boards in a given area. In these situations, the vacation club will sit on both boards in order to help closely monitor future budget decisions. A good place to start is with the backgrounds of the people serving on your board and/or those that are up for election.

You should see if the people serving have professional backgrounds in some faucet of the legal, auditing, accounting, finance, construction management, and marketing industries. All of these backgrounds are very important in making large capital expenditure decisions. The time to be concerned is when the board is up for reelection and very few people choose to run. This could mean there is a great deal of apathy toward the property, and/or there are many problems associated with the resort. In most cases, these boards are run pretty well and there tends to be a steady supply of newer candidates. I would be careful if someone has been on any of these boards for over 10 years. These are supposed to be temporary positions and should be filled with professionals or retired owners who have appropriate backgrounds, not lifetime members where too much control can be dangerous. *"That's the way we have always done it"* is not an answer to a financial question.

All of these boards are required to maintain board minutes which you are entitled to review as an owner. If you have any trouble getting the board minutes, that is a red flag, and you should make sure you are not investing into a property that is undermaintained. The obvious answer in this case is to walk the property and note any deferred maintenance. The majority of Category One and Two time shares tend to be very well run, and normally, we only see issues with smaller time share companies that are falling into a Category Four property.

Be aware of any time share that is priced well below the market or is being sold for a few hundred dollars. You could be on the hook for a future assessment that is right around the corner. Most of today's larger points-based systems use complex allocation models for all of the eligible properties inside of your vacation package, making the likelihood of your plan getting assessed much smaller as these plans tend to carry a much-larger reserve and insurance requirements, making an assessment almost a thing of the past. I have not received an assessment in over 10 years when my company migrated into a points-based system.

Carefully examine the vacation club property portfolio: The large time share companies all have different resort portfolios, and each offer something different. Many of the smaller brands concentrate on a regional area with a small cross section of desert and beach locations located on one or the other coastlines. The larger time share operations have operations around the globe and focus on both domestic and international travelers. Other operators like Hilton Grand Vacations, tend to build multiple properties in one area, like Hawaii, and offer more choices in a much-smaller footprint. Some operators like Hyatt and Four Seasons offer only a few locations that tend to be purchased by owners who love a singular location.

None of these are necessarily better than the others because the level of luxury, locations, and benefits is intended to fit a certain segment of the market. The important thing is to make sure your current and future plans will work with your family over the long term. I have bought time shares for the single reason of getting into one location and have bought others just to have more points to trade. The plan you decide to purchase will likely allow you to stay in many resorts under the "Points or Exchange Rights" that come with the plan, but make sure you understand how many people have booking priority ahead of you as trading from one high season location into another high season may sound easy but could prove to be difficult. The best way to know for sure is to see what vacation options are available by making your sales executive try and book a villa right in front of you if you are serious about a certain plan. I would routinely do this right in front of the client and it helped close many deals. If your salesperson is not willing I would request another sales executive or ask for the manager and let them know you want to see in real time what works and what does not. If they refuse, you are looking at the wrong plan or company. Of course, our booking and reservation tips and tricks (Chapter 17 and 25) will prove useful over time, but even with clever efforts, "sold out" can actually mean "sold out" in some but not all cases.

Trading platform hierarchy: Think of your membership as a large pyramid with about 10 lines drawn across it like the picture below. This example is not intended to reflect any of the top seven time share providers but is just an estimate of what a time share booking pyramid might look like. The actual hierarchy will vary between the top time share companies with either more or less emphasis put on one layer over another. What is important is that as an owner, you understand there is a relationship between customers, and even within the same company, there are layers that have inroads into reservations that may or may not come from different inventory allocations. In some cases, one layer may or may not have preference over the other but could simply live in a different database, leaving a lower layer open where a top layer is closed, or vice versa. By understanding the reservation pyramid, it is easier to understand that the large global time share companies manage a complex array of inbound reservation requests, and often, the front desk may not even have control of some of the data banks. This is why someone may not be able to secure a room at the front desk and someone else might be able to book a room through a different source. I have found that understanding this pyramid helped me navigate around tight booking windows because I was able to book a time share reservation as a hotel customer, and thereby, I was able to extend my sold-out time share reservation.

Over long periods of time and with the right questions, you can build your own software pyramid which will help pinpoint openings that occur within different reservations windows. In other words, it is possible for occupancy rates to go up and down as owners convert points right before deadlines and release reservations to make room in their point bank to apply toward a newer and more desirable choice. Some time share reservations might cancel when certain events occur like a lack of snowfall or many PGA players missing the weekend cut. A large projected storm that routed into a different direction can also change demand almost overnight. The last day for converting a legacy week into points also might open that home resort because it suggests that many owners are likely to visit a different resort, especially if the point exchange is less expensive than the week they just gave up. Knowledge of these things going on can put you in the reservation queue well before the phone calls come in to grab that next open reservation if you are adept at using your operator's automatic booking options.

Understanding your operator's pyramid reservation stack

Sample pyramid reservation stack for a large time share operator

TOP VIP	Generally called Chairman or Platinum, but this is the highest ranking in a time share company
Tier Two	Sometimes Presidential or Gold, equal to second highest
Tier Three	Sometimes Silver but usually third-highest ranking

Tier Four	Initial owner level for first-time purchasers. Intranetwork trade. This is a home-to-home trade that has priority. This grants an internal customer the right to trade within the same company
Executive VIP	Could be high-ranking hotel customer or executive within the company. Reservation could be from a different data bank
Promotional Bookings	Home company looking for new customers. May pull from the same or different data bank with allocation model
Hotel Crossover	Hotel partner importing into time share reservation bank
Rental Pool	Developer using allocation model for rental income
Employee	Employee perk to stay at discount based on allocation model
Out of Network	Foreign developer looking to inbound into competitor reservation pool
Friend/Family Rates of Employee	Employee perks granted to open rooms or small allocation pool. Reserved for family/ friends. Likely to have larger villa pool during off-season periods.

This is a good way to understand what could be a theoretical stack for a time share customer priority. The above example is intended to reflect an example rather than an actual stack from any one company. I am not going to talk about one specific company here since that would be unfair and could be inaccurate since different developers will have different software priority stacks. Each company has their own rules and booking priorities. However, it is fair to state that although they are different, they also have some similar practices that tend to favor their top customers, not unlike most businesses. The top of the pyramid will likely represent the VIP customers, those that have spent at least $100,000 and as much as $350,000, or even more in some cases. These people have special booking rights and in extreme cases, can book at the last minute into top resorts that hold rooms for them. This is expensive and this customer pays for this right by purchasing a very expensive vacation plan. The next three or four tiers down might represent various levels of membership. They will usually have some type of ranking with each tier having better booking windows, special discounts, and certain guaranteed times and location preferences over the tier just below them. Usually many top time share resorts rely on different databases for different inventory, and they may or may not speak to each other. This is why we say to be sure to understand ALL of the tier structure because even one level up can make a huge difference in your overall vacation experience over the years. While a bit ironic, it may also be true that the more you spend in some cases, the more you save, meaning that in the long run, your RRC ratio and payback indicator will improve dramatically if you owned a plan that provides for bigger discounts and helps you book prime seasons. This is one business where spending more to be a top customer can pay off. When you factor in you do not have to maintain your villa and it is waiting for you all the time, suddenly, your maintenance fee can look very cheap compared to actually owning a prime vacation home.

As you glide through the pyramid stack, you can see that most all of the large developers/operators have several inbound reservation pools, all vying to book a villa. You can imagine the demand that comes in with fresh snow or that prime July weekend. Notice that as you go through the software stack, there are still several reservation pools awaiting an answer to book a room. As you near the bottom, you will see that the industry actually works together to take each other's guest when rooms are open. In reality, this is a fantastic idea, but first-time buyers need to know these trades can be almost impossible in prime seasons. Each resort has its own way of making sure they have given all of their time share customers and even hotel customers plenty of time and notice to book the resort. It is only after these windows have expired that the reservation pool expands for foreign trades to come into the system. Some operators will keep a small pool of rooms available for foreign trades, but they tend to be the less desirable rooms with reduced views.

Some operators may keep a very small inventory open just to make sure they honor any contractual obligations, but it is safe to say these rooms are at, or near, the bottom of the priority stack. This is good news if you like your home resort but can be difficult to trade into another resort and sometimes even within the same company. Notice, however, that by using any combination of family rates, if you have a relative in the business, hotel relationship through your rewards card, or just plain jumping into the rental pool, either within the resort or even with another owner, you have multiple paths into that vacation if you really want to be there. Often, other owners will list their vacation weeks in the top Internet sites because they may be on another vacation and do not have the time or funds to use their week. I was able to put together a monthly rental once when I only had 3 weeks to rent by paying a premium for the fourth week. I lost money on that week but made a nice profit by packaging a 1-month rental in the summer for a willing customer. The stack helped me make the deal because I knew the rooms were there if I knew where to look for them.

Your return on investment through the payback indicator: Remember our rule is that your time share should have enough economic value after your payback indicator has expired to net you back your original net purchase price in the form of rental savings. This will mean about 8–9 years for most people, which includes maintenance fees. In the medium term (5–10 years), time share has typically resold for about 50% of what you paid for it, assuming it is a Category One or Two time share during the first decade of ownership. Over 20 years, you should make a small profit on what you paid, assuming the original purchase allowed for ownership via a deed in perpetuity. Remember, we have been in a period of relatively low inflation for the past decade. The higher the inflation rate, the better a time share will perform because it becomes a bigger hedge against rising rental rates. History has shown with inflation around 3% per year, you will likely get back your purchase price and perhaps a small profit after your payback period has expired twice over, about 18 years for most time shares in Category One or Two. In real economic terms, the price has likely at least doubled, so a 50% discount, plus a small premium in 20 years, will have most owners out of their Category One and Two time share at a small profit.

This assumes you bought a deed with your ownership. This is also assuming the industry does not change and adopt an electronic trading system. If this occurs, we expect prime Category One and Two time shares to trade much closer to new prices if the industry can remove the high transaction cost now apparent in the resale market. Both, discounts and incentives will be able to shrink as both liquidity and lender capital become more transparent and there is a ready and able bidding market. While there is a secondary market at present, the spread between asking price and the bidding price is too wide, and secondary market transfers usually do not grant all of the original developer rights, further confusing the marketplace.

It is worthwhile to ask before you purchase what trading and legal rights will transfer with the deed. You can also ask them if there is a secondary purchase option and what the terms are. In most instances, you can expect a fairly large discount to current prices as the developer is not primarily engaged in the secondary market as a for-profit concept. They may buy at bottom prices to maintain control of the deed, but more importantly, it is just good business practice to buy your own product back at below what it cost you to produce it. This is actually a better use of shareholder capital if the company is public.

Can thee rent thy villa? As we have discussed, renting your time share out to third parties can be tricky, and you should realize what works well one year may or may not work as well the following year. It is true that certain high-profile two- or three-bedroom villas located in Category One or Two timeshare projects will likely be rented in high season every year and will usually have a consistent demand for them. I have found my time shares do rent well during high season, during prime sporting events, and when the resort is very likely to be sold out in most or all of the rental and reservation buckets.

I have also had other times when it just does not rent, although these times tend to be more nonpeak, and there can be a lot of competition. That said, always check your time share's policies and fee schedules to make sure you can execute on your plans and understand your prime rental windows. Oftentimes, the best time to rent is during high season when demand cycles are at the highest level. Another good test is whether you would rent your own villa at the price you are asking. If the answer is no, you may have your sights set too high. If you do not want a hot summer month in the desert, it is unlikely anyone else will really pay up for it either.

We have found using any of the top online rental companies works best. Some of the best we recommend have very reasonable fee structures. Make sure your fees are performance based, and you only pay for a successful rental. I have had great success with several of the larger Internet companies that specialize in home and villa rentals. We recommend some of these companies and how to rent your villa in Chapter 20, "How to Rent and How to Not Rent Your Villa."

New product pipeline: It is always a good sign if your company is in the process of opening new locations. New locations keep your vacation club exciting and also divert reservations into the new property for a while, allowing all of the owners a bigger reservation pool until the cycle repeats itself and more memberships are sold. While this is a constant process, opening new resorts in top locations will only make the vacation club more successful because it can offer newer state-of-the-art facilities in locations that have been in progress for years. It takes a long runway and lots of time between acquiring the land, getting all of the zoning in place (entitlement process), and then constructing the project. The large developers now prefer larger resorts if the land is available because it is usually more economical to build since it will help reduce the cost per unit, which, in turn, can lead to better pricing. We all have a vested interest in the clubs using as many new products as possible to keep operating costs in line. Check if your sales executive knows about other new projects in the pipeline. You should only rely on projects that are either under construction or have been publicly announced. In changing economies, projects can be delayed or cancelled if the economy takes a turn for the worst.

Look at the CEO/chairman of the board of your Vacation Club: While it may seem like a long way from your purchasing decision, reviewing the track record of the CEO and the board of directors can provide clues about the longer term for the company. If a new CEO is on board, take a look at his or her background. Does he/she have acquisition experience or construction experience? He or she may have come from a legal or accounting background. Usually, a board of directors will hire a new CEO that has strong expertise in the area they have to focus on. For example, if the company is adding staff to the development team, it might signal they wish to go on a new development path and add several projects. If the company has been suffering from losses or missing their numbers, they might bring in a CEO to focus on cost cutting, not exactly a positive sign for a lot of new projects coming online.

If the CEO has been there for a while, the company does not seem to have any large class action lawsuits (all companies get sued; it is the large lawsuits that can hurt them), and they are opening new projects, it is likely the company is doing very well. Ask about any debt within the parent company or go online and review the balance sheet. It is not likely your sales executive may even know how strong their own balance sheet is. A strong balance sheet is a sign of a disciplined management team that knows large-scale projects take time and waiting in the wings with cash may be a smarter strategy as they can move fast if prices start to fall. Running a large time share company requires multiple skill sets, and anyone is likely to need help in some areas because the skills required to manage construction, management, acquisitions, and marketing cover a great deal of special knowledge in the time share business. While the business is now quite large, there are only a few names around the world that can truly say they have vast experience in all of these needed skill sets.

This is why a CEO with a strong track record is hard to find. A well-rounded board of directors is the best way to ensure long-term success.

Know your Operator's Balance Sheet: : Since most of the larger time share operators are public, it is fairly easy to get ahold of their balance sheets. Another way to analyze their future is to read the analyst reports that are available. These reports are generally well researched and have a great deal of valuable information about the company. You want to look for trends, new product offerings, expansion plans, and also take a look their financials. If their stock price is up year after year for most years, it is a sign the company is well run. Time share is a very capital-intensive business, and investing into a time share company is very different from investing to purchase one of their products. If you plan on acquiring a large time share portfolio, you should avoid overexposure by also investing in the same company's stock. This is particularly true if you want to sell your primary home and follow some ideas in this book and live in time shares part time every year. As time share owners, you want to see a strong balance sheet and stable management. Most every large time share operator will, and does, get sued for a variety of reasons. The main issue for time share owners is to make sure the company does not have any, or very few, large class action lawsuits. These suits can drain much time and money from an expansion plan and is a sign the company needs to be more transparent. A solid track record of growth with a pipeline of recent projects is what the ideal time share operator should look like.

You may not be able to ever get enough information on any public or private board, but a quick review of backgrounds and history of senior management is usually very worthwhile and can provide a clue on how the company will be managed, at least over the next 5 to 10 years. Since a large investment in any time share plan could be in your family for generations to come, it makes sense to do a little homework and understand who you are partnering with to run your vacation portfolio.

The new staycation model—what is it? As the industry continues to evolve, we can expect to see the large operators roll out some new products designed to capture just the weekend, or short-term, traveler. We expect to see more and more of the larger hotel chains offer some type of "Vacation Points to Stay" program in what was traditionally a typical hotel room or suite. The new staycation model is for owners who want to use a hotel for a small, 2- or 3-day stay, well located, and likely in or around a downtown, beach, or other top draw location. These types of hotels may or may not accept the regular hotel loyalty points, or likely will reserve a larger block of rooms for time share owners seeking to use their currency for a short term hotel stay. These programs will be geared around vacation points used in the operator's vacation program. Marriott Vacation Club is just beginning to roll out this program, and it has been well received by those who have stayed in one of these types of hotels. I stayed in the San Diego property at 701 A Street and could not have been more pleased. My suite, although much smaller than its time share villa counterpart, still had a small kitchenette complete with a microwave and mini dishwasher, along with a reduced supply of dishes, glasses, and silverware. This was just enough for a nice 2-day stay.

The suite had a separate bedroom with a sliding door, a small kitchen, and adjoining bathroom, and had a small but well-appointed living area with a large-screen TV in both the living room and in the bedroom. In a pinch, the regulation couch could have accommodated an overnight guest. Best of all, to book it involved just a few mouse clicks, and the price per point cost and therefore converted cost in dollars was at least half what a twenty-seventh-floor hotel room should have cost. The suite I enjoyed was larger than a regular hotel room, which just added to the bargain. This new time share model is now in five cities with Marriott, and they expect to open many more. We believe this new time share option is a perfect complement to any vacation plan and definitely gives Marriott a leg up for those that may have downtown travel needs in the United States. This product is also perfect to enjoy numerous sports and entertainment events that tend to populate the larger downtown areas. The benefit of escaping the taxes and resort fees were very pleasing, helping to drive a bigger gap between the alternative downtown hotel rooms and this new type of "minivilla in the sky." It is easy to see this trend looks like a real winner.

CHAPTER **15**

Luxury Beachfront Resort versus Luxury Beachfront Time Share

COST SAVINGS IN a time share versus hotel resorts Many of today's megaresorts with multiple buildings spread out on 35 acres or more now boast mega pools, tennis courts, golf courses, lazy river pools, indoor and outdoor spas, and have upgraded food and beverage services. It can be difficult driving by one of these megaresorts trying to figure out what is the difference between that and a mega time share resort that has nearly all of the same features and most of the same amenities. It can result in the same experience . . . until you examine your bill at checkout. The time share traveler, however, recognizes the actual hotel room or smaller resort hotel suites are almost half the size, or less, of a two- or three-bedroom villa with a full kitchen. The other obvious feature is that with the time share product, many of the pesky fees just are not there. While many of these fees may not be significant over a few days, they can really add up over a longer 2- to 4-week stay. Let's look at what happens when you compare a megahotel resort with a mega time share resort.

A 2017 cost comparison of occupying a beachfront Time Share versus a luxury resort hotel in the summer 30 day stay

Newport Beach, California

Notes		**Monthly**	**Daily**	**Monthly**	**Daily**	
		Lux Hotel	**Lux Hotel**	**Lux TS**	**Lux TS**	
Hotel Charge	Newspaper	$0.00	$0.00	$0.00	$0.00	
$8.00 for 2 per day	Coffee	$240.00	$8.00	$0.00	$0.00	
$1.00 day	Ice	$0.00	$0.00	$0.00	$0.00	
Suite	Heat	$0	$0.00	$0.00	$0.00	
Air Conditioning	Air	$0	$0.00	$0.00	$0.00	
Water Bill	Water	$0	$0.00	$0.00	$0.00	
Gas Bill	Gas	$0	$0.00	$0.00	$0.00	
Cable Bill	Cable	$0	$0.00	$0.00	$0.00	
Wi-Fi Value	Wi-Fi	$150	$3.00	$0.00	$0.00	
Save from dinner out	Kitchen	$0	$0.00	$0.00	$0.00	
$20.00/night	Parking	$600	$20.00	$0.00	$0.00	
$200/day X .06%	Room Tax	$1,260	$42.00	$0.00	$0.00	
$25.00 day	Resort Fee	$750	$25.00	$0.00	$0.00	
no charge	Local Phone	$0	$0.00	$0.00	$0.00	
$250.00 1 USE	Dinner Limo	$250	$8.33	$0.00	$0.00	
Maintenance Fee	$1300/week	$0	$0.00	$5,200		
Charges		$3,250	$106.33	$5,200	$173.33	
Hotel Rental/Suite	$700 per Night	$21,000	$700	$0.00		
Cost of Mega Resort Hotel for 30 days in a one bedroom suite		**$24,250**		**$5,200**	**Mega Resort Time Share in 1,450 2+2 villa for 30 days**	
Time Share Savings				**$19,050**		
Assumes Time Share is Paid for.						

We have also noted that with a long-term stay (1–3 months) in a time share, you could actually reduce the cost of your primary home expenses by a small but meaningful amount. If you are going to stay for a month in a time share in July, you do not need to use your air conditioner at home, you will not be taking showers at home, you could just cancel the newspaper, drink coffee in the unit, and you will not need the same amount of gas or electricity. While not a great deal of money, we ran the numbers above to look at just how a luxury time share resort can be cost beneficial when compared to a like kind luxury resort hotel. . Notice the difference with the monthly savings from resort fees, parking, and taxes that a time share provides over a megahotel. While these are just external charges, the real savings is, of course, with the cost per day in a resort time share versus the room rate per day of a resort hotel. We can see from a simple comparison that the luxury time share will save over $19,000 per year versus just paying for the luxury resort hotel. This assumes 30 days a year of luxury hotel or time share stay regardless of how long any one stay might be.

CHAPTER **16**

Understanding the Time Share Sales Process and Rationale

THE TIME SHARE sales process—the same-day close rationale: Time share is one of the most fascinating businesses in the world because there is nothing quite like how it is bought, sold, and used in today's fast-paced economy. For starters, for many families, a time share could rank as one of their largest investments behind a home, certain automobiles, and possible other investments like a rental property or larger stock portfolio or 401(k). Most financial analysts would likely argue that a time share is really not an investment but rather an investment in your family and the memories that come along with the time share. We would tend to agree this is a fair point for the vast majority of buyers who buy a time share.

The interesting thing about this rationale is, what do you call a $40,000 purchase that is clearly not a home or automobile that is supposed to save you money? If it is not a financial purchase, what kind of purchase is it? Nobody buys a time share so they can spend more money on downstream vacations. Well, if the purpose of buying a time share is to save money, then it seems that a vacation club operates like a large coupon, offering the chance to buy goods and services in the future at a lower price. This debate could go on for some time but suffice it to say, there is a financial reward to buying a time share which usually takes 7 to 10 years under most situations (excluding off-season and short-term discounts) to realize this payback. However, the intangibles like convenience and flexibility for new locations and new products also make time shares more relevant and useful today. Perhaps most of all, having that family vacation on the calendar every year forces us to get out and take time off. If church was scheduled every 10 days instead of once a week, most of would likely go three times a month instead of four.

The reason that salespeople are under pressure is because they are compensated and trained to close on the same day they meet their client. Most of the industry is not set up to accommodate most time share decisions over multiple meetings. Some large operators have adopted this method, and it works well for them under a more relaxed program. This is generally a commission-only business, and it takes great skill to meet a stranger, get to know them, and then build a trust profile sufficient to close a $40,000 sale in 90 minutes. The large operators know precisely how many tours the average person takes before they buy. They also know if they don't close you today, a competitor may well close you tomorrow, perhaps on the back of a competitor providing a much-better presentation that got the ball rolling. Now it is 6 months later, and you are in Hawaii, more relaxed, and you decide to go to lunch at that new megaresort with the grand opening balloons guiding you through an array of beautiful waterfalls and lush gardens. You walk in for lunch, and there it is, that convenient vacation desk sitting right out in the lobby while you await your reservation for lunch.

Now you get to tell your spouse you get a free restaurant dinner for two at your favorite steak house if you just endure a 90-minute presentation. Sounds pretty good. You go have a nice relaxing drink at lunch with an umbrella and a large pineapple wedge on the glass rim, and the next thing you know, you are beating yourself up for not owning more time shares so you can stare at the ocean, relax, and enjoy life. Three hours later, you sign what seems like 20 documents, walk out with a phone book of vacation choices, and you are now either a new member or you have upgraded into perhaps a higher membership status. What are the odds that salesperson could have called you on the phone at work, scheduled a meeting to discuss your vacation goals, and then spent 4 weeks trading legal documents in the mail? The time share industry knows what the odds are . . . and they are near zero. The vast majority of time shares need to be sold while you are likely on vacation because it takes time to unwind and get out of the stress routine, free up your mind, and then ask yourself what is really important in life. Vacations are not important if your job is on the line and you are under pressure to meet deadlines.

The free gift shoot-out: Nothing is more interesting than a couple getting ready for a time share tour. I have heard stories of couples writing on their villa mirror in lipstick "we're not going to buy," couples vowing to each other that no matter what, they will stick together and they are just going on a tour for an "update," and, of course, that free gift usually worth $50–$150 for a 90-minute tour.

Magically, every year, the time share industry books billions in sales from people who "were not going to buy." Why does this happen? The short answer is because vacation plans, in general, make sense, provide a disciplined method of vacationing, and remove cost surprises. In some years, if it were not for a prepaid vacation plan, it is likely that many families might scrap the family vacation to save money. It is not unusual for families that do not own time shares to just skip a vacation for many years at a time. The problem with that is you do not get those years back again, and if you have younger children, you will never be able to recapture their childhood. In time share presentations, and those that are most impactful, it is usually one of the spouses who points out that it is not about the money, it is about the memories. This combination of emotion combined with huge financial incentives has proven to be a very successful model for the industry.

Time Share- A commission-based industry: Selling time shares can be extremely rewarding for the right people. It can also be very hard on those salespeople who cannot make that critical connection to convince a client to spend $25,000 to $60,000—or more—based on a presentation. While skilled discipline is needed to maximize presentation awareness, success comes to those salespeople who can communicate clearly, stay on point, and create enormous trust, all in a time span under 90 minutes. Like many commission-based business models, the time share industry is like real estate itself; that is, the top 20% of those in the business make most of the money, while the rest work toward retooling their skill set or moving into other industries. For this reason, it pays very well for the few who can master the art of painting a vacation picture in simple words and connecting with their customers. If you find yourself on a time share tour, you should be aware these are people who rely on sales to earn their income, and regardless of your impression of the product or their effectiveness, it is always appropriate to be honest with them, let them know your issues, and most of all, avoid making up reasons why you may not be able to purchase today. Just go with the real reason. This is one time where admitting you are broke is the best way out, if that is your situation.

The best way to handle a time share tour—be honest: The best way to respond to a time share tour should just be to tell the truth. If that means you do not have the funds, then letting the salesperson know that saves a lot of time and frustration in the long run for everyone. If you are being open and having an honest exchange, you may well find that a particular time share tour is a very good fit for your lifestyle. Time share salespeople are some of the best trained salespeople in the world. They know emotion, have budget awareness, and can sense, usually, when the truth is being told. If you cannot, or do not want to, make a purchase, it will be easier and much faster to get to the point quickly; otherwise, you force a salesperson to go down a road to answer an objection you really do not have but chose to use as a reason not to buy. Using the real reasons to explain why you cannot purchase today is always preferred and will help the sales associate avoid countering reasons not to purchase that are not valid. For example, I used to hear on occasion the reason a client chose not to buy was because they wanted increased flexibility to make vacation choices.

When you represent a program with thousands and thousands of travel choices, offered in over 100 countries, that can be booked 24/7 with as little notice as 30 seconds to 13 months ahead of time, it is not logical that one would turn down this type of time share purchase due to a "lack of flexibility." This type of illogical answer forces the salesperson to spend another 10 minutes or longer reciting all of the possible choices one can have in the program to counter the comment on flexibility. All this method does is delay the inevitable, force more closing attempts, and leaves the salesperson in a never-ending banter contest that serves no purpose. Keep your answers real, short, and to the point, and try to engage in reality. This will allow your tour to reach the proper conclusion one way or the other, and in the end, serves your interest much faster.

The typical time share business model requires running as many tours as possible in a given day. This creates a full schedule with a predictable number of closings per day that can then be staffed with legal and contract experts who can produce all of the necessary paperwork in usually about 45 minutes or less. If the process involved thinking about whether to purchase later, the problem is, when is "later" supposed to occur since most salespeople prefer to fill their day being on tour? The more tours one gets, the more closings one can earn. The tour process itself does not allow for much time to meet two or three times with each customer. This would result in fewer tours per salesperson, which, in the end, would result in lower incomes. Most time share people realize to make a very good living, you need to turn as many tours as possible. This is particularly true when many compensation programs are designed to pay out higher rates to salespeople when certain benchmarks are achieved, making it all the more important to spend more time on more tours, versus meeting the same client over and over.

While there are always extenuating circumstances that can delay purchases and closings, the time share industry is generally not designed to provide a relaxed approach to purchase. There are programs that do provide for a more relaxed approach, but these programs generally produce lower volumes than the higher-pressure approaches that require same-day closings. Time share operators have a large vested interest in using proven approaches that produce the best results. The time share business also faces enormous overhead to deliver quality projects and therefore relies on gathering constant data and feedback to see how and where they can improve the customer experience.

Have you ever been on a time share tour where time is never free for your tour guide? On behalf of all salespeople who work on commission, please be aware you may not wish to be on a time share tour but think about going on three or four 90-minute tours a day and being under pressure to close a deal so you can bring home a paycheck to your family. While you might be on vacation, the person you meet with is very much trying to make a living, so honest and productive feedback is always appreciated. If you received great service, send your sales representative a short e-mail and thank them and/or provide them a referral. Your one referral may just make their working an entire month worthwhile.

CHAPTER 17

Understanding Time Share Software Rules

UNDERSTANDING TIME SHARE software rules—why this is important: In today's hectic Internet world, few methods of reserving anything can compete with a few keystrokes on your mobile phone. Time share reservations and, to an increasing degree, all changes, upgrades, cancellations, etc., are also made through software reservation applications. Before we begin to deconstruct what can appear to be a mysterious world, let's take a crash course on how basic reservation systems are tied together, or in most cases, *not* tied together. We will also discuss various methods proven over time that can sometimes land that sold-out reservation.

Network computerized reservation systems: The average person might assume when you access a reservation system from your mobile phone it is the same thing as accessing the same network from your laptop or desktop device. While both methods are supposed to deliver a seamless and speedy transaction process, they can be very different. This is because the application layers are different, and so are the rules for programing, formatting, and scaling, meaning one or the other method could be superior at any given moment in time.

First, you have the application layer which is the place you go online to make a reservation. It is essentially a powerful Web site (sometimes called an e-commerce site) that can access many other software platforms in order to get something done, like making or changing a reservation. Think of this as an airport where information lives. Also remember, many other people are landing and taking off through different paths than the one you came in on. They also need to move through this information network and may likely compete with you to get what they want, in this case, *your* same reservation.

For any large-scale network to be effective, the application layer must consult with the actual information on where the reservations are being stored. This is normally called a database program, essentially an electronic library that stores how many rooms are open, which are booked, and which are available at any given time. Keep in mind the data bank only knows what it is told to know. Let's say, for instance, the resort you are staying at has 450 villas. The layperson might think that means at any one time there are 450 villas to book in the coming year. This could be wrong as the database software may have been programmed with 380 villas. Therefore, on renting the 380th villa, the resort is sold out. Well, then, how can other people still get reservations? The answer lies in they are communicating with a different software program that controls a portion of the other 70 villas. In software, never assume anything.

Now, let's review how the time share reservation systems have evolved. We know that time share software is really very much like hotel software. You access a data bank, find an open room, and fill it with a customer, and then in computer speak, mark the room as "booked." The reality is that the hospitality industry did not start with time shares. It started with hotel rooms. The information that is accessed, stored, credited, and debited with a time share reservation is very different from a hotel reservation. This means for the two to work together, a whole new software generation needs to blend the two different concepts, or operate independently of each other. Take, for example, when you book a time share, you have to have a way to pay for it. In the time share world, this means deducting either points or weeks from your inventory. Hotel software does not know what a point or a time share week is because they were programmed to understand a Visa card, not points sitting in an account. This is not to be confused with hotel reward points for staying at the hotel. We are talking about vacation points, the currency now used to book a villa in most of today's time share vacation clubs. Hotel reward points involve a whole new database issue and have been around for years. Their logic and ability to process can be very different from vacation points. Think of each one as almost a different language that sometimes needs to talk, or even yield, to one another. The methods on how these two languages may yield is referred to as software rules, essentially an organized method designed to allow one or more systems to work with each other, when, at some point, a decision on who overrides whom has to be made. In this case, the software might be forced to rule and in a way, is the judge for who gets what when too many inbound reservations are competing for a dwindling supply of rooms or villas.

Different strokes for different folks: Today's device manufacturers have their OS systems built into cell phones like the iPhone, Droid, and Samsung Galaxy. You may use one browser on your iPhone and that may be different from the one you use on your laptop. You may have a combination of several. In a perfect world, system upgrades, future versions' releases, software patches, etc., would all work in a perfect, seamless, one-size-fits-all architecture. We all know that is not the case, but we should all recognize that software is like a system of tunnels. It is possible some tunnels could close or open under different environments, especially when working with different browsers. You may have your settings on high alert telling your OS system to stop access, when your phone may or may not have the same settings or restriction issues. I have often been shut out or granted access to certain Web sites depending on the browser I used to make the introduction; i.e., my computer, cell phone, or laptop trying to open into a Web or e-commerce site.

Cell phone software is different than laptop software at the operating system (OS) layer. Phone software has to deal with small screen and format issues that larger platforms were not concerned with. Furthermore, the software teams that built the gateways and handoffs for your cell phone device may not be the same team that built your laptop OS and access gates. They are supposed to be in sync but for many reasons, one or the other could fall off due to system overloads, denial of service attacks, or even device or software failure. Just know that while all driveways should lead to the reservation server (the final stop), some could be down or have detours along the way to get your instructions to them. Some of them may have different inventory balances for a period of time, or even all the time. Now can you see how two people can have two different experiences at the exact same time when booking a reservation?

Understanding booking software intelligence: While the largest time share operators work hard to manage ever-changing reservation issues, they must also manage multibillion-dollar construction budgets, expensive land acquisitions, new health plans, and then balance Wall Street's concerns for more profits, all the while having to budget for software overhauls and upgrades that can easily run over $100M for replacing old legacy systems with the newest Web-based technology. This is sometimes referred to as a "Fork Lift" upgrade because it means the owner is replacing most of the prior systems. This can take years to design and implement.

The industry requires developers to keep reinvesting in next-generation software that can process requests faster, through more devices, and these newer systems have to understand how to manage multiple types of reservations inbound from servers that may or may not speak their language in the same way. Reservation systems from 10 to 20 years ago were not designed to speak with the brand-new Web-based 2.0 software of today, and they do not understand modern-day database management and communication. As a result, a whole new industry developed, often called "middleware software." This is software designed to help application software talk to other software programs, like database management software, by creating common ground in the middle and using standardized handoffs and signals to overcome prior software deficiencies where communication was not possible. Think of it as software for software. Some middleware products are so sophisticated they can help delay expensive upgrades for years, often providing interim solutions to more complex network problems. Middleware software when well executed is like a really good Band-Aid that can actually be a very good fix for a particular set of problems. In other cases, it might only work for a while, or only solve certain problems but serves as a much-better short-term solution when the budget may not be there to start over with a new system.

Now, let's take a third bucket and fourth bucket of information just to keep things more interesting. In the above example, a resort may choose to rent, say, 30 rooms out of the remaining 70 rooms for those customers who do not own timeshares but rather just pay the rack rate for a prime summer rental for, say, 5 days. In this case, this room could not be booked by time share software, even though it is the same resort. So as the 30 rooms fill up and the dates get closer to arrival, the software is trained to recognize the resort is running out of rental rooms. What does it do? Well, for the most part, it cannot just call the time share data bank and borrow rooms. Those may still be needed. More than likely, it just rents out the last room, and then another software bucket gets sold out. In each case, the application layer is talking to a different database for each customer because they serve different markets and the reservation request is very specific as to the currency it uses to actually book the room. The one thing that all of these systems have in common is the "show me the money" part. Inherent in every type of booking software is how to pay for it, whether by time share credits, cash, electronic currency like credit cards, or by pay with points.

Now, in bucket number three, a customer calls into a reservation line and wants to book a room using hotel reward points in lieu of vacation points. We are down to the 40 rooms left, but let's not forget there are many other separate databases still vying for those last 40 rooms. The resort may leave a few open for other time share companies accepting trades from competitors for their time share customers. For this to work, five to 10 rooms will need to be set aside because they run on a separate reservation system that can access and handle the inbound trading requests, which, you guessed it, all run on different software systems. Now, we have employee, promotional, time share, trading, cash, hotel points, and vacation points all competing for a shrinking inventory at the same resort. From strictly a software point of view, it might be much cheaper for the resort developer to cut the resort into five or six smaller resorts rather than trying to blend five or six software systems designed over the past 20 years to learn how to speak to each other. So, in other words, the actual 450 villas might look something like this:

A random look at 450 open villas and how a large resort might book your reservation

1. 380 rooms dedicated to owner pool via vacation points or week owners
2. 30 rooms dedicated to rentals by the night
3. 7 rooms dedicated to third-party exchanges
4. 9 rooms dedicated for hotel point exchanges
5. 4 rooms for employees in training or on vacation
6. 10 rooms under renovation or repair
7. 8 rooms for customer promotions at reduced rates
8. 2 holdbacks or "in case" rooms

The average person does not think about how villas are allocated in a software system. The advantage to understanding the software architecture comes from being able to do things that other people cannot do with a reservation. The careful and studied person knows that understanding how reservation buckets work means you could have seven other ways to strike out versus just one, even though the resort is "sold out." It may be sold out for most people but maybe not for the few that know how to open up other reservation paths.

The irony here is that the person answering the phone or booking you into the resort may not be aware of some, or all, of these types of reservations because he or she only books rooms from one or two of these systems and may not even have access to the other systems.

I recall a friend of mine who was really frustrated when airlines switched to charging baggage fees. This is now advanced to charging not only for a large suitcase, but in several cases, airlines also charge for additional carry-on bags. Pretty soon, we will have to pay to bring our wallets on board. Why not? Many women now have to pay for large purses that cannot fit under the seat.

Frustrated by getting charged for junk fees, my friend figured out that his first-choice airline would allow him to use his cell phone to check into the flight, thus, avoiding any kind of check-in line. During the reservation process, he was prompted to answer whether he will have any bags. He routinely replies no. When he goes to check onto the plane at the gate, the cell phone confirmation application on his mobile phone only displays a bar code. There is no confirmation for the status of his payment for luggage. If he had checked into the service desk, the computer would have been able to confirm whether the bag was paid for because *that* system can display this information. If he checked in at the front check-in line, the gate agent could ask him about the bag, and he could just say he changed his mind, but either way, the gate agent has the responsibility to charge for the bag whether or not they do it. The point is, he never sees or conducts business with the check-in desk. He goes straight to the gate. The cell phone application receipt process was not designed verify baggage fees. He has saved $30 a bag per trip for years now because the cell phone application is not designed to audit bag fees.

This is what we mean about different protocols for the same process using different rules. In theory, checking in for a flight, whether at the front desk, using a kiosk, or cellular phone, should all get you to the same place, on the plane. They just have different rules depending on what driveway you take to get into the reservation bank. Time share reservation paths can also be different and can yield different results.

So, can any reservation system that has multiple pathways into booking a villa because they may just have separate inventory data banks that may not always speak to each other.

Keep in mind our examples here do not represent any one time share operator as these are just examples of how software gaps and rules can create opportunity . . . or frustration . . . for the customer. Our research shows that even within large time share companies themselves, they could have different rules and booking policies, as well as exchange and rental priorities that, in some cases, can change or be adjusted, all affecting real-time reservation windows that themselves are constantly changing.

The Internet versus the phone reservation—Are they really the same? How does booking a room on the Internet compare with booking a room over the phone? Do you just assume the odds are exactly the same? You should not. I have, on rare occasions, tried to book a room online, only to find out the system shows the rooms are sold out. It should be clear after our above examples why the telephone live agent, or preferably, the reservation manager, is the best last hope for a villa when the resort is sold out. The main reason for this is they are likely the first person to have access to information the computer systems do not have yet. I have also had luck asking the manager to please call me if a villa opens up. When I was on-site, I usually followed up with a pre-paid Starbucks coffee card as a thank-you as I was leaving the desk, or, in some cases, I just threw one in the mail if my desired reservation was many months out and I had time on my side. I would say the coffee card and a nice written thank-you has worked slightly more than half the time and this was well before I had top VIP status with my timeshare.

Different software applications have different hand-offs and connection abilities: Having helped to co-found and finance three different software companies, I learned over a long period of time to stop thinking like a person. One of the top complaints I got when listening to a potential time share customer was "I can't seem to ever get the time I want when I make my reservation." My standard answer was, "I bet you are thinking like a person." After a brief discussion, we began the process of undoing what human nature assumes versus what computers actually do. Unlike humans, computers are not emotional. They just want to be fed an X or an O, and they will perform like a champion.

I would then explain that people no longer make reservations; computers are in charge of that. If you are going to communicate with a computer, you need to act like one. This, of course, would draw a lot of blank looks, but it did increase awareness on starting to change how they thought about making a reservation . . . more importantly, *any* reservation.

Once people understand that reservation windows and software paths are controlled by multiple runways and have different rules, it becomes much easier to understand how I might get a reservation 5 minutes after you are told the resort is sold out. The answer is, I am likely pulling a room from a different inventory bucket, or I did not get a room that day, but I positioned myself to get a room when one opens up, which, for me, in many cases, was the same as knowing I will have a room. It was just a matter of waiting for my confirmation number. We provided an example above on how and why cell phone application schemes are very different from other applications and, therefore, are designed by different people with different programing skill sets. What might work easily on one system may not work on a cell phone application the same way . . . or even at all.

When you compound this fact with over a dozen software paths trying to book a room at the same resort, it is easy to see that by thinking like a computer, you can usually find a way around the blocked path you started with. You might have to get creative. If you review the pyramid slide we show in the above example, you can figure out that if your tier one or two status does not get you a room, how about an employee rate from someone you know that works at the resort? If you start tipping someone really big there, you will soon have a friend. How about going on a tour? Most resorts actually conduct tours on Christmas Eve and the day after Christmas.

Call the sales desk and ask for a promotional tour. Some overseas tours like Hawaii will give you 4 or 5 nights at 15 to 20 cents on the dollar just to take a 90-minute tour. Now you can waitlist for an extra 2–3 days and follow our tricks and tips on clever ways to add to your vacation. I tell people the game is about getting any kind of stay. It is much easier to add on to an existing reservation even if it means moving down the hall or down the street than it is to get a new reservation in high season when the resorts are sold out.

I recall one of my last trips to Las Vegas. I was planning on meeting my son there so we could catch up and watch some football games together. I could not get past the National Rodeo Finals that had consumed the town in early December. It seemed like every other person had a cowboy hat on when we arrived. Never mind it was my fault as I had decided to go for a week 3 days before the trip. I went online and could not book a week, but I did get 3 nights at my timeshare resort and 3 more nights for the end of the trip. I also got a nice short-term booking discount. Not discouraged, I kept checking to see if day 4 might open up. It turned out it was sold out, but I was able to book 6 of the 7 nights just a few days before departure.

We headed up to Mesquite on day 4 for a day of pools, spas, and golf. We came back the next day and checked back into our regular time share to finish the trip. Building in flexibility saves money. If your town is sold out for a night, many times, the next town down the road is open and cheaper. There is usually something fun to do in almost any town of any size. In our case, the golf, dinner, and the room discount probably saved us over $350 from doing the same thing in Las Vegas. I do not recommend this approach for everyone, but often, a 6- or 7-night stay can be had if you can just find a way around the 1 or 2 nights that are sold out. I suspect that some of the cowboys that left early did not make the finals and therefore just went home. This happens a lot when competitive events are in town. That opened up the inventory for the end of the week. We already had 6 of the 7 nights booked, so getting the last night would not have mattered much one way or the other. The trip was much cheaper, more fun, and there are almost always other options if your first choice is sold out. I told my son we might have to take a time share tour, and he laughed, knowing that was Dad's way of getting us a nice suite if we needed it at a competitor's resort.

The point is that many sporting events can change the occupancy numbers overnight. The PGA tour is the same way. Over 30–60 golfers leave town every Saturday morning if they do not make the weekend cut. What is sold out on Friday night could open up on Saturday morning. This process is also true in Vail every summer when soccer teams from around the country come in to play in some national tournaments. All of the teams need rooms if they make it to the finals, but the fact is, over 90% will have to go home as the finals get closer. Therefore, many rooms will no longer be needed. Given the convenience of wait-listing technology, many time share operators will now book your reservation on their systems in the early hours of the morning while you are sleeping if a reservation opens and your request is sitting in computer land, ready to close a new reservation. I have booked dozens and dozens of reservations over the years by wait-listing into sold-out rooms.

Computers get cranky too: I remember when I was in New York on business and needed to stay an extra night to finish some negotiations. I went back to my hotel, only to find out the hotel was sold out . . . or so everyone thought. I remember watching the body language of the gal at the front desk who was trying to find me a room. It felt like she had typed a novel as I stood there watching her type for 5 minutes. I finally sensed something was wrong, and I asked her a question. I asked her if she had access to the latest inventory count. As if she could read my mind, she said no, the system won't let her in. I figured what happened is she was just reentering the same information over and over and getting the same result. I then asked how she knew the hotel was sold out, and her answer was that the last time she checked the system, there were no rooms left. Never mind I had not even begun to work around which inventory bucket she was using. I patiently asked what time she thought that was, and she said about 9:30 a.m. It was now 11:35 a.m., and most of the line in the lobby was from people checking out. I thought if just one of these people has to leave early, that information would not be reflected in the latest inventory count. I then asked her would she be in trouble if she turned off her computer and unplugged it.

She thought my request was odd, but since the manager was right next to her, she asked the manager if that would be OK. I sensed the manager was having a lot of issues with the reservation system, so she was actually in favor of anything that might help. I told her to exit the reservation system before she turned off the computer, and then unplug and wait for 60 seconds. The check-in, checkout line was now getting much longer.

She then turned on the system, and within 30 seconds, an inventory screen showed up with two open rooms. The look on her face was amazing. It was like she discovered gold in the sink. She lit up with a huge smile and now felt very compelled to move on with my new reservation. The manager came over and told her to give me the suite for the room cost, something my credit card status was supposed to do anyway, but I was not about to ruin her upgrade news. I thanked her very much and checked into what New York calls a suite. In Colorado, we call a suite a regular hotel room, since that was about the size of it. In any event, remember, computers get overloaded too, just like people. The computer system just chose to just shut down when too many instructions were pouring into the system from different pathways. When it rebooted, it worked fine. I guess computers need coffee breaks too sometimes.

Why humans beings still matter: My last story on getting reservations has to do with a dating service that called me with news of a very pretty client the service wanted to match with me. She was a very successful CEO who liked my profile and requested a date. She phoned me up, and we agreed our first date would follow some old-fashioned rules. I asked her if she would mind making us a reservation at a very popular steak house on the beach and that, I, in turn, would be happy to pick up the check. She was very impressed with this arrangement and went forth to make a reservation for that day. I got a text around noon that the restaurant was sold out, that she had called twice and even talked to the manager. Being a CEO, I guess she was not used to hearing the word no. I promptly told her not to worry but rather to meet me at the location on the beach at seven. This was hugely problematic for her. I even got a call from her after the text, trying to make sure I understood I was asking her to meet me at a restaurant that she herself had confirmed was sold out. She called around 1:00 p.m. and assured me there was no way I could get a reservation because she checked and the restaurant was still sold out. I again told that I appreciated her concern but not to worry as I would take care of it.

The funny thing about this story is I got off of her call only to take a second call, and then forgot about the fact I was meeting her at a restaurant that was sold out. This occurred to me around 4:00 p.m., just a few hours before we were to meet.

I then called and left a message for the manager. I said I was a regular customer, was in a real jam, and I knew he was the only person there that could help me. I asked if he would not mind calling me at 4:45 p.m. as I was going to head out of a meeting to take his call. I tried to make him feel more important than me.

I got a call at 4:45 p.m., about 30 minutes from when I called him. I explained what happened, leaving every detail exactly the same. I further let him know I was about to look like a complete moron, and he was my only hope. He burst out laughing on the phone. I told him since my request was not only unreasonable, would it also be a problem for him to arrange for a printed reservation card with my name on it, and could he please put that on my table that is otherwise not available.

He laughed again, and to my surprise, he said, "John, I will see you at seven." I hung up the phone now just as excited about the entertainment value of my date rather than just the date itself. I decided to get there at 6:45 p.m. There it was. A small table in the middle of the room that was a bar high table, exactly what I asked for because it was near the bar and the music, perfect for people watching. There were so many people there they were standing in between the bar tables, and a few people were using my table to set their drink on. The table itself was empty with a picture frame on it with my name not only printed but stored inside a glass picture frame.

The bar was packed so I ordered a drink and just watched her come in. She came into the bar area and quickly realized the place was packed and it probably would take a few minutes to find me. She walked further into the bar, and then saw the table with my name on it. She almost looked disappointed as I think she had the "I told you so" speech all ready to go. She sat down and proudly cleared away the people leaning on the table and let them know this was Mr. Botdorf's table, and they needed to give us some room. Then she texted me, and I told her I had just arrived and was walking in. I went around the main entrance and through a side exit so I was in position to enter from the main door. I walked in and met her with a nice smile.

She complimented me on coming through with a table. She spent the next 3 hours very cleverly prompting me to give up my secret. How did I get the table? I guess she will have to read this book as I never told her how I did it. It was nothing more than being honest with another guy who recognized the "guy code of honor" and also felt my approach was either too genuine or funny to ignore. I am quite sure the "gal code of honor" would also work in these types of situations where honesty and humor combine to make people do things they would not otherwise do. Real guys will always help another guy try to impress his date if he can. I slipped him an Andrew Jackson when I saw him, but it was well after he had come through. The guy code was honored on both sides. The point is, treating people with humor or kindness can sometimes lead to them overriding a computer. Take advantage of it now before computers become the bosses. That fact is closer than you think. When computers begin to mimic human emotions and can laugh and take bribes, this old-fashioned human trick will become outdated. Imagine your computer saying it will get you that table provided you upgrade its memory by next week. How about your computer suing you because it wrote more of the book than you did? Think 2030. It is right around the corner.

Software hierarchy: Hopefully by now, we have learned that software hierarchy, in some cases, can be the difference between getting a reservation and not getting one. The more complex the business, the more likely that more than one reservation system is involved. The key to understanding how to outsmart a reservation system is to first determine how many ways there are to book a reservation. This concept is universal to all reservation systems. Once that is known, you can determine what the likelihood is that you can try to book a villa from a different software source. This will allow you to ask reservation questions you may not have understood before. Remember, though, the person you are asking may or may not know about other reservation paths, or may not be able to access a particular path. In this case, you may need to call another number or find a way to access someone who has access to unbook rooms or villas. It is also actually statistically possible to "unbook rooms" in rare cases because, sometimes, managers have access to information that rooms on the system are going to open up. I have been able to land a reservation about 20% of the time when I just leave my phone number, and then let the person know I have a nice tip for them, just between the two of us. They feel connected, and when something pops up, will usually call because, after all, they are helping fill the reservation.

Once you can really understand all of the reservation possibilities, you can travel with much greater confidence that your choices are bigger than ever. It may take several weeks, or even years, to understand your software hierarchy since this information is not published and is not something that is necessarily shared with just rank-and-file reservation clerks. Only a few people at the very top of the resort headquarters may truly understand the software hierarchy, so you will go a long way if you just quietly gather this information and use it to your advantage when necessary. That makes life more fun for those of us who get it. It serves little purpose to talk about it since the very people you are discussing different reservation paths with may not even understand what you are talking about.

Discount time share reservation windows—the magic key? Nothing is more fun than a week at the beach . . . unless you get another week at the beach, at little or no cost. The secret to time share is to take advantage of the rules you are subject to whenever possible. None of us can change our maintenance fees. They are what they are. But we can change the price we pay per night for the maintenance fee. The beautiful thing about discount windows is they do not come with daily maintenance fees. This is the reason I got excited about time shares, and the reason you can lower your cost of staying in a villa to well below what your vacation plan might originally cost you when you purchased it. In other words, if your annual maintenance fees are $1,500 a year, and you get to stay for a month instead of a week, your average cost per night goes from $214 to $50. This is not possible under any other rental scenario. You can't lease an apartment, condo, or hotel for a month and get a free week every few months. This *is* possible with time shares if you know how to maximize the discount windows offered by many plans. The key to a great retirement is to get your cost per day for both your home and your travel as close to zero as possible. This will help you retire with an offensive retirement plan and really enjoy the rest of your life in style and on the move.

Premium conversion windows: Many time share companies offer an opportunity to convert points into hotel points or will let you book your vacation points at certain times of the year at a discount. Increasingly, we are also seeing extra travel benefits like cruises, luxury homes, and even guided tours offered at discounts or reduced cost during slower times of the year. If you are willing to put in some time understanding all of your choices, you can find some bargains. The important thing is to look for vacation options you want to explore anyway, but doing so at a reduced rate is an even better way to use your points. Whether you use hotel or vacation points, be sure to ask how and when they may offer better terms. These windows can change, so you need to stay on top of your program to take full advantage of your vacation plan.

Credit card points for vacation travel: Many of the top brands encourage you to qualify for a credit card that includes vacation or reward points on the card. In these cases, you can really help lower your travel cost by using one of these cards for everyday purchases. Many offer extended credit card rewards if you use the card checking into their resorts. Some also allow you to make payments or club purchases on their branded card as well. This is a very good way to accumulate air and hotel travel points on something you might be doing anyway. Be sure to ask your vacation advisor if they support a certain credit card to take advantage of this bonus. This is often on top of the incentive bonus you will also earn for completing the transaction. Getting points on top of points helps reduce your payback indicator since the value of all upfront gifts reduces what you are actually paying for your time share. In extreme cases, I have seen this card purchase worth over $25,000, equal to two first-class tickets for airfare and a 7–10 night stay at a 4.0 star, or higher, hotel, just for buying a time share on your credit card. If you spend around $100,000 on a higher-end time share program, what kind of math genius do you have to be to get paid over $45,000 in up-front incentives for the right to have future discounted travel? This is one of the greatest deals available today using a credit card today. This could be on top of the incentive purchase bonuses. If you do your research on this subject, you will be enjoying one of the best vacations of your life . . . on the house.

Hotel versus Time Share booking priorities-conflict or benefit? One of the hardest things to understand in the time share industry is how the affiliated pieces of the puzzle fit together and who might get reservation priority over whom. In simple terms, the time share company is required to set aside so many units, and then dedicate them to the owner pool when talking about using or staying at vacation clubs. In addition, the same time share resort may also offer rooms to the general public or to preferred hotel guests looking to stay at a top time share resort. While this may feel unfair, the allocation models work both ways and work in your favor by usually providing significant hotel upgrades in many cases to your vacation membership if and when you stay at an affiliated hotel. Many of the larger hotel operators now control 35 brands or more, so you may have upgrade privileges at hotels you have never heard of or where you have never stayed. This is why understanding the hotel affiliation and what brands are in your hotel bucket can provide many more choices when looking at international or national travel plans.

The simple way to manage the process is to make sure your hotel membership and rewards number are always handy, and just confirm your hotel rewards number is currently registered and up to date. You should also be receiving quarterly e-news or mail advising you of updates and summarizing your hotel point status. If you are not getting something like this, you should call and make sure your membership is on active status.

CHAPTER **18**

Buying a Time Share on the Secondary Market

Buying a Time Share on the Secondary Market-Back door genius or caveat emptor?

PERHAPS ONE OF the top questions that surfaces when evaluating time shares is, why don't I just purchase my time share on the Internet and save a lot of money? Well, there are pros and cons to this strategy. The existing developers would prefer to sell you their product(s), which is why the industry offers a number of incentives to help you make a choice now versus later, albeit at a higher price. Even after these discounts, resale values, for most time shares, are still below net purchase prices. That said, the developers do use and reserve primary choices and perks that only apply to their direct customer base. Some of these special benefits include choice booking windows, preferential status on room choice, stay and availability windows, and status toward higher membership that, by itself, can have an effect on your RRC ratios and payback indicator.

So, in essence, it may be punitive to one customer to buy in the secondary market and accretive to another purchaser looking to save money on the front end of a time share membership. It depends on your goals and intention for vacationing and whether occupying a preferred resort like your home resort is most desired versus trying to obtain a low trade into another resort where your priority is too low to ever really get into. An owner may have a lower trading priority in the second case because the membership status, if purchased through a nonapproved broker, may likely not count in the developer priority stack. This could mean your trading rights are now diluted and have little real trading value. An owner could also lose some of the hotel conversion perks (like vacation points used for hotels), discount rebates for short-term bookings, and upgraded status perks if you own a week that is not recognized as registered and purchased through the developer. In the end, it just may cost you more as missed bookings and discounts begin to add up. It is best to forecast your intentions over the next 20 years, and then decide if the money saved is worth the perks given up. These tradeoffs are going to vary among the different operators, so be careful not to make assumptions on one based on a different program.

Why your time share profile changes on the secondary market: Many people have told me that they were able to purchase a prime time share from a major developer from a third-party broker, and then they claim to have paid around half of what the developer was quoting for the same right. While the information on the surface might be true, in many cases, this analysis is flawed because it does not take into account the value of the perks that often come with a developer purchase. If I sold you a used 2013 Camry for $20,000, and you showed me one in the paper for $12,000, it may not automatically mean I paid $8,000 more than you if, in the glove compartment, there is an envelope with $8,000 cash in it, and it is mine to keep.

If I get 30% off due to my status on all future stays in a vacation club scenario, booked under 45 days, I could book one trip to Hawaii for 40,000 points while you book the same trip, but it cost you 60,000 points. In essence, over time, the up-front advantage may cost an owner a lot more in the long run than if a larger purchase was made through the original developer.

Furthermore, this could be from the same developer, during the same week, for the same unit. Now, who is ahead? Is it the savvy Internet purchaser, or the buyer who paid retail from the developer? What if the next five vacations were booked with a 30% discount? When the math is reviewed, the more expensive developer purchase might be over $10,000 ahead on a dollar-for-dollar basis after those vacations are enjoyed. How does that $8,000 saved look now? The point is, while one might save 30%–50% on an up-front time share purchase you found on the Internet, it may not count toward your membership status with the developer, and it may not provide the same booking rights. On the other hand, if you bought a time-share for the right to occupy just one or two locations, and you feel your booking priority is high enough to get the reservations you want year after year, then a secondary market purchase may be worthwhile. I have found a combination of the two could also work, but if you are offered a chance to "enroll or register" the week you bought from a third party without the original developer, it can be very worthwhile if the original developer will grant you full rights. Note that the fees from the original developer may vary from time to time, so let your time share salesperson know when or if they may waive this rule. You will likely need to purchase some more time share points in conjunction with the developer waiving any registration fees or granting you full rights on a third-party purchase. This formal process in the end may well entitle you to additional discounts or other benefits that could really help your RRC ratio and your payback indicator. This can be a very worthwhile thing to do if owning a great deal of vacation time is important, and you want to stay on or get to the top of the ownership pyramid.

It is all about that basis—reducing your payback indicator using the secondary market: I have been asked many times whether purchasing a time share on the secondary market at what usually appears to be a heavy discount is worth the effort. The short answer is that it depends on why you are buying the time share, how much the discount is, and are you fully aware of the benefits you will forgo if you avert the original developer through a secondary purchase. It also depends on whether you ever intend to purchase more time shares since additional developer purchases could prove beneficial toward increased membership benefits. You may not gain increased membership benefits by buying time shares on the secondary market. In that case, your purchase could prove to be punitive to you when you try to combine it with time shares you have already purchased.

A good review of the math is always a very good place to start. The great thing about the time share industry is that while it is a form of temporary housing (we predict a long-term time share market will develop), it is really a housing derivative and is somewhat like a stock option. This is to say that when you buy a time share, you buy the right to occupy a piece of real estate for a certain price at some point in the future. So far, that is just like a stock option that grants the right to own a stock in the future. The time share provides the right to stay every year, while the stock option just gives you an outright 100% ownership after the purchase is made. The point here is that while the price of stocks and housing is fairly consistent, that is, the prices of like-kind homes and stock tend to trade within fairly consistent trading ranges, time shares do not. If time share is a real estate derivative, meaning it is only for a period of time within any one year, what is owning a year of time share called? Would this be "temporary" housing or "permanent" housing?

Furthermore, how can a year of housing in a top-tier time share be so out of tune from the same thing in the form of a house? How could one cost up to four times more than the other? Are you not just living in 1,550 square feet with large-screen TVs, cable, two bathrooms, two bedrooms, with a full kitchen and dining room either way?

The notion of living in a time share full time versus the cost of home ownership. This is a very interesting topic because at some point, common sense always shows up in a comparative analysis. The obvious issue of whether it is practical to live year-round in a time share is something that has already surfaced in the industry as a few people have figured it out. The challenge to the industry is what they are going to do when many others figure it out. After all, in order to live year-round in a time share, you would, by definition, have to be one of the largest customers in your membership. Management can hardly afford not to accommodate their most loyal users. This is why we predict the industry will migrate toward the long-term time share (6–12 months) as a way to embrace this market that was not initially forecast but will likely become a by-product of the pricing mismatch that now exists with home ownership versus year-round time shares. This is fueled by the current Beachfront Index that proves living at the beach in a time share year-round is substantially cheaper than owning a home roughly the same size at the same beach. If this is true in one of the most expensive housing markets in the country, it follows that other markets could also produce a Beachfront Index well over 2 to 1, with many neighborhoods running over 4 to 1 at the beach. While the location may not be at the beach, the concept is the same. This is a pricing dynamic that can create a whole new marketplace and will be driven by the following factors:

a. Lower operating costs can be achieved through economics of scale versus a private enterprise business coming to your home to mow the lawn or fix your appliance.
b. The time share model is divided by 50 owners a year, thus lowering the per week cost of utilities in many cases since high use times are spread out over a 12-month stay versus 3 months in the summer when air-conditioning can be expensive.
c. Off-prime beachfront locations will help lower the cost of dirt when the purpose is to provide quality timeshares without the need for a prime ocean or ski mountain view.
d. Housing price increases have nothing to do with time share values, thus allowing the spread between the two housing solutions to rise to illogical levels where out of the box thinking will enter the decision process.
e. Living in a time share year-round will require new marketing to praise the new product as a real live solution that increases the quality of life.
f. Developers will need to use new technology like family video walls and pictures to remove a prior family and replace the pictures with the next one with just a push of a button, making the villa more like a real home.
g. These new time shares will need to offer private storage lock-offs to make annual moves, seasonal, and 6-month moves a normal process. Since this will involve a fee and a new profit center, this concept will evolve to include automobiles, boats, golf clubs, clothes, and artwork.

2017 Home Price Comparison of Prime Beachfront Housing versus undiscovered Beach Alternative

We believe these sleepy beach towns could hold the key to the next big ocean front area's for time shares

	Expensive Beachfront/near	Median Price 2017	Best Alternatives Beachfront/near	Median Price 2017	Alternative Beach Home Value Prop
1	Hilton Head , NC	$377,900	Myrtle Beach, NC	$159,900	Lots of restarants, golf, boating
2	Palm Beach, FL	$861,600	Pensacola, FL	$115,000	Top 25 Beach
3	Key West, FL	$749,000	Matlacha, FL	$184,800	Located on or near beach
4	Key West, FL	$749,000	Matlacha, FL	$316,000	Waterfront Condo
5	Waikiki, HA	$399,900	Waianae, HA	$364,600	NW of Honolulu/larger home
6	Miami Beach, FL	$397,800	Hobe Sound, FL	$228,000	Located on or near beach
7	Laguna Beach, CA	$1,690,000	Los Osos, CA	$418,403	Lowest Beach Median in CA
8	Martha Vineyard, MA	$633,000	Block Island, RI	$422,500	40% off for east coast island.
9	Malibu, CA	$2,887,500	Oxnard, CA	$446,800	Prime beachfront much higher
10	Hilton Head , NC	$377,900	Ocean City, ML	$289,000	New Prices much higher
11	San Padre Island, TX	$299,000	Gulf Shores, AL	$240, 300	Listing-Median-$329,950
12	Martha Vineyard, MA	$633,000	Rehoboth Beach, Del	$412,361	Prices moving higher
13	Cannon Beach, OR	$569,000	Cannon Beach, OR	$569,000	Number One but affordable
14	Naples, FL	$334,700	St Petersberg, FL	$176,800	New Listings much higher
15	Santa Cruz, CA	$795,100	Monterey, CA	$732,900	Top Beaches and Golf

Given the rising cost of time share land combined with the over burdensome process of entitling beachfront property, we believe the next move is to locations that will be considered prime in 20 years. These sleepy beach towns offer prime sunsets/sunrises where land can be purchased at much lower prices than the current list of prime beach towns can provide. Many of the homes in these towns currently trade at 50 to 75% below their famous beach town counterparts, often less than 100 miles away. These towns represent the next trend in time share as it is forced to redesign its model to keep up with retirement, millennial, and boomer time share demand for beachfront living at affordable prices for 6-12 months stays. Keep your real estate glasses on as these towns could see a nice resurgence in values over the next two decades.

Sources: US News and World Report/Zillow/Realty Trac/John C Botdorf, Broker

Pricing Disclosure While we believe these figures are accurate and come from reputable sources, we cannot guarantee these median prices can remain stable or not decline under certain conditions as a number of economic factors including but not limited to pricing variables due to seasonal shifts and demands, economic and toruism flows, overall employment conditions, and significant differences in some neiborhoods could cause these numbers to vary. Although these figures are considered accurate from reputable sources, all readers are advised to hire their own advisors before making any investments. Current prices may adjust upward or downward due to a number of economic changes in the US economy.

The One Year Time Share Life

One of the theories we have suggested in this book is the fact that it is possible to live in a time share at little to no cost over any period of time. It is just a matter of knowing which time shares can rent for a large premium and then using the balance of the time to enjoy no cost housing. In the case of moving against the herd and staying in off season locations it is very possible to rent out about two weeks of prime season and then have about 3 months of time share time to live in. In essence if one owned enough time share to rent out about 45-60 days a year, you could live year round in a time share and cover your annual operating costs. Estimates can vary widely but a combination of primary and secondary market purchases costing between $350,000 and $600,000 would yield enough time share for this type of result and in some cases be slightly over or under what is needed. There are a number of variables that could affect these figures but we have done it enough to know it is possible. We are not suggesting this is practical, as most people would have to enjoy travel and living very light for this to work. We are suggesting the math is there because the numbers are the numbers. We have assumed a generous time share acquisition budget because many of the weeks or points would need to qualify for a Top Presidential, Platinum or Chairman Status in order to own enough booking priority to make the discount travel possible and therefore would need to be purchased through the developers. That said a combination of purchases from both a developer and from the secondary market would save about 35-35% if a plan were used to assemble this type of portfolio. It is food for thought because even if one owned a $600,000 home you still would fact operating expenses of $20,000-$30,000 a year assuming the home was paid for. In our model the annual operating cost for $500,000 to $600,000 is zero.

The Hybrid Housing Model-

We looked around the United States and found 15 major beach cities (source: Zillow) on both coast lines where 2016-2017 trades were showing the median prices of homes near the beach gong for a low of $115,000 to over $1M, with the median prices of many cities around $300,000, all well below their much higher priced and more established neighborhoods where prices were running two to three times higher just 50 to 100 miles up the coast line.

We have speculated it is very possible for many couples to consider selling their brand name home in a well known city in almost any state, and then purchase for cash a smaller home in an up and coming beach city. We believe these cities are likely to appreciate relatively faster over the next ten years and the cash saved from downsizing to this concept could pay for some Catatgory One or Two ime shares and allow for extra cash to be invested into additional retirement funds. This assumes a couple or individual has at least $500,000 equity in their existing home. The concept could work with a smaller amount of equity but you would have fewer choices. In both cases if the new home and time shares were purchased for cash it would be possible to retire much earlier, debt free and enjoy three months of travel or rental income per year. We hope this book can help some of you realize this dream. The numbers are there, the deals are there, and the cost per day to live could be much lower than your existing situation if the right plan down size plan were put into place. The enclosed Zillow spreadsheet is just one example of where beachfront living is possible at much lower costs, which combined with the right time shares to fit your life, could provide a much more enhanced and lower cost retirement. The balance of our book is dedicated to this concept.

CHAPTER 19

How Do I Sell My Time Share-21 Things to Know

How do I sell my time share?

BEFORE YOU SELL your time share, be certain *why* you want to sell it. This is important because it will help you understand how to sell your time share. If you do not wish to pay the maintenance fees, for example, and that is the primary driver to sell, then perhaps you should consider renting your time share, assuming it has rental possibilities. In some cases, you could rent your time share and pay the maintenance fees for 2–3 years, this way, enjoying every other year or every 2 out of 3 years at no cost. If you do not feel comfortable doing so or you are unable to successfully rent your time share, then selling your time share, like renting, involves a number of key steps.

Steps to take when selling your Time Share

1. **Contact your developer or current operator to confirm their selling policy and any right of first refusal**: You should always start with calling the company that sold and manages your time share property. In some cases, they will either have a formal resale marketing

program or may even agree to purchase your time share back from you. You should also confirm with them what the rules are on registering any buyer you may find. This is information you need to have before you start your selling process. Many time share companies have a right of first refusal to buy back the time share so the last thing you need to do is to sell your time share at a fire sale price, only to find out you now have a claim from your time share operator for violating the right of first refusal rules. Take careful notes, ask for the name or ID number of the employee, and make sure you use the proper transfer form and have requested all of the paperwork you will need when you find a buyer. You may have to wait until you find a buyer to submit the paperwork for approval. You might be able to submit a request to sell your time share for a certain amount, and then submit that request and see if the time share company will respond. Always get this approval in writing for your records.

2. **Contact your HOA president** : While this may seem unnecessary, it is important you also understand what is going on within your time share property. Now, if you have a large points-based time share, you may own a portion of a large trust, in which case the local environment or home resort "issues" may not be all that relevant. However, if you belong to a time share with individual rights to a particular property or belong to a portfolio of just a few properties, contacting the HOA can be very important. First, they may be able to help with your sales effort and/or may have a recommended list of brokers they have interviewed in the past to sell other time shares in your building.

Second, they will know if you have any upcoming or pending assessments that could negatively impact the value of your time share. This would be far better to know *before* you sell your unit. If this information was available to you as a member and you failed to disclose it, you could be sued for lack of disclosure. The courts have increasingly been ruling against sellers and their brokers for failing to disclose any well-known monetary issue affecting real estate of all types. This is particularly true if a simple check with your HOA or board would have revealed this information. Be sure and keep copies of all correspondence and make sure you get your answers in writing so you can rely on them.

3. **Understand concepts with transfer taxes-do you have them?** The concept of transfer taxes can be very controversial because in some ways they are just another form of property taxes which already consume a large part of real estate ownership costs, even those associated with time share real property taxes. Transfer taxes have been around for many decades and, in fact, in many parts of the country that have high value vacation homes, it is not unusual to see some type of transfer tax. Several ski resort towns have transfer taxes of up to 1.25% of the selling price of the home, often meaning these taxes can run over $100,000 in addition to other taxes like property and capital gain taxes that can also be triggered by a real estate transaction. These taxes go to support local activities like year-round decorations, lighting and artwork displays, shuttle services, restaurant delivery and pickup, as well as some local recreation centers and off-site parking that keeps the

residents happy. In reality, many of these services are used more by out-of-towners coming in to ski than the local populace. In any case, these programs are usually well run and make the areas very nice to visit. While the more traditional form of transfer taxes may or may not be as relevant for time shares, the tax is very real and could have a major impact on your net selling price. You should be wary about signing any listing or agreement to sell without understanding what this tax is going to be.

The important issue regarding time shares is to understand what these taxes do and what they cost since they affect your resale value. In many cases, the transfer tax can be based on your square footage, the price of your resale, or just a plain price per transfer. Some time share operators may charge a minimum fee equal to $2,500 or more. The transfer taxes combined with the brokerage fees and escrow cost could consume up to 70% of your cost, meaning you could end up with $3,000 on a $10,000 resale. Escrow fees will run around $900 to $1,000 to open escrow and close the sale on top of brokerage fees and transfer taxes.

These high transaction costs are very hurtful to the industry and consumers and are the one area within the time share cycle process that needs improvement. The majority of sellers are either older and cannot travel well or younger families who have suffered a setback and need to liquidate their time share holdings because they cannot pay the maintenance fees. For most of us, if you own a time share for at least 10 years, you have likely recouped your investment, and over a 20-year period, you have received all your money back twice if you owned a Category One or Two time share, making any money recouped on a sale just additional savings. That said, we would like to see these taxes greatly reduced in those cases where they are excessive.

It is important when you decide to sell that you call your operator and ask them what all of the fees are that they charge for any sale of your time share. Normally, in most time share sales, the owner will absorb the real estate commission of around 25%, and the buyer will pay the escrow fee and closing costs. Figure around $1,000 for closing costs, not including transfer taxes, with about $350 of that amount going for title insurance. This is important for both parties as it shifts the burden of delivering a clean title to the title insurance company. This guarantees you were the owner of record and that the title is free from all liens not disclosed in the title report.

Given the complexities of time shares and the fact that any time share could have had multiple owners, you should always opt for the title insurance. The only possible exception might be that the cost of the time share is less than the title insurance, in which case you should get confirmation from the developer that you are the new owner and realize if a problem with the title ever arises, you have not lost much. Clearly, at some point, buying insurance for more than something costs is a little silly and probably a waste of money.

4. **Check for past, pending, or future assessment possibilities**: The larger, publicly run time share operators have almost made assessments a thing of the past because they have large, well-run boards in most cases, with audited statements, and have strong reserve practices in place. You may find that you bought an older time share or bought something 20 years ago and are in a footprint with just a few properties. It is possible, although not as likely today, that you might be subject to assessments. A letter from your HOA will help absolve you of any disclosure liability and should be part of the paperwork you turn over to any buyer. Make sure you also have all of the CC&Rs (covenants, conditions, and restrictions), bylaws, HOA regulations, resort board minutes, and any other rules or documents your developer requires any new buyer to review before you start the sales process. If you have to, you may need to go back to the developer and request this information. If you own an older time share, your rules may predate any newer rules, so you will need to track down the older rules to make sure you are selling the exact time share you purchased, not the newer points-based regulations that may have taken over your resort. It is also possible you could have some "grandfathered" regulations on how your maintenance fee is calculated or how your booking rights lie in comparison to any updated or newer rules.

This one fact alone could mean the difference between a long and weary sales process and a quick sale, because you could have a rare, tactical advantage. The older your time share, the higher the probability this may be the case. Remember, time shares are regulated by your state's Department of Real Estate, and thus, are subject to a litany of disclosure laws. While your broker may not be aware of any older rules or preferences, it is *you* that can be sued if you sign off on a disclosure checklist representing certain facts and they turn out to be detrimental to your buyer. These documents at one time would have been filed within the Department of Real Estate, inside of their subdivision or time share divisions. They should have copies of all of the documents that were required when you bought your time share so you can check with them if you cannot locate your records.

5. **Research your market before you sell your time share**: The best way to figure out how much effort you will need to expend on selling your time share is to ascertain what category your time share is in. If your time share is a Category One time share, while it will not sell itself without some effort, it is really about not overpricing or underpricing your time share relative to what your exact time share has recently sold for. This can easily work against you since the sales price is more a reflection of the last person's need to rid themselves of their time share versus what the true economic value might be.

   If you have a Category Two timeshare, it is likely there will be some demand for the unit; however, economic factors like unemployment rates, interest rates, and whether the economy is growing versus slowing down could impact the sales process. In this case, you will want to take a few extra steps to make sure you can get to a closing within 3 to 6 months.

If you own a Category Three or Four time share, it may take over a year or longer to find a buyer, so this will require aggressive pricing and a strong marketing program to get your deal closed. It may also be your time share has a negative value. In this case, you will need to follow our instructions under **Selling your time share with a negative value** discussed at the end of this chapter.

6. **Selling your time share—the marketing plan**: You should be able to contact an escrow company or time share broker that specializes in time share sales and have them provide a work sheet for the closing. This is not difficult. The tricky expense is the transfer fee. Some transfer fees are as low as $25 for deeded weeks, and some newer transfer fees can be $3,000 or more. You do not want any surprises, so calling your operator and getting this nailed down will avoid any chance of that. Generally, the owner pays the brokerage fee and the buyer pays for closing and title insurance. Your closing statement should look something like this if you are the buyer:

Transfer Fee	$900
Escrow Fee	$220
Processing Fee	$125
Title Insurance	$300
Fed Ex-Misc.	$75
Total Expenses	$1,620
Prorated Maintenance	
Fee ($900 per year) June Closing	$450
Net Closing	$2,020

7. **Calculating your sales price:** Most time share companies require you prepay the next year's maintenance fee at the end of the prior year so if you are up to date on your maintenance fee, you will get a credit for the time you did not use. You now have the estimated closing cost and can now move toward pricing your time share. Remember, if you list your time share for $9,000, you will have to pay the brokerage fee so you may actually net $6,750 or so after commissions, and far lower if you have a high transfer tax. It is very important you understand how much the closing costs are because, in some cases, they can be higher than what you are selling your time share for. You need to put these costs into your asking price because the buyer only cares about the total cost. You also should be armed with all of your documents that impact ownership at your time share so you do have a delayed closing while you search for them.

   The next thing you should do is create a one-pager that defines your booking rights, how far in advance you can book a reservation, what the cancellation policy is, if you qualify for any discounts, and what the off-season savings are. If you have multiple properties, then figure out a range, i.e., 15%–25% off of high season. Note any special features like a fixed week or holiday week. Define how many weeks or days a year the membership provides or provide a range. A list of other locations is also recommended. You might also provide any tips or tricks you may have on getting your favorite reservation. Your goal here is to get all of the summary information on *one* sheet of paper. List the last 3 years of maintenance fees and any taxes or other fees. You should also list a rental range for the times you used your time share, and then list the RRC ratio and payback indicator that will be realized if they purchase your time share. Disclose any estimates that are not guaranteed and may vary in your own disclosure.

The new RRC and payback indicator should be quite a bit higher if you are selling your time share well below what you paid. If you are listing your time share with a broker, make sure you are both in agreement with all of the information on your one-pager. Now you can review comparable sales from your time share operator, the Internet, and at least two other brokers. Some people must sell in a hurry, and therefore, one or two comparables may not reflect what a patient sale might bring. You also need to know how many other time shares in your resort or in your program are for sale. There are a shortage of prime Category One time shares on the market and generally a surplus of Category Three and Four time shares on the market. We recommend you speak with at least three or four different brokers to come up with a market value. You can then recheck and make sure you are in the ranges of the RRC ratios we recommend in this book in Chapter Five. While our suggested RRC values have significant economic value, it does not mean that a cash buyer is sitting around waiting to pay what your time share should be worth. This is an industry that trades on downward cycles and comparables based on someone else who just wanted closure with their time share. Most of us are only as good as the last comparable. That said, do not be afraid to list your time share for 25% higher if there are very few competing time shares on the market.

As we discuss in great detail in other chapters in this book, you will need an RRC ratio around 2.2 to 1 or higher to have a real shot of selling your time share. If you are below this number, you might just donate it, gift it to someone who will use it, or follow our instructions on selling your time share if you have a negative value below.

8. **Understand your selling options- why there is little motivation from others.** One of the challenges in the time share industry is selling your time share. The problem is that the amount of time and effort it takes does not make a lot of economic sense for brokers unless they can get a 25% commission. Even then, you end up putting your time share into a very competitive bidding process that continues to favor downward pricing because the product is the exact same for everyone, making the price the only reason to buy from one seller versus the other. There is not much difference in most like-kind time shares like a bigger garage or a larger patio that might bring you a premium over your exact time share being sold by another seller. This is another reason the secondary market favors buyers over sellers. The problem is further compounded by the fact that eventually a seller just gives in and breaks the next lowest price, now creating a "new comp" at, yet again, lower prices. The madness stops when inventory gets scarce and the price rises to the next highest price, finally creating a short-term bounce. The fact is the economic value of these time

shares is generally much higher than they sell for, but because the market is highly inefficient on *how* time shares are sold, it makes it very hard to capture real economic value.

This is why we believe an electronic market is needed to reduce brokerage fees, title insurance, and escrow fees, which, in turn, would increase the equity in all time shares. Until this happens, we will continue to see very high transaction costs in the industry. For this reason, the more work you do on the front end, the higher chance you have of selling your time share yourself. If you do want a broker, we recommend you consider a broker with a long established track record in time share sales. If you cannot afford to use a broker, then we recommend you consider selling to your operator as they do not need a broker and you may end up netting close to what you might have got with a broker but without the need for a commission.

9. **The blueprint is already here—the need for a real electronic network for time share.** : One of the huge wins in time shares is how fast, how efficient, and how successful the electronic marketplace for rentals has become. This is because the market is not slowed down by weeks of paperwork, often requiring a right of first refusal through the mail to approve or disapprove a sale. Rental programs take only minutes to conduct and thousands of dollars changes hands, smoothly and without any problem. The market is proven, well established, and the old days of charging a rental commission of 30%–40% have been replaced by 5%–8% electronic commissions which take

seconds to transact. Computers have the capability of clearing a right of first refusal in less than a second if they were used. The resale market could allow for payment to brokers in 24 hours versus the weeks the industry takes now to complete a transaction. Broker fees would come down because a deal could be made in one meeting, just like it takes now to buy that same time share at a much-higher price from the original developer. The time share industry needs to address this challenge because the product is one of the best forms of real estate ownership and offers millions of families a proven way to vacation at a much-lower cost. That said, the time share market and its ability to grow are negatively impacted by this lack of liquidity. Using transfer taxes and other forms of tariffs to regulate the secondary market only serves to hurt the very people they are trying to win over, those of us who believe in time shares.

When a typical couple purchases a time share in their 40s, and then buys again in their 50s and 60s, the industry wins, as do the owners. Now after spending 30 years building trust, faith, and confidence in a product, the industry does an about-face and leaves the consumer hanging to try to sell their time shares because they are now in their 70s, and traveling is not practical for many older people. The number one complaint I heard in many cases was "I do not want to burden my kids with my maintenance fees." An electronic market would instantly clear this issue. So would building retirement homes where the asset could be used to provide temporary housing for the same customer who traveled around Europe for years on their time share and now needs a small villa to live in during their retirement years. Taking care of parents in retirement villas are the very same people that worry about paying maintenance fees. This would, by itself, turn lemons into lemonade because their time share can be rerouted into a long-term retirement time share designed for this use, and the maintenance fees would go toward their care.

The worst part of this process is that some children grow up hearing about maintenance fees issues and the fact there is no way out of a time share, creating a negative experience for some new customers. Others families pass down to their children the joys of time shares, and they enjoy the time share process without any worries. It is the percentage of unable or unwilling families that do not want this liability that haunts the industry. The irony as a multimonth owner in time shares is that my kids cannot wait to inherit my time shares because they are very Internet savvy and understand how to make time shares work for them.

10. **Finding the best time share broker**: This is far more difficult than finding a broker to buy or sell a home because to be successful, a broker will need to close over a hundred deals a year. Even at a 25% commission, a broker may only make $1,000 working on one time share deal for a month or 2. The key to success is attracting buyers and preferably through both an Internet site and an old-fashioned brick-and-mortar office. The first thing to do is figure out why you bought your time share. It is likely you really enjoyed a location you stayed at and figured out you would

like to stay there every year or every other year. Draw a circle within 5 minutes by car around your time share, larger, if needed. This is where your best broker may be located.

Now, drive to the nearest shopping center with a market/drugstore and head to the nearest mall or to a nice outdoor shopping mall. Once there, take a look at the stores and see if you notice a real estate firm that advertises they buy and sell time shares. The few brokerage offices that exist and specialize in time shares tend to office as near a time share resort as possible. In cases like Palm Desert, Calif., there are over 20 large time share resorts just within the Palm Desert area. The people who stay in time shares have to go to the supermarket. They have to eat out at restaurants nearby, and they love to shop, in many cases.

These time share real estate offices have access to valuable walk-in traffic because owners cannot help wandering in to see "what their time share is worth." Many want to sell their time share. Many want to buy more time share and want to see if they should buy it from the developer or perhaps from a broker. Most potential buyers and sellers feel more comfortable dealing with a real person, someone who has been in that same office for over 10 years. This feels safer than trusting the Internet with a sale because the Internet does not have one big trading platform run by the top operators (like we predict it will) but rather just dozens of operators with pages of advertisements offering time shares for sale. How do you know who is real and who has your back? People want to be able to hold someone accountable if there is a problem. They want an office where they can drive over to, to handle a problem, not an 800 number to leave a message. After all, you are buying a piece of real estate not just sending flowers through the mail.

The good news is that this office probably trades on all types of time shares so you might own a particular brand in Hawaii that also has property in the desert. It does not matter if you are from out of town because one of your time shares is not; it may be across the street. You can certainly track these offices down via the Internet, but that does not compare to visiting and talking to an actual broker eye to eye.

The public is getting wiser to the industry, and they will know they can buy your week in Hawaii and stay every year in the desert or vice versa. Most now have the same maintenance fees if the sale is "points based." You may also want to buy a legacy week at a cheaper resort if they use an older maintenance formula and that week can be traded into higher fee markets like Hawaii. The point is, you want to deal with a firm that has a long and established data bank, and most important, benefits from daily walk-in traffic. You want a firm that may have a buyer in their pocket. This will not come from the sales office in the resort; it will only come from the time share office across the street or a few minutes away, as the case may be.

11. **Your time share value may compare to the last sale in your building-how to dodge the pitfalls.** Negotiating to buy or sell a time share at some point has to involve

common sense. People tend to sell their time share at the lowest bid because that is way it is always done. You may be better off making up your own marketing package and coming up with your own mail out. It all depends on what your time is worth. Clearly, a time share that rents for $4,200 a week should be worth more than $9,000, but if the market sells that same unit for that price, that becomes the price until inventory becomes scare and a higher comparable can replace it. Don't be afraid to just tell your broker that you are not interested in a price of $9,000, but if a buyer comes along at $12,000, you would be interested. See if the broker writes your number and name down and wants to register your deal or sign a broker/sale agreement. If not, you won't sell it there at that office anyway. If a broker won't write your name and contact information down because you are off on price by a few thousand, it is not a broker worth having. You need to weed out the lazy and weak brokers anyway Be aware that another office in another city may have sold a time share in your building for $12,000, which is why it makes sense to understand where your buyer is coming from, and more importantly, where your comparable sales are coming from. The data does and can vary widely. This data is not usually shared between the real estate industry, so your same unit could easily trade for 25% more in another, unrelated data bank, than where you are getting your information for comparables. As we have said, the time share business is not always fair or rational; hence, the time share-informed people tend to do better, both buying and selling.

12. **Get aggressive and sell your time share with a rental in place** You should now be able to pinpoint your high season rental and search for a renter before you list your time share. Usually about 60 days before high season is a good time to be marketing for that summer rental. Clearly the reverse is true for prime ski time shares. This is typically the highest RRC ratio, although certain outside events could provide a nice rental window outside of the high season. If you can rent your timeshare before you sell it, you will jump to the top of the buyer list and will command a small premium. You can also prove your time share has economic benefits, and that it will likely only take 2–3 years to recoup your investment, making a purchase at $12,000 a bargain. It may not matter to a buyer that there may be a better deal, as, at some point, saving every last dollar is not important to everyone . . . just getting a week at the beach purchased is good enough. You should be able to rent high season out 60 days in advance, and you could then let the buyer keep the rental income. This, of course, might reflect in a higher listing price, but both the broker and the buyer will feel very comfortable your unit has clear and established economic value.

13. **The time share creative sale—consider trade, note, rental split and/or tax donation.** If you are not getting the traction you need to book a rental, you may need to consider trading your unit. There are several concepts involved in trading, but the main one is that the larger the trading pool, the less important any one smaller element in the deal may have in concluding a transaction. Let's provide one example. Assume you have

decided to buy a house and find one to make an offer on. The home is priced at $480,000, and you decide to make an offer. You offer is $475,000 with $75,000 down. They counter at full price. You let them know you cannot raise your price or come up with any more cash. However, you will give them your time share worth $8,000 to make up for the $5,000 difference. In this way, they may take the deal, figuring they could take a trip, and then sell the timeshare for $3,500. They may do better, or worse, but at least you get your time share sold. They also take the deal because you are qualified to get financing, and they want to move on. In this situation, they were not looking for a time share, but because the time share is such a small portion of the overall deal, they may take it.

14. **The art of the trade**: I had a partner in college, and we used to buy cars at the auctions or from *The Recycler* magazine when I was in college. We ended up owning a very nice Vanden Plas (looks like a Rolls-Royce) we paid $8,000 in cash for. We probably made $20,000 driving it for private parties looking for a limousine for the night. We ended up trading it for about $150,000 in appraised gemstones 2 years later. We got out of some upcoming maintenance issues and split up the gemstones 50/50. I then ended up with two prime Super Bowl tickets in Pasadena and a used Porsche 911 when trading the gemstones plus used them for jewelry gifts for over 20 years. Not sure but the trade probably made me over $40,000 on a $4,000 investment. (See the full story about this car in the last chapter, "The Art of the Time Share Life," A note from the author.)

This is just one of many examples and clearly only works if you are willing to think outside the box. Other possibilities include advertising your time share for a trade for a car, boat, or other asset. Trading can be very good for both sides if you can find the right trade. Again, this is not a preferred method of selling your time share, but if you own a marginal time share with little economic value, you may need to get a little creative when looking for the right buyer.

Other methods might include retaining title by agreement until the buyer pays off the note and you sell the time share for $500 down and a certain monthly payment that works for both the seller and the buyer. If you find someone with good credit, this may be a very good option for a working family looking for a discounted vacation plan. There is always a danger in carrying a small mortgage, but if you retain title until the time share is fully paid off it can help with your maintenance fees as a worst-case scenario.

15. **Time share brokerage and listing dos and don'ts.** : You may fall into a conversation about having a "time share" company offer to list your time share for sale for a small marketing fee. Don't even think about it. These companies are not in the real estate business, and you have a better chance of standing on the freeway with a "For Sale" sign than you do paying anyone to list your property for a small marketing fee. Selling time shares is a tough business and anyone successful at it will demand a high commission because that is what it takes to get people to move on your behalf. If the company gets a fee for selling your time

share, and the fee is paid out of the closing proceeds, then that is fine. Skip the fee for services and use that money to market your own time share. You would be better off putting a nice three- or four-page brochure together and getting ahold of a Canadian phone book. Your buyers are in there if you own a time share in the sun. You may have to go through a few thousand, but they are definitely in there.

If you do decide to list your time share, be sure to focus on getting a time share broker with an office suited for high-volume walk-in traffic that specializes in time shares. Although there are not many of them out there, there are usually a good handful in or near every major city. Make sure you have your listing paperwork reviewed by an attorney or competent professional so you are not signing something with any hidden surprises.

16. **Be your own local agent**: You may be able to put up a few signs at local churches if your location is in a vacation town. Many towns have churches that have services for four or five religions and share the same building. The visitors tend to be from out of town and many own time shares. Sometimes the churches will have community bulletin boards as will some of the local markets or local coffee shops.

17. **Reverse engineer how your timeshare is used to find your buyer**: The best way to understand your market for buyers is to learn where they come from. If you ski, for example, just ask everyone you meet on the ski lift or at the local bar where they are from and if they can

recommend a favorite place to stay. You might find out they are in your building. In any case, if you discover a large group of people are coming from certain areas, that is a clue you can place an advertisement in that area. If four people that day say they are from Canada, ask about the local paper. Every paper now uses the Internet when you buy an ad. It is just that you will be marketing to a very targeted area. We are, of course, big fans of the Internet, and you or your broker will likely use the high-traffic Web sites, but it never hurts to go old fashioned sometimes because few people bother any more to go old school, making your advertisement stand out. It is likely you will be the only person on the board if you target a smaller local area out of town for your rental or sale of your time share..

If you are looking to rent your villa out every year, it may be worthwhile to put more time into understanding your market because the results will be easier to repeat with follow-up business. You need to know what the local hotels charge, how big their rooms are, and if they provide breakfast. Look at the cars in the parking lot. Do the people come from the rent-a-car lots, or are they coming from out of town or out of state? You may be in route to a more popular destination and your rental could have value as an overnight stay. In that case, it may not be a great multinight rental.

Check with your local community and tourism offices and see what is on their calendar. That will give you some clues on who may be coming to town. You can do the same thing with the sports calendar and confirm what teams will be in town. A regular football, baseball, or basketball schedule is generally not a great rental unless the game is a bowl game, a huge rivalry, or a once-a-year event, like a PGA golf tournament. The sports rental is often for only a few days, but if hotel rooms are scare, the well-placed time share can be a gold mine for just a few days.

Lastly, look at the local convention center and see what is up for business. In some locations, a huge convention could cause a big squeeze on room rates. I have seen many companies relocate their sales conventions into small ski towns during the off-season to provide a new environment for their employees and save a great deal of money. You might be surprised that although that great ski week is always a good rental, you may have a shot or two if you know a medium-size company is bringing 100 to 500 people into town. You can always expect that 5% of any tour group would prefer larger digs for a few days. The closer you are to the actual convention, the better your chances. Look at the largest hotel or resort in your town that has the largest convention or ballroom space. They built it to fill it, and the on-site hotel rooms have become commonplace for many companies to host large sales events. The top executives in that company may find your time share next door more desirable than the actual hotel if you have a Category One or Two time share.

18. **The proper way to e-mail blast to friends/family/neighbors—keep your marketing positive**: The old saying, it is not what you know but who you know still matters. Many people that lose their jobs are afraid to

reach out to friends and family to let them know they are looking for a new job. This is usually because they do not want to be judged or appear they are soliciting them for work. That makes sense. On the other hand, these are the only people who know you and would have any possible interest in helping you. They are far more likely to respond to you then sending out 1,000 résumés through the Internet. You become one in a million when you do what everyone else does. Selling a time share is the same thing. You just need to send out an e-mail that is positive and not negative.

A positive statement is something like this:

After 19 years of enjoying our time share in Vail, Tom and I have decided to hang up our skis and soon retire to a warmer climate. We expect to sell our house in a few years, and right now, we are going to sell our time share in Vail. It has provided us with 19 years of precious memories. It is a well-appointed 2+2 villa that is 1,450 square feet. This time share is now priced at $36,000 from the developer. We are asking $18,300. It cost around $450 a night to rent this same villa in the winter. We own the right to occupy it for 7–10 days a year. We are offering a $1,830 referral fee or 10% to anyone who refers us to a buyer. Our brochure is enclosed. Our thanks for your passing this on, and please look for our Christmas card. We miss all of you and know how busy life can get.

Sincerely,
Tom and Ann Taylor

A negative statement would read like this:

How are you? Tom and I have decided to sell our timeshare as we just can't find the time to use it anymore. We wanted to let our good friends know before we list it. We are looking to get around $18K, which is about half what the developer charges. If you know someone, please refer them to us and we will pay you a referral fee. It is a 2+2 villa located in Vail.

Kindly,
Tom and Ann Taylor

Note they both convey the price, but the first one sounds like a caring neighbor while the second one sounds like you are just trying to unload your time share on some poor fool. It is not that the second one is insulting; it just does not have a nice "ring" to it. Also, you may decide the referral fee is $150 and the neighbor might feel entitled to 10%. You end up putting yourself in a tough spot. Notice we used $1,830, or 10%. In case you end up selling for $8,000, you can adjust the fee to $800. Paint a picture but do it in one sentence. People don't want your life story or pictures of your dog.

Just get in and get out. This was a quote from one of the best teachers I ever had in high school when taking his final. His name was Mr. Gopel, and as far as I know, he is still teaching in Los Angeles. Stick to the facts, make your point, and go home. Clearly, you can adjust this message based on age, location, and your future, but do tell a story in one or two sentences. It gives a welcome feel and sends a sincere tone.

19. **The best research is right under your nose**: Given the wide ranges of time shares and their locations around the world, it is not possible to provide a single model for renting out a villa. Rental practices and patterns can, and do, vary widely, even within the same resort. One year you could have four or five rental leads for that great ski week, and the next year, you could end up without any calls, even with more advertisements. Sometimes the economy and other variables could play a role, so we always advise not to count on rentals until the money changes hands. That said, the more research you do, the better your year over year results will improve.

20. **Interview local hotel clerks—they know where the guests are from.** Local hotel clerks or the person running the concierge desk can often be a wealth of information. If the front desk is slow, you can often get a great deal of valuable information from the people who interact with the guests every day. They hear their complaints and understand their needs, so if you are a bit clever, you can ask and receive valuable information. One great question is always too ask how business is. You can then work your way into when the hotel is the busiest and figure out why is it so busy. If the hotel is sold out or is always sold out for some of the year, there is your clue. It takes a bit more work to get to it, but generally, you can also get some basic information on where the guests are coming from. The local concierge desk is also a great place to garner what guests like to do on holiday. For example, if you find out the best place to go horseback riding, you could visit that place and see if the owners will let

you place a small ad in their changing room or sign-up room. Large family events are great places to find renters who need more space than just a hotel room.

Larger time shares are much-better choices than cramming families into two or three hotel rooms. The same is true for local restaurants because they have the small daily newspapers out front in many cases. If not, visit the local grocery store because they usually will have the local real estate magazines or papers. These are easy and very affordable to run ads in during your rental season. I would always read the out-of-town newspapers when I was in town just to get a sense of the local markets. These are easy sources of valuable information. You need to remember, as a rental, you also compete with every home that is near your rental as they can be a local hotel as in Airbnb if they offer rooms or entire homes for rent. People will gladly rent an entire home over the cost of your villa if they get a better deal.

21. **Selling your time share with a negative value**: The first step before you consider just dumping or walking away from your time share is clearly to make sure you do not ruin your credit if that can be avoided. Going through the steps to properly transfer legal title to another owner is always the best way to conclude any issues you may have with your time share. We are assuming that your villa is not rentable as just renting it to either pay off the loan or have a source of income to pay your maintenance fees should always be a priority. This may not be an option if you own a Category Three of Four time share. In this situation,

you want to make sure you have also examined the trading power of your time share. I reviewed a time share portfolio from a couple that complained to me they cannot afford the maintenance fees anymore, but to my surprise, they were able to trade year in and year out for Hawaii and the beach locations. We have always advocated that renting villas a long way from home can be tricky because you have little recourse if the renter does not show up, other than to salvage any remaining days you might have left, assuming you have last-minute cancellation rights. These rights can vary a great deal in Hawaii since it is a destination location, and it is hard to find last-minute renters.

I discovered the reason they could not sell their week was because it had an old maintenance fee formula that when converted into certain types of trade, had a very low conversion value, thus making a trade for the whole week the only option. The good news was when they converted into a beach week off-season, or got a week in Hawaii, the maintenance fee was in line with what those weeks cost at the time of year they could trade for and get a reservation. Since they had many years of travel ahead of them, they like the trades they got every year, so the best solution for them was to do nothing since they admitted if they sold or just gave away the time share, the cost to replace the vacations would run about 2.5 to 1. They had a 2.5 to 1 RRC ratio, which is very healthy. They just had to go through the back door and trade their week every year to get there. When I asked how they would pay for a vacation if they got rid of their time share, they answered they just would not go on vacation. While doing nothing in this case was an easy choice, going through the thought process is always worthwhile.

If you cannot trade and do not wish to trade your villa, you cannot rent it, you are down to just getting rid your villa through a legal process. This must be done correctly so as to avoid any damage to your credit rating.

a. **Give your time share back to the developer**: The first place to start is with the original developer that developed the project and/or the current owner if the resort changed hands. They have the best handle on current value. If they are not interested in your time share at any price, then you will need to proceed with some other options.

b. **Donate it to charity**: See if you can find a real estate broker to write you a letter stating the value of your time share. It is important this come from a time share broker on their letterhead with an address and phone number. You can then see if your favorite charity might accept it, but you will likely need to pay the first year or two's maintenance fee. While not ideal, this is a good way to either sell the time share or find a good charity to accept it.

c. **Hire a time share or law firm to represent a disposition of your time share**: We have researched a number of quality firms that represent owners looking to get rid of their time share. We had intended to provide a list of these firms but feel that each time share case is unique and the owners should first explore other options in this book before retaining another firm at additional cost to liquidate their time share. We also believe the industry has received quite a bit of bad press about time share tactics, which, while present in a very small number of cases, is also blown out of proportion. We do not have advertisements to "get rid of your home" or "help undo your automobile purchase," so why all of the fuss about time shares? We believe this negative press has hurt the industry, and we, therefore, would prefer to focus on a preventative approach going forward where the consumer does their homework ahead of time instead of deciding 3 years later their purchase was unwise. By all means, if you feel you were cheated, you have a number of firms on the TV channels and all over the Internet that, for a fee, can help you. For the vast majority of us, we should hold ourselves accountable, do the research, and treat any time share purchase like any other large purchase: do your research, make a choice, and go enjoy what the time share has to offer. All of the top operators have products that, in the long run, offer at the very least, a place to unwind and enjoy life, not to mention that most all programs have some type of value proposition over ever-increasing rental rates. As we know, not all marriages work out, but that fact is not a reason to forgo ever getting married.

CHAPTER 20

How to Rent and How NOT to Rent a Timeshare

CAN I REALLY rent my timeshare and make money? The concept of renting your timeshare to another party is not new, nor is it illegal in most cases, although it could be subject to restrictions and/or taxes. It is important if this is a concern that you review your time share documents very carefully. From a fundamental point of view, renting property you control really is a basic property right dating back hundreds of years under British common law first originating in England. The real questions are whether the idea is worth the effort, and can one actually make money. The short answer is yes; however, it is important to realize that rentals can be fussy and demand can vary for seemingly no reason from one year to the next. That said, there are certain patterns and rental windows attached to a small number of premium time shares that do tend to provide, year after year, demand for rentals. It should not be surprising that these tend to be the luxury and top-tier time shares yielding the most demand.

The best rental windows tend to occur around the holidays or when certain high-profile events are in town like the X games, a PGA event, a high-profile concert, or just controlling a two- or three-bedroom in prime summer season in July or on the slopes over Christmas. These rental windows have continued to rise faster than the rate of inflation, and in some top-tier locations, I am seeing RRC ratios running at over 7 to 1, i.e., seven times the daily cost of ownership. Remember, these are rare and most time share rental models will likely run around 2.0 to 2.5 to 1 in the first 5 years of ownership, assuming there is rental demand. The higher RRC ratios come from savvy time share owners who have learned how to cover their maintenance fees through rental, have paid-up time shares, and an average daily cost under $25, so getting $400 to $500 a night can bring them over a 20 to 1 RRC.

What are the economic realities of time share rentals? When we refer to rentals in this section, we are referring to whether you could make money by reserving your villa, and then renting it out to a third party instead of occupying the villa yourself. We will, of course, always advise you to check your particular timeshare's rules and policies and further advise that you become aware of any national, state, or local laws regarding short-term rentals. Certain places like Hawaii actually tax rentals in time shares, so you must be careful to pay attention to zoning and income laws when considering this option. Even the IRS has a limit on this area, but under certain conditions, does allow the timeshare owner the right to rent out a timeshare for up to 14 days before any income becomes taxable provided you are not otherwise in the real estate rental business. Not a bad freebie as our tax code is increasingly limited on free passes for income of any kind. Be sure to recheck this fact before you file your return as limits and/or restrictions can and do change often, even within the IRS code. I have found that relying on IRS publications (position statements on taxable events) generally can provide a good guideline on where you might stand in this issue.

The general answer for the United States and most other countries is you can rent out your timeshare subject to any taxation laws. The bigger question here is, does your timeshare have enough economic value to create a market for itself? Remember, the larger your RRC ratio, the more likely you can create a market for your timeshare because market rents should be far higher than your ownership cost (maintenance fee) per night. I would suggest you will need at least an RRC ratio of 2.5 to 1 during the season you seek to rent, and if you are 3.0 or higher, then renting becomes much easier because the supply of available rooms will likely be smaller in prime timeshares during peak season. If you do not have these ratios in place, I am not sure based on historical data you will make money renting your unit, but you can at least cover your cost if your timeshare is a class two or even class three unit during high seasonal demand.

You can expect to use the following as a general guideline on rental rates:

> **Category One—luxury to top-tier time shares**: You should be able to get up to 4.0 times your average daily cost for luxury time shares and around 3.0 times for top-tier time shares, assuming you do not use stretched points in the maintenance calculation, so if your maintenance fee is $200 per day, your top rate will be around $700 to $800 per day. Another rule of thumb is about 70% of what the resort charges per night, so if the resort is $800 a night, then $560 a night is in the ballparkfor most, with some ultra luxury

Cat One villa's with 3 or 4 bedrooms commanding in excess of $4,000 a night for prime holiday rentals. Usually, the lower of those two numbers is the most accurate. In some prime locations during high season, you end up with the same number, especially with owners who have lower maintenance fees than the rented resort, and were able to up trade into the high season into a top rental market. Hence, this is why some owners could get 4.0 times. Keep in mind these rates reflect only about 25% of all timeshares and are truly luxury villas. If you have to ask or think about whether your time share is a luxury villa, the answer is no. It is likely a Category One or Two time share. Once you stay in a truly luxury time share, there is no question you are in one of the most sought-after time shares in the world.

In other rental cases, owners stretch their points so their maintenance fee per day could be far less than a new owner with just 1 or 2 weeks of ownership. This will cause a dramatic swing in your RRC ratio because your cost per day is well below the average for that same villa. This is why we spend time discussing your vacation portfolio, since it takes extra time to make rentals really pay off because you are spreading down your overall cost of ownership. Remember, you cannot change your annual maintenance fees from the resort developer each year, but you can change in many cases, what your cost per night is by obtaining extra nights through discounted booking windows. These extra nights do not have extra maintenance fees, and that is where the magic lies in cutting your average daily cost.

Note that low seasons in the desert resorts where extreme heat is present will not command these rates, and, in fact, your time share is not likely rentable unless there is a major event in town or you are down to 1.5 times, or less, on your maintenance fee per day. The best rates are always in prime beach areas or in the mountains to escape summer heat around the July 4th holiday. In the winter, of course, prime ski locations follow the same rule, especially over holidays where family time is at a premium and demand far outstrips supply.

Category Two—secondary level time shares: You are looking at 2.0 to 3.0 times your average daily cost based on your daily maintenance fee as a general guideline. This maintenance fee is for a 1-week owner, not someone who has multiple months of time share and has averaged way down their daily maintenance fee. This also assumes high season, and there is demand for your unit. Usually, there will be demand if your resort is running at sold-out or near sold-out occupancy, where the only way into the project is through renting from existing owners. Please note, while many Top Two Tier resorts are very nice to stay at, rental rates can fall dramatically within the same month. While summer months tend to rent at a premium and winter months tend to do the same during prime ski season, you still need to have a marketing plan to set your rental apart from the competition. We review these practices below.

Category Three—midlevel to the top 75% of time shares These time shares are not likely to have much of a rental market unless you are very near the beach or a popular ski resort, and even then, it can be short lived, primarily working the best in high season. These projects can rent, but you will command 50%–75% less per night than the Category One and Two properties. That will mean you will hover somewhere between 1 to 1 up to 2 to 1 over your average nightly cost, depending on the time of year. Prime rental windows will be shorter and could be just Christmas week and July 4th without much extension into the summer and winter seasons. That said, your cost basis is likely much lower than Category One and Two properties, so obtaining less than half the rent of top-shelf properties could still provide a nice return and cover your maintenance fee when funds are tight.

Category Four—economy priced time shares- the bottom 25%. : These can be older buildings with some visible signs of outdated designs like cottage cheese ceilings, even avocado carpet in extreme cases, and they likely have older kitchens with marginal appliances. That said, if they are located in an expensive town like Vail or Aspen, the chances are they have been upgraded and repositioned as a boutique hotel or upgraded to Category Two or Three time shares. Some of them, however, just seem to hang around because the location brings in renters who rely on a big discount.

If they remain a Category Four, then your rental window will likely be to high school or college students, young professionals, and young families looking to pack five or six kids in a small villa and use it to wake up and ski all day. Damage issues and repair issues tend to run much higher in these types of rentals. You will also not receive much more than your maintenance fees per night. Right now, that might be $50 to $75 a night. Many students pool their money and each kick in $25, with some kids sleeping on the floor. That said, some of these units may have undergone a nice remodel, could be well located in a popular town, and can be an exceptional bargain. That would be more the exception than the rule in this category. As in life, one usually gets what one pays for, and although these Category Four time shares can pack a lot of surprises to the upside, this is one example where disappointment will win most of the time.

How do I rent my timeshare? In some cases, renting a time share can be relatively easy, like in a high season with a Category One or Two timeshare. It more or less involves posting the time available, unit size, photos, and location online, and all it takes is answering a text or phone call and you are good to go for a rental. Filling out the online forms can be complicated for anyone not used to dealing with the Internet or Internet shopping, but for most of us, it usually only takes about 20 minutes to open an account with your preferred Internet vacation site, fill out the information, and post your advertisement. Most Internet rental sites suggest uploading pictures of the grounds and unit, and some sites require it. I have found pictures have a much-higher hit rate, and combined with a brand name like a Westin, a Marriott, or a Hyatt property, will also attract renters because, unlike a home, the renter pretty much knows what they are getting in terms of quality, space, and amenities.

Many people that call or text may have already rented in the same place the year before. Do not assume just posting an advertisement will result in a rental. It sometimes takes a great deal of practice before you can master which site, which properties, and what times of the year work best. Remember the 10–10 rule. The top 10% of time shares rent very well 10% of the time. It takes work and patience to get good at renting time shares, but the rewards can be substantial. We have found five sites that do a good job matching renters with owners.

Proven Rental Web sites for Time Share(s)

a) Airbnb www.airbnb.com

b) VRBO www.vrbo.com

c) RedWeek www.redweek.com

d) HomeAway.com www.HomeAway.com

e) Booking.com www.booking.com

If you want better results, you might try using up to three sites, although you will need to be very diligent and cancel and update your listed dates after you rent your villa. As we have suggested, do not take anything for granted. Be sure to call the local vacation resort directly and make sure your renters are acknowledged as guests. You should also follow up with the resort and make sure they checked in. This is important as some programs allow you to cancel reservations up to as little as 24 hours in advance. If your guests fail to show up, you can at least recoup your unrented days with many programs subject to their cancellation rules. Most guests do arrive because their Internet rental site requires an up-front deposit, and in many situations, you get to set that up in advance. We recommend a 50% deposit up front with the balance charged on check-in.

The most important thing in renting out a timeshare is to ascertain what the real level of demand is for your unit. This can be tricky and also may vary from year to year. If you have a lot of competition and you are trying for a rate that is equal to or above the rate offered by the resort, you are not likely to get great results. I like to use the above sites because they are performance based and only collect a booking fee if your reservation gets booked. We do not recommend using fee-based services that charge up front to list your vacation rental. These firms are not in the rental business in our opinion and have little incentive to perform. Internet services that collect the rent after it is booked must go to much further lengths to make sure your rental is presented well and is within reach of current market trends.

We recommend listing your villa as soon as you know you want to rent it out. If you can list your rental at least 3 months in advance, and longer, if you can, it is always best to get the most amount of rental hits. If you are not getting at least a few hits 30 days before your check-in date, it is likely your rent is too high or you have unrealistic expectations about the rental market. Remember, you are competing with homes, rooms in homes, apartments for short-term stays, hotels with weekly and long-term stay customers, and even relatives and family that start to look attractive versus paying $800 a night to stay at the beach. Almost all of these options may likely be cheaper than what you are asking.

How to increase traffic to your time share sales effort The first thing to understand is that you must be competitive with your surrounding area for the dates you may wish to rent out your villa. I can tell you from practical experience that 2+2s are the best rental villa in terms of size. You can get a premium for three bedrooms, but it usually involves a family dynamic or a group of people wanting to ski or go to a concert. It is not that this group is not out there, they are just not as prevalent or large as the 2+2 market, or you may not get as much of a premium for the third bedroom. The exception here are three bedrooms during holiday weeks. Large families love to snap up these apartments in the sky for those weeks. Studios are generally too small to rent for many big football games, concerts, or vacations, but they do serve a purpose for an individual that may prefer staying at a time share resort. The 2+2 gives two couples or two friends a much-larger unit than two comparable hotel rooms provide, and over the years, has proven to be a better sweet spot for the average rental. Large families will pay up for a prime three- or four-bedroom, but they represent a smaller portion of the overall rental pool, and many families looking for this type of rental are budget conscious, and just doubling the price for a four-bedroom over a two-bedroom will not lead to near as many possible renters.

The most important aspect when renting a time share is to understand what is going on in town, and that is a good time to figure out where your renters will come from. The electronic Web site does a very good job of pulling traffic, but remember, they are also renting out rooms, apartments, and other time shares at prices well below what you might be asking. They control the flow of information and in general, cheaper rooms and apartments sell faster than their expensive resort options.

Most time share renters seeking top seasonal rentals are people in their late thirties, early forties, and younger fifties, as a general rule. These are people who are in their peak earning years, may be alumni in town for a huge football game, or a small group traveling into town to see a very large performer like a top-ten global band. In other situations, it is people who live in alternate climates, have high incomes, and are looking to get out of the heat or cold. Then, of course, you have people looking to get into the mountains to ski. Whatever the profile, it is important that you fine-tune your advertisement to your audience.

For example, if you feel you want an edge over people advertising on one of the top Internet sites, then go to where your renter is coming from. So, if USC is playing in the Rose Bowl like they did in 2017 when they played Penn State, one of my prime beachfront time shares had alumni in town for the Penn State game at the Rose Bowl. Anyone looking to rent that week could have put an advertisement in any one of the campus or alumni papers several months prior and had an exclusive audience since most people would not have made the effort. Another good choice would be to call the university and ask for the alumni association president and see what ideas he or she might have. They likely would know of several people interested or may have a better way to reach them. Even better, put an advertisement in the local Penn State newspaper in the city around the university. This is just one of hundreds of examples.

Going against the herd: This method of going after your renter can prove very successful; however, it does require some effort and a bit of detective work. Most time share owners do not need or wish to spend their time trying to chase down a few days of rent per year. Other owners do not mind the effort as it can make the difference between owning and not owning their time share because unexpected bills can pile up, and often, using your time share can produce some much-needed cash. I have had years where I was grateful to have the opportunity to raise a little cash to meet unexpected bills, and renting out my time share was a better option than selling other assets. The key is when competition gets tough, get aggressive, go out of town to find your customer, and don't be afraid to get creative.

If you have access to your time share at or near a convention center or large downtown area, most all of the large hotels host different companies in town almost every week.

You can find out who is coming to town and call the CEO of the company. You will be routed to the very person who likely has access to, or is in charge of, booking reservations for the CEO and possibly some other vice presidents. These assistants are usually very busy, so you want to get to the point very fast and offer to send that person an e-mail. Make sure your marketing slick has plenty of photos and stress your rental high points, whether it be views, pools, golf, etc., and look for the amenities, restaurants, etc., that will complement your target renter. In some cases, you may just be doing the assistant a favor because, in the end, they get the credit, or the blame, for a bad reservation, so they are always looking for better value, flexibility, and convenience . . . the very thing most resort villas offer.

Event-driven or seasonal-driven customer-which is it and why it matters. It is important to understand why there is demand for your unit at the time you want to rent because it gives you some clues on how to rent your villa. For example, is your renter in town for a specific event or do they just want to enjoy the beach in a prime summer month? If you have a seasonal renter coming into town, then your market is much bigger because the demand is there day after day during the whole season versus a few days before or after a big event like a football game. The top Internet sites do a good job of managing global traffic because their marketing arms drive renters to their site looking for prime rentals in high-demand vacation spots. That said, you can also cover and increase your odds by advertising in multiple sites and offering something beyond just the rental if you understand your customer profile. You can also charge more rent if your packaging is on target.

For example, a gift card at a popular steak house nearby separates you from the five, 10, or even 20 other rentals perhaps in your same resort. If you make sure your fee is $25 a night lower, and you offer a $100 gift card, the chances of you renting soar. You will not know when the last rental will book and some of the advertisements expire without getting booked. It is also possible someone may be interested in your villa but might end up canceling before they book, or make three or four bids, and then accept two, and then eventually accept the other bid, even if you make the top two. It is always better to leave a little money on the table and provide that gift card because, until the unit is booked and a deposit becomes nonrefundable, you could end up wasting 3 or 4 days and end up losing the one renter you had on the line. Renting time shares is like being a plumber. If you want the business and you are a plumber, the first callback always has the advantage.

One way to attract high rental demand involves packaging a rental with either event or sporting tickets. This really only works well with high-demand sporting or concert events, not run-of-the-mill regular season games. We recommend this type of rental for things like the playoffs, high-profile PGA events, or nationally televised rival games with college football, particularly if a bowl game or college ranking is at stake. If you have access to these kinds of tickets or any of your network or relatives can get them, this package can work out very well. You need to market this type of package to both teams and should start at least 3 months in advance when out-of-town guests start to make plans. You can advertise with the large rental companies and just have the customer inquire about the tickets. It is always best to sell the tickets for face value and put a premium on the rental as long as you stay at, or below, what the resort charges.

If you have access to other assets, like clubs or your brother-in-law owns a small limousine company, don't be afraid to come up with something unique. If someone is paying you $650 a night for a week, and there are two advertisements competing for one last rental, that $200 dinner card combined with a $300 limo ride to and from the restaurant may just make the difference. In many towns, like Scottsdale, Ariz., you can call for a limo to take you to dinner, and then call back 3 hours later for a ride home. Often, this is only $75 or so each way, less than half the cost of paying a limo driver to wait for you to finish dinner. This limo/dinner package may cost you $500, but it may have been what landed you a $4,550 weekly rental you might not have otherwise landed. Be different and make a difference, and your rental clientele will show up for you.

Your advertisement needs to be complete: When crafting an advertisement, the rule of thumb is do not assume anything. Do not assume your renter knows the property, the area, how to get there, what the inside looks like, or even that it contains a kitchen. Spell it out for them. The more information that is cleanly presented, the better the experience will be, and the faster you will get a deal done with a deposit. Taking the extra step to include directions or letting them know it is a 15-minute ride to the airport are details that really matter to someone out of town. Letting them know it is 20 minutes to the big game, if there is one in town, or 5 minutes to the beach by shuttle lets them know if your rental is what they need and helps take out the guesswork. Many rentals may be coming from another state or even another country. They will jump on an advertisement that walks them through the unknown and does a better job than you did, even if it means paying a little more.

The advertisement needs to read like you are there: Make sure you can provide a detailed picture, drawing, or description, and preferably all three of what the inside of the villa looks like, how the rooms are separated, and what the patio or balcony view looks like. The more you can take out the guesswork, the more likely a rental will come from your ad. All of us have booked something, only to be disappointed, so remember, they may not trust you but will trust a lot of photos. A backup sheet you can e-mail that includes phone numbers to call for nearby restaurants and information on traveling around town makes you look professional and helps keep your rental from cancelling at the last minute. . Renters looking to pay $400 to $600 a night want details, lots of them. If you can provide a map, including inside and outside pictures and a description of local restaurants and shopping, all the better. Remember, these people may have saved up all year to go on the trip you are advertising, and they do not want surprises. Make sure you know how late the pools are open, if there is a spa on-site or nearby, what time is check out and check-in, etc. These things go a long way to avoid confusion. Inserting this info into your advertisement (or letting them know you have a four-page rental kit) gives a higher level of comfort to the renter than your request for $500 a night is worthwhile, and they will feel proud after they check-in.

Understand when the market is not there: If you are not getting calls, there are only three possibilities: you are either not reaching your target audience or your unit villa is either overpriced or there is just not any rental demand. We have always seen rental results run much higher when you select a few rental windows that are very special. The average time share does not have a lot of demand most of the time, some at any price. Since you likely have the option of special knowledge about your favorite time share city, an upcoming concert or event, a special PGA tour, and so forth, take advantage of that. Remember when Tiger Woods was on the cover of almost every golf magazine? Attendance soared when he was in the lineup to play and fell by 50% or more if he cancelled. When the St. Louis Cardinals were hot and the Cubs had Sammy Sosa and the Cardinals had Mark McGwire chasing the home run title, every game was sold out in the final 30 game stretch as they headed into the history books with over 70 home runs. Today's travelers are smart. They love to go to a city and knock off two or three fun things to do. Combining a ski or golf trip with a ballgame, and then driving another 100 miles to visit a friend or see a new opening is no big deal anymore.

Every year will be different. Someday a woman is going to be the favorite to win the Indy 500 or Daytona 500. Good luck getting a rental in Daytona when that happens! We will see any number of teams set a precious record over the next 10 years. Some bands will host a few reunion tours. Whatever it might be, you may have the keys to land a premium rental. In time share, it only takes one or two rentals a year to cover a large portion of your maintenance fees, dramatically dropping your cost per night. Putting in a little effort into this process can pay off big, year after year. If you follow our advice, you will be successful.

Remember, any rental over your maintenance fee is a good rental. Don't try to take every last dime off the table. People know if the market is $700 a night and they are paying you $550 a night. They know you are helping them and most people appreciate it. Everyone, no matter how rich, wants to feel like they made a good deal. Give them one and they will keep your number and you have a good chance they will call you back or refer you to a friend. Renters tend to rent year after year, and owners tend to buy more time shares over the years. Based on the models we have run, there is an argument that neither one is necessarily better than the other. It is just a matter of what is right for each of us at the time.

There are a lot of people who will happily pay that $550 a night instead of buying a time share year after year rather than purchase a time share. Those of us who have figured out how to benefit from them also win by netting much more vacation time at little or no cost. This is the fun with time shares and why, if you are a math fan, the right vacation portfolio can help pay for your retirement while you are lying on the beach, taking that text for a rental.

How NOT to rent your timeshare: The biggest way to absolutely fail at time share rental is to jump into a market you do not understand. A beachfront market in Mexico is very different from Newport Beach. Myrtle Beach is not the same thing as Daytona Beach. Each beach city has a very different vibe, and renting requires you know what that vibe is because it affects the way to craft your marketing campaign. It also affects ***where*** you look for your rental and how you design your marketing campaign. Renting to people who like to ski is a very different process than renting at the beach if you take the task seriously. Snow rentals, for example, fall and rise with just a few inches of snow coming in—or not coming in.

For most of us who do not own a Christmas week, renting means you need to be smart, invest in what you are doing, and understand that putting an ad in Airbnb is not going to work all the time. Perhaps your renter does not use Airbnb. Ideally, you should have at least four or five ways you are seeking a renter, and one or two of them should be very different from "what everybody else does." I hear all the time that I would never want to go through all that work to get 2–3 days rent. My answer is . . . then don't do it.

If you do decide you want to rent a few days a year, understand that like everything else in life, a great knowledge of what you are doing goes a long way. It only takes a few hours of research to design a campaign. Once done, you can use the information year after year since, if your campaign drew at least four–five renters, then it is likely you did everything right. It might take a few years to understand what works and what does not work. You have to put the time in now for the first few years, and then the magic will work for the next 25 years once you master it.

Think of renting a time share like trying to fish for the first time. You drive up to the lake, you stopped at the local bait shop, and got the right fish food because the guy at the bait shop that sold it to you said so. You then head over near the rock outcropping because that is where the fish always bite. How do you know that? You know that because that is what the guy next in line at the bait shop told you. Now armed with all of this knowledge, you sit on a rock for over an hour and nothing happens, not even a single bite. While you sit there, you see an old-timer walking up to the lake from a trail that runs deep into the mountains. Your first thought is, does he live up the trail in a cave? He is not that clean, has a really old fishing pole, and he is not carrying a bag that says "Harry's bait shop." He pulls what looks like a bug out of his pocket, rolls it into a tight roll, and then puts it on his old pole and sits down about 100 feet below you and drops his bug into what looks like a deep crevice. You know what happens next.

After 5 minutes or so, he pulls a large trout out of the lake, pulls a newspaper out of his left pocket, cuts off the fins and head like a trained sushi chef, drops the remains back into the lake, and then rolls his trout up in what was likely the morning paper and heads back up to the trail. We will pretend he was going back to his cave because it makes a better story.

Now you sit there on your perched rock shaking your head, wondering, what the heck am I doing wrong? Remember that the art of renting a time share starts off with product knowledge. You need to know who is at your time share when you are trying to rent it. Have you been there at that time? What do people dress like? Is it families, singles, or mostly couples? Is the parking lot full of rental cars, or do you see a lot of Jaguars, Porsches, and BMWs in the parking garages? What is the resort charging for the night you are trying to rent? You need to know this because you need to be below that number, sometimes *way* below that number.

You also need to know how full the resort is. Resort management today is very sophisticated. They know a year in advance within a few rooms how full they are likely to be. They can change pricing by the day, and often do so. They know how many people will call or just drive up and rent within 48 hours with a high degree of probability. This information helps them drive what is a long software process, unleashing villas for employees, VIP tours, exchange trades, third-party exchanges out of network, etc., all based on predictive modeling from prior years. While you cannot know all of this, you can at least try to understand these dynamics because they provide clues on where to find your renter.

We will dismiss with the obvious here. If Penn State is in town and playing USC at the Rose Bowl and half the lobby is wearing college sweatshirts with their team's logo, this would not qualify as detective work. This is what we call the "no-brainer" and one reason why with this knowledge of where many wealthy alumni stay makes great rentals. Of course, you ran ads in the Penn State and Newport Beach areas where the higher-priced homes were 3 months ago, didn't you? By the time you figure out what goes on, the information will be outdated if you are not in the game the year before doing your homework. History tends to repeat itself. It is not likely USC and Penn State will play in the 2018 Rose Bowl, but we know now there will be two teams that do play. This will be a small but very powerful rental window because the two teams may not be known until 3 weeks ahead of time. It does not hurt to run a few ads in four cities where the teams might come from. This type of rental window will more than pay for the ads.

Dismissing the obvious rentals, however, is where you can gain an unfair advantage. This is why thinking outside the box will pay off with a solid rental deal. Some examples of this are looking at what is not so obvious. Who or what is coming to town? This would be an event-driven rental and is a different campaign. High season is not an event rental, it is a seasonal rental where demand is driven mostly by far more people wishing to occupy than the available supply of rooms. This is a much-easier rental and providing your pricing follows the rules, running three or four advertisements on Internet-marketing sites usually works pretty well.

An event-driven rental requires pinpointing your target rental audience because they are likely driven by a single event to seek a rental villa. Often, concerts in the desert in the fall like in California or the Daytona 500, or a significant golf tournament like the Masters, all would fall under an event-marketing campaign. These are obvious choices and tend to match the economic reach of the people who have the time and money to travel to these types of events. In these cases, a combination of target marketing and demand-driven metrics work best where Internet advertisements combined with some target marketing will produce the best results. For example, a list of sponsors from last year's event will give you a perfect mail out list for next year. You will need to make 40 or 50 calls to confirm the addresses, names, or e-mails, but once you have a list that works, you can use it over and over for the same event in the following year. When you put all of the people that respond onto your own rental list for that rental, you can see how easy this process becomes after 5 years or so.

Don't assume an event-driven or even high-season rental will just take care of itself. Renters often get a false sense of what is available because other people are doing the same thing you are, listing their villa on three or four Internet sites. This creates a false reading on what is really available since many people are trying to rent the same villa over and over through different ads, even though they only have one villa to rent for that week in most cases. This is why when you get a call or text, being professional and prompt is the best way to close a deal. It can be frustrating trying to close a rental, and often most renters are talking to three or four owners at the same time. You should always do whatever you have to do to close your deal on the first call. You should also assume you have a renter who verbally agrees on a potential deal but fails to follow up with a credit card deposit. This usually does not happen with Internet sites because they require a deposit to hold the reservation. Remember, just because someone inquired about your rental does not mean they will rent it. Make sure this process is completed as soon as possible and you have your confirmation from the rental company before you cease marketing your rental.

Can renting a time share be a business? It is unlikely that many people rely on renting their time share to earn a full-time living unless they own a time share rental company or perhaps a local real estate company that specializes in time share rentals. Given the streamlined cost of online rental services, this business or type of rental is not practical for a 1-week rental and makes more sense as an online business. The vast majority of time share owners do not own enough time shares to justify renting their own portfolio year-round. As with any type of opportunity, the bigger the opportunity gets, the more likely someone figures out how to assemble a large portfolio, and then offer it into a different market. An example might be buying a lot of beachfront time shares in Hawaii, and then specializing to offer this rental in Japan. The operator might package this with a tour or dinner incentives.

While it is not likely this will represent a large percentage of owners anytime soon, it is only a matter of time before the price of gold can get so high before someone decides to market silver in a different package. We predict a very small niche will develop over the next 10 years where the top 15% of the time share market will specialize in Category One and luxury time shares. These operators will also rent them at a premium because availability windows will be harder to book, and like Super Bowl tickets, there will be a market to buy a ticket for those willing to purchase on the secondary market. In this case, however, it will be at a premium, not a discount on the rental side and will be highly deliverable once an electronic market emerges into a full service model, an easy and normal evolution resulting from the last pieces of the puzzle going into place.**How can I position my rental for maximum gain?** The best way to achieve maximum gain is to start with maximum exposure. You should list your time share in at least three of the top Internet sites for rentals. We do not recommend any more than that because if you are not getting any action, is it because your time share just does not have a lot of demand? If this is the case, adding more ads is not going to solve the problem. You may need a more targeted approach to proactively find your buyer by marketing directly to a club, association, a soccer league, or any other type of group that gathers in your town at the time and place you own. The top Internet sites draw traffic because people love the beach or want to ski, and there are thousands of people who use these sites.

There is no reason you should not catch your share of fish unless your price is too high or your villa is a Category Three or Four and is located in a lower-demand market. Your location may not have a lot of nightlife, may have few surrounding restaurants, and may not have the large resort pools, clubs, and entertainment that comes with megaresorts. When people spend good money to vacation, they want something more than they get at home. Even if your market value is $200 a night versus $600 a night, the people paying $200 want to have a good time, have plenty of options, and want a fun and safe environment for their kids or guests. Make sure you are marketing your villa to the right audience and matching your advertisement campaign to where your buyer will see your ad. It may not be on a high-traffic Web site. Positioning into the right rental pool is the key to success.

Knowledge is power-the time share matrix: Knowing the neighborhood during the time of year you are looking for a rental is the key to why people want to rent. Is it the snow, the lake, the beach, or the town? Is it a nearby sporting event, the proximity to local hiking, or a festival that is in town? Remember, most time shares are like hotel rooms in the way they rent. They rent for a lot more money per night, although they tend to be a lot bigger and offer a lot more value. With all of that said, however, you still need a reason why someone is leaving their house to stay in yours (albeit it may be yours for just a week).

Don't assume it should rent because the company that owns it has a global brand name. That is a reason to trust the rental, not a reason to pay a premium to be your time share at any given week. There must be a compelling reason for people to spend their hard-earned money on renting your villa. This is why we suggest that not all time shares are good candidates for rentals if they are near a major attraction. It also helps if there is not a lot of competition. Most beach towns are very crowded and large ocean view villas are hard to find in the summer; therefore, there is an oversupply of eager renters wanting to enjoy that magic summer. If you own a great time share 3 hours away from a major airport located in a small city, while it may have terrific views, if there is no compelling reason to be there, demand for your villa could be fairly soft all year-round. Know your market before you decide if a rental market exists.

Knowledge is power-the time share rental matrix: As you know from this and other chapters, knowledge is the key to successful renting. Do your homework on what comparable properties rent for and remember that your time share competes with surrounding homes that can also rent for far less than your time share on a rent per foot basis and offer more sleeping space. You must also know how to target your customers and where they come from. Once you master each of these disciplines, you can often enjoy season after season of rentals that could become part of your retirement and vacation plan. Everyone wants a bargain, and everyone wants to be treated well. Offer more than your competition and follow up often. You are, after all, if only for a moment, in the hospitality business.

Packaging your time share rental for success: One surefire way to stand out from the crowd is to offer either tickets or other items (Disneyland passes), etc., and package the tickets with the villa. Sure, you will take on extra risk, so the best plan is to plan on going to the event if you do not succeed. If your game or event is special enough and tickets are hard to come by, you will usually collect a premium on the rental and likely, on the tickets. Be sure you are in line with all local, state, and federal laws on ticket scalping practices. The point here is not to scalp your customer but to offer a hard-to-find package deal. I have even thrown in limousine service and done quite well on these special occasions. Again, since this is a premium service, do not take anything for granted. Your job is to overcommunicate to make sure every detail is perfect.

Other time share package ideas:

If your time share is on a lake, offer a kayak coupon or fishing bait.

If your time share is near the big game, offer a dinner card to a top steak house for a round of drinks or for dinner.

If your time share is near the beach, throw in a beach kit with sunscreen, crackers and cheese, and imported water, juice, or soda.

If your time share is near Disneyland or Disneyworld, throw in a sweatshirt from there.

If your time share is near a ski area, a bottle of wine and some cheese works well.

Focus on your core strengths- The time share game is not rocket science. It is about being transparent, offering brand name recognition, delivering a value proposition, and making sure you take care of the customer. Sounds like you are a major hotel operator. Well, you are in this sense. Where else could you be a partner with a name like Marriott or Hilton hotels without even an interview. Managing your time share can be very fulfilling if you know what you are doing. The big names take care of the maintenance, the check in and out, clean and replace the sheets and are there to repair and replace a myriad of items with just a phone call, even if it is from your customer. Why would you want to blow this type of relationship? Once more your partner really does not even charge you to handle these things for you. It is buried in your maintenance fee of course but when your RRC ration starts to run over 5 to 1 and you make $600 to $800 a night, this opportunity starts to look pretty attractive. The only thing you have to do is your homework, be savvy about follow up and always double check things to make your customer feels like the original customer. Follow the 67% rule, look to acquire Category one and two time shares only, and use long marketing windows with out of the box marketing techniques and you can be the time share King on your block. This business is not going away and a when your time share is paid up, there is no such thing as out bidding you. You can list your time share for one half the market price if you had too and still make plenty of money. Follow the rules and the world is yours to stay in, at little or no cost once you build the right time share portfolio.

CHAPTER **21**

The Time Share Beachfront Index

A Time Share Condo/Condo/Home Comparison

COST TO OCCUPY a time share, home or condo for one year at the beach. The world population is fast approaching over 8 billion people. The United States has only 360M people, or less than 4% of the world's total population. The United States, despite some of our problems, continues, and will likely remain, to be one of the most desirable vacation choices in the world. There are few cities that can compete with the energy and excitement of New York, the beaches of Florida, the climate and sights of California, the islands of Hawaii, the city of Boston, the lights of Las Vegas, and many of our historical landmarks like Mt. Rushmore, the Grand Canyon, Moab, Utah, and the Rocky Mountains, with pristine lakes and some of the most outstanding mountain sunsets and waterfalls. Travelers from all over the world pour into our country every year, with most wanting to return or even move to the U.S.

We have developed our coastlines for over 200 years and continue to see net migration into the beach cities with inland properties even 5 to 10 miles inland now seeing higher-than-average appreciation from families wanting to be "near the beach." In many parts of Southern and Northern California, a small 1,400 square foot home on or very close to the beach now commands well over a million dollars, with new three- or four-bedroom homes well over 3 million that are close to the beach.

This has now placed a home of even 2,500 square feet simply out of reach for over 95% of the population. Yet, prices continue to rise for beachfront properties year after year. When you examine this trend, we see family generations often inheriting some of these properties, with the balance being sold into the market to a combination of foreign and domestic buyers choosing to park their cash into prime beachfront property. Even in real estate downturns, beachfront property falls in value the least of all homes and tends to recover faster when the economy in housing picks back up.

If you analyze the entire West Coast and include Washington and Oregon, you can clearly see that most areas that have beachfront access have been developed, are too rocky to be practical, or the property is owned by the state. In many other areas, building permits are not possible or it could take 15 years or more just to obtain zoning for a multi unit project, something that is beyond the horizon of 99% of all developers. In addition, there is not enough built-in infrastructure to just go in and support a large 1,500 home project. There are not even a handful of potential sites along the West Coast that could accommodate

1,500 residences of any kind, including high-density projects like condos or apartments. We are essentially sold out of beachfront property on the West Coast unless a small site could be rezoned for a high-rise use and somehow pass the dozens of regulatory, environmental, and coastal issues that usually stop this type of project in today's business climate.

The California coastline is more coveted because its southern location closer to the equator makes the weather much warmer with less rain than either the Oregon and Washington coastlines. Most of us today will not ever see a large-scale resort project built again on the West Coast unless a developer is successful at rezoning land from industrial or commercial use back to residential.

If we view these statistics from another angle, something interesting appears. The vast majority of dwelling units along the California coastline, except the city of San Francisco where high-rises are the dwelling unit of choice, are homes, and most range in price from at least $1M to over $25M. While calculations about the total number of beachfront homes are difficult to come by, just driving along the coastline, you could get to over one million homes on or very near the beach if you include the entire state. It just depends on where you draw the line from the beach, but within a quarter of a mile, it will generally fall into either beachfront or at least be considered a beach home if it has even a partial ocean view.

Now, let's do the same for a time share. I have reviewed the portfolios of the top seven global brands and can report there are not even six properties among the industry that truly face or are on the beach itself. Is there something odd about this fact?

Let's put this observation into simple math. We have over 40M people living in the state of California using the latest 2017 poll numbers, which include net migration into the state for 2016. We have as many as 1M homes bordering the beach or having at least a partial ocean view, yet we have only six time share properties among the top developers that face or are very close to the beach in the whole state of California. Which one of these seems scarcer? We could also make an equally compelling argument for the great state of Florida, essentially made by God for people to flock and retire with beachfront access and views.

Recall that we have more visitors to California every year and more net migration flocking into an already crowded state. This is evident by the growth of homes now spreading into the desert areas, the only place left where large land tracts still exist.

It is not out of the ordinary to find the cost of a small beachfront home exceeding \$3 or \$4 million if you are looking for a small 2–3-bedroom home that is situated on the beach. In many cases, the home is more likely to be near the beach if you are talking about Newport Beach, Newport Coast, Corona Del Mar, or Laguna Beach. In our analysis, we wanted prime ocean views but did settle for comparables very close to the beach with very good ocean views. This is in line with the Marriott time share comparable in Newport Coast that has fantastic ocean views. We will therefore just use prime ocean views as the standard within a very close walk to the water.

Most real estate brokers in the Southern California market might laugh if you told them you want to purchase a small 2+2 bedroom/bath home on the sand for about \$3M.

After looking around this area, we discovered we could acquire a condominium for around $1.6M, with small homes around 2,500 square feet on small lots running over $4M.

We found home inventory for a home coming in at around $4.6M in 2017 that had an extra bedroom and bath and great ocean views. We assumed we had just under $1M to find our beachfront time share, condo, or home that would provide for living in it all year-round. We have, for the moment, assumed we could book the villa in the time share for a year, if, for no other reason, then just to do this comparison. As a side note, this is an area where ocean view lots can sell for $5–$20M or more, where the buyer intends on tearing down the house to replace it with a larger and more modern home.

We further assumed using $975,900 as the down payment in all three situations leaving the condo and home purchase needing to acquire a loan of $652,600 and $3,645,100. Both had down payments of 59% and 21% respectively. We also assumed the time share purchase was for all cash, keeping the net investment in each deal the same. We assumed a 30-year loan at 4.75% for this analysis, given the rising interest rate environment with the Federal Reserve having just increased interest rates again in March of 2017.

The Beachfront Index Results

June, 2017-Newport Beach, Calif-Vicinity to purchase Beachfront Time Share/Condo/Home

		One Year Time Share	2+2 Ocean Condo	Beachfront Home
		Assumes substantial ocean view from many rooms.		
	Notes	**Time Share**	**Condo**	**Home**
	Sq. Feet	1,550	1,550	2,100
	Price/Foot	$629	$1,050	$2,200
	Bed/Bath	2 + 2	2+2	3+3
	Cost of 52 Weeks	**Purchase Price**	**Purchase Price**	**Purchase Price**
$12K/Week	Weeks 1-28	$336,000	$1,627,500	$4,620,000
	July 4th	$55,000		
	Christmas Week	$65,000		
$14K/Week	Weeks 30-42	$168,000		
	Weeks 41-51	$350,900		
	Total Price	**$974,900**	**$1,627,500**	**$4,620,000**
	Cash Down	$974,900	$974,900	$974,900
	Percent Down	100%	59.90%	21.10%
4.75%	Loan Amount	0	$652,600	$3,645,100
	Monthly Payment	$0	$3,420	$19,014
	ANNUAL EXPENSES			
30 Year	Loan Payment	0	$41,040	$228,168
1.20%	Taxes	$15,360	$19,530	$55,440
	Insurance	$0	$3,120	$6,825
	Trash	$0	$0	$1,345
	Pool	$0	$0	$1,625
	Electricity	$0	$850	$3,180
	Gas	$0	$620	$1,215
	Water	$0	$850	$1,850
	Cable	$0	$1,200	$1,850
	HOA	$0	$7,200	$11,500
	Main Reserve	$0	$1,200	$4,500
	Maintenance Fee	$68,500	$0	$0
	TOTAL COST/YEAR	**$83,860**	**$75,610**	**$317,498**
	Summer Rental	**$63,000**	**$42,000**	**$75,000**
2018	**Beachfront Index**	**1 to 1**	**1.67**	**4.74**

We can see the time share at just under one million produces the lowest cost to own. It is possible the maintenance fees could be slightly lower depending on how the weeks are acquired, but even under optimal circumstances, the maintenance fees would be at least $73,000 a year, about the same as the condominium. All of these have at least two bedrooms, two baths, and two parking spaces. We are not suggesting that for most people, purchasing a time share is a viable alternative to a home. That said, as the Beachfront Index continues to rise, pushing more people out of the buying pool, at some point, silver starts to look like a better deal than gold. History has proven this with both metal and real estate.

It is an interesting conversation to try to explain which of these three potential assets has the best chance to double in price over 10 years. We project the condominium and the time share will each double by 2026, and the home will appreciate much less than double its price over the same period. Note that the home is not only over four times more expensive, it costs 3.5 times as much to own every year. In 10 years, the owner will have also spent close to $1.4M more in cash to own the home, about the cost of the condominium for a relatively small increase in overall square footage.

We believe the time share option is not only a better value, but has more upside. We are fast reaching a breakpoint that when less than 99% of the population can afford to buy a house at $4M-plus, how is this statistic supposed to improve if that beach house currently at $4.6M goes to $8.8M over 10 years? We believe we are headed into a decade of very slow appreciation as most millennials head into their prime earnings years and want to remain free, mobile, and out of debt.

The gold versus silver analysis-when does one price create a bargain in the other? Over the past 200 years, economists have measured the price relationship between gold and silver, constantly pointing out when the price of gold becomes historically more expensive than silver. Tennessee bullion expert Franklin Sanders is credited with measuring this relationship dating back to 1792. For the next 130 years, the price for an ounce of gold was about 16 times its counterpart in silver. Then when the Federal Reserve was created in 1913, this ratio had risen all the way to 96 to 1 at times. In recent years, the ratio has stood at about 51 to 1. There are some historians who believe that silver will again fall back toward its historical norm.

It is even more amazing when you consider there is about 10 times more aboveground gold as there is aboveground silver. Silver, because of its conductivity properties, has many more uses in modern-day technologies ranging from dentistry, automobiles, and many high-tech devices, along with hundreds of tech components that rely on silver.

Economists have reasoned that while each metal has unique properties different from each other, they both offer metallic, physical, and financial benefits that run closely together such that if the price of one were so inverted relative to the other, a correction or rebound could create enormous profits for those people who can wait out the temporary market imbalance. Time and time again, this ratio has proven to work with silver always going up in price or gold coming down until a more normal trading premium was once again reached.

We also believe, like gold and silver, that prime time shares aligned along beautiful coastlines that offer spectacular views and warm climates are also going to have to align themselves closer to the price of homes of similar location and utility value. As next-generation time shares specializing in 3–6-month stays become more commonplace, the gap between homes and time shares of similar utility value will become more apparent. Already, those of us who have lived in high-rises understand that while they have higher operating costs, the units are very much the same. It is the lifestyle and views that attract this type of customer, along with the ease of coming and going in a secure building.

We predict the real estate lines that define high-rise ownership will start to blur more and more as developers start to capitalize on this new trend toward longer-term time shares. Given the shortage of viable land options, some city councils will be forced to look at high-rise options to help solve demand for more housing of any kind. This will also be needed to make deals pencil in today's very competitive environment for prime locations. This bodes especially well for two- and three-bedroom products that closely mimic the year-round housing model. We have already seen a trend in several timeshare projects where the same group of customers gather for months at a time to escape the cold winters of the United States and Canada for the warmth of the desert and Hawaii. Many of the older Hawaiian properties have seen the same set of customers get along so well they have bought more and more time and now consider their fellow time share owner's neighbors since they all meet for 1 to 3 months every year at the same time, and have for decades. This trend has been established for many years and is already well in motion for a 6–12-month time share model to avail itself in formal presentations. Given the strength of this trend to stay longer in prime-time shares, it is only a matter of time before this silver investment in real estate heads toward the gold standard of a beachfront home, and in doing so, will outpace the home alternative at the beach for price appreciation over the decade.

CHAPTER 22

The Next-Generation Time Share Model(s)

ONE OF THE next time share models—long-term guaranteed stays: We believe one of the new products that will be released over the next 5 years is what will be called a "long-term stay time share." These will be new real estate derivatives that operate just like a regular time share except the resorts themselves will be a little different and more designed for people on the move who want to stay about 3–6 months in one location. They will also operate at a slightly lower cost than their 1-week cousin, the traditional 7-day time share, because these types of time shares do not need to be located in top-grade vacation locations; instead, they will offer luxurious settings and a whole list of additional benefits we will describe below.

The driving force behind this trend will be the Beachfront Index will work itself into the primary home market where the cost of staying in a timeshare becomes more favorable than a traditional primary home, whose average daily cost is currently added onto the cost of traveling or staying in a time share.

Under the new time share trend, we predict some people will sell their larger home for a smaller one and drop their average daily cost by 65% or more. We believe they will also buy more time shares to augment this new mobile lifestyle.

This will be done in a number of ways, including downsizing what is today known as the primary home, and then paying cash for a smaller patio home and couple it with either a time share home or related time share product where the owners are looking to occupy a long-term time share for 3–6 months a year using a combination of patio homes, townhomes, and long-term time shares to complete a 12-month living and travel plan.

We predict as the next cycle of real estate appreciation continues to push more homes out of reach for even more buyers, the market will need to find a new answer. The new answer will be the trend to acquire small townhomes or patio homes that yield lower operating costs and pay cash for them. These homes will likely be located in growing areas well outside major metro cities, where land is much cheaper, zoning laws are more favorable, and these homes can be produced at a much-lower price per square foot.

The owners will then have the cash to pay for a 2–4-month time share that becomes very affordable as many buyers will now have little or no mortgage debt because they sold off that $1M home in favor of a small patio home in a Class B city, where Class B is simply defined as more affordable not necessarily less desirable. Certainly, all of the parks, libraries, and public transportation will still exist. It is just that the need to live in areas where the land value is equal to 50% or more of the value of a property is no longer affordable for many people generally over 50 years of age. They do not need to be near primary employment centers; they need to live in areas that are much cheaper to live in on a daily basis where utilities, taxes, cable, trash, and water prices are much lower and entry prices for homes are equal to what a down payment is for their former primary home.

Next Generation Design Footprints: In order to drive down the cost of longer-stay time shares, these next-generation time share concepts will need to acquire large tracts of land at much-lower cost than the traditional primary beach sites in Hawaii or the Caribbean. Since land cost can be as much as 30% or more of the cost of a time share, by getting rid of the need to be on the beach or the base of a ski slope, this type of land should cost about 25% to 50% of what traditional time share land costs to acquire. The goal will be to construct a new urban real estate project with a small retail and restaurant section surrounded by a well-designed mega scale time share project with heavy emphasis on landscaping, street scaping, and design elements like water features and small park areas for the surrounding buildings. Ideally, new and more inviting outdoor kitchens will encompass the landscape and be near every building. This type of project can offer both patio homes, midrise, and even midhigh-rise products depending on the area, view plains, and realty economics. The irony here is that the same developer could offer the same project in two different cities, with the client preferring to spend 8 months in Arizona during the winter months, supplemented by purchasing a long-term stay project in Utah or Colorado or Wyoming or even affordable homes in California in the desert communities or in Florida in second-tier cities. The combination of these ownership products could allow many couples to retire much earlier and create an offensive retirement portfolio in the process. We predict this new model will be the biggest trend in housing over the next 20 years.

The Retirement Time Share Model: This product does not exist today, but the economic reality of so many underfunded retirement plans will force developers to rethink housing solutions that fit the needs of most people. The baby boomers are now reaching 62 years old in record numbers, and the vast majority do not have enough money to retire but do have home equity and some savings. According to Boettner Center for Pensions and Retirement Research, in a study done in 2013, it was predicted that in January of 2017, 10,000 baby boomers will retire per day and this trend will continue for the next 19 years. What is worse is that according to the Employee Benefit Research Institute, the amount of 401(k) retirement plans has dropped since 1980, having dwindled down to just 15% of retirement workers in 2017 versus 39% in 1980.

This same source also predicted that 22% of boomers will likely owe more on their house than it is worth in the time period from 2013–2016. This predicament has led to an estimated 51% of baby boomers predicted to retire in a lifestyle either well below or somewhat below what their previous standard of living was. This is why over 75% of boomers will start to draw Social Security at 62 rather than wait until age 70, when their payout would have increased from an average $1,200 a month to over $2,000 a month if they could have held on for 8 more years. It is further estimated that today, a single male will need an average of $187,000 to fund out-of-pocket medical costs, with a single female needing $213,000 because of the longer life span for females. Given that most retirement-eligible people have less than $15,000 saved and about two-thirds have less than $150,000, the need for more affordable housing is going to far outweigh any of the current options of today. Our country has a 100% chance of facing a severe retirement housing crisis in the next 20 years with the need for smaller and less costly housing quickly outpacing any other sector. This spread for lower cost housing is going to widen significantly over the next 20 years, but most boomers are going to want to retire in a community that feels and acts like the same lifestyle they had before, with a preference toward more—not less—luxury built into the product mix.

If you watch television, have you noticed how many commercials now favor the reverse mortgage? Imagine sitting down with your children and letting them know you have just signed a reverse mortgage that allows you to draw $3,500 a month against your house, something your kids might view as **their** future house. If you are in your early 60s and you live well into your 80s, how are you supposed to reconcile the financial car wreck that has to occur before you pass away? Under this scenario, if you live to be 82 in 20 years and are in reasonably good health, you will be facing a *$1.3M mortgage* with a new loan payment that could rise to well over *$10,000 a month* by the time you reach 83 years old. Reverse mortgages should be for people that have an 80% chance of living only 5 years or less, not 5 years or more. Just the stress of a reverse mortgage will kill off many people, so, in some cases, the problem will resolve itself. This is not a way for anyone to enjoy what is supposed to be a "quiet and enjoyable retirement."

There is a better way than retiring and betting you will die before you run out of money. The alternative is to force your retirement plan into an offensive mode, retire out of debt, and buy a patio home and combine it with a long-term time share plan. We recognize this plan will not work for the alarming number of people that have worked for over 40 years and have no savings or home equity. This is not something this book was written to address. We can help those with a net worth of $500,000 or more by lowering your cost of living rather than your standard of living. This can be done by repositioning your monthly housing outflow of funds so you can essentially reduce your overall housing cost by 75% or more over what was considered your primary home.

The next generation of long-term time shares will start to address this need to travel, escape the heat or the cold, and provide a meaningful environment to enjoy life. It is noteworthy that this trend will also favor millennials who are now shunning the idea of both home and car ownership. The trend in microhomes is exploding with nearly every state now offering homes that fit on a trailer and can be moved. While living in 85 to 100 square feet might work for some of us, the majority of us still want a nice kitchen, a separate bedroom, a possible guest room, and at least two bathrooms. This is the blueprint of many time shares with some offering three and even four bedrooms. This trend will also continue into the long-term stay model.

We are involved in designing megatime share resorts for next-generation developers looking for a new housing model to accommodate up to 3,000-plus units. The size of these projects will help create the economies of scale to offset and help lower the delivery price per square foot. This type of master plan can also be built over 10 years, providing a long-term profit center for the developer. It does not have to mean a bare bones product. Some of these megaresorts will be designed for those that want luxury at a lower cost and are willing to pay for it. Many couples retiring from a 3,000 to 6,000 square foot home or larger are in favor of not only a smaller home, but one that is actually nicer inside than the large one they are leaving. This means 11 foot ceilings, high-tech screens with artwork, superefficient and green appliances, extra closet spaces with interior space designs, and two to three bedrooms that are larger than the typical suburban home. Smaller, grander, more efficient with lots of mood lighting, and heavy landscaped yards with water features and small outdoor kitchens that use a small footprint, but every foot is maxed out to entertain and help provide a cozy and private outdoor experience.

Who is going to build these projects? Given the vast majority of skill sets required to acquire, design, and implement this type of project, it is highly likely that this model will come from one of the top seven developers over the next 10 years. While the large national home builders are also good candidates, it might be the large time share companies are better suited for a portion of this type of project, while the large home builders could handle the year-round patio homes that are sold to just one owner. In this regard, a possible partnership with each side working on a common model could prevail. Given the statistics for this type of housing, it is almost improbable that this type of resort would not be built. It may end up with different arms and legs, but the notion of a 90-day to 180-day time share makes sense, saves money, and most of all, could allow a developer to sell the same home for 120% of a normal sale, charging each side 60% of what a patio home would otherwise sell for on a traditional sale. The owner saves money because they get the house for 40% off and only pay operating expenses for one-half of the year.

The New Time Share Village Concept

Some of the upscale features of this next generation time share model will include:

> **Interior design new products—high-tech revolving photo walls**: The new long-term time share model will need to focus on two concepts to be very successful. The first is that since one or more families will be constantly moving in during the year, it is important that the patio home, apartment, etc., reflect a strong personal and family touch. The current time share market does a very good job of hosting and receiving families, so they are already set up to provide additional

features. The main one should be the inclusion of family photos, shark or fish tanks, and revolving artwork, all depicted on screen TVs sprinkled throughout the unit. This technology is already here and will add a strong personal touch to the time share apartment. Now a family can preload photos up to the cloud, and when they arrive, they can walk in and see pictures of their family throughout the villa. This concept can also produce a number of moving screens that display fish tanks, artwork, and even short videos of the area. This will have tremendous impact and separate their stay from the ones before they arrive and after they leave.

The second theme will be the need for extra cabinets stored either inside the unit or nearby. If the owner plans to stay every year, and the unit is designed to host four 3-months stays (actually four 87-day stays to accommodate maintenance, etc., then one room in the house should include four separate lock-off closets. These can also be stored off-site in another building. This would help the owners that drive in from another city, and they would avoid hauling their artwork, golf clubs, clothes, etc., back and forth. This design addition will help remove a great deal of the pressure to get packed and ready every year.

Vehicle Storage and Maintenance Yards: This community for long-term time share stays will be set up to allow for owners to use golf carts throughout the entire resort, including trips to the town square, golf course, gym, and various social buildings throughout the complex. Owners should be able to either rent a golf cart or store one in the vehicle maintenance yard all year-round. This would allow them to fly in and shuttle to the project and have a car waiting for them or have use of the golf cart when they are on-site. A pool of golf carts could also be made available for a separate charge, once again, dramatically lowering the cost of owning either multiple cars or a golf cart.

Time share car and bike lot: In this new urban design work/live/play/retire lifestyle, the need for a car will be replaced by Uber, golf carts, and time share cars. Owners can walk or drive over to the time share lot, get in a car that will beep when they clear security, and take the car for 1 hour or 1 month. They will receive a bill every month for their car use. This new form of ownership will likely run around 50% lower than the cost of owning one car and closer to 75% lower than the cost of owning two or three cars. Once more, owners can have that fast sports car up to Las Vegas, and then get a Honda for that long drive to see relatives where getting gas every day is required. More flexibility, more spendable cash, a lower cost of living, and a better life. We are very excited about this next-generation home and living design and are already hard at work driving this concept to reality.

Protected parking spaces: As this new economy unfolds, the irony for some is they may be able to afford that new Tesla after all because they do not have a mortgage. Some of these people will want to park their new car in a covered garage, away from the elements of sun and weather. These new time shares will need to offer some garage spaces to accommodate this lifestyle shift. These garages can come in different sizes, and, of course, will be a separate add-on cost that can be leased for 3 months using your points. Garages will ideally cost about 15%–20% of what the villas cost in points per day.

Garage rental—on-site storage: This will open up the market as long-term owners will require a small storage garage to store items they will want to use during their 3–6 month stays. This will also allow the developer to collect fees for providing this service.

Discount shuttle transportation: Given the scalability of a larger project encompassing over 400 acres with several different types of time share and fractional ownership products, the developer could afford to price in shuttle service to and from the airport, even if it involves a discounted fee. This would allow owners to use cars in the auto-share lot and avoid the expense of a rental car. This savings alone would fund the discounted shuttle service in the form of a discounted fee for transportation to airports and restaurants.

Seasonal clubs: This new model could support short-term classes and clubs that run 3 months or so, allowing owners to pick up new skills in computer classes, art, and other classes in demand for that area.

Outdoor kitchen, fire pits, social gathering rings: This concept is already well underway in many larger time share projects; however, with small fractional pods, the developer could afford to create small outdoor kitchens that can be used on a first-come basis, with others that can be rented for the evening. This will make hosting small lunch and dinner events for celebrations very enjoyable for the owners.

Small amphitheater: The larger projects could support a small amphitheater to host local music, lectures, movies, and other big-screen events for owners looking to share entertainment. The more benefits that can surround the long-term time share, the greater the demand will be to live there every year for a portion of the time.

The six-hole golf course- times four: Half the grass, half the cost of lawn maintenance. With just 24 holes, a developer could create 12 different combinations of 18 hole golf with just 24 holes designed to switch out in four separate (six) hole pods. It would be like creating 12 golf courses but only paying for 1.33 times the cost of just one. The golfer gets 12 different combinations of 18 holes, making the resort feel much bigger with different golf challenges built into each six-hole pod.

The project could then be built along a combination of landscaping and water features with 24 holes of golf contained within the project. Every weekend would sport a different 18-hole course with a separate option to play just six holes of golf. This could be easily designed with a large X as the axis with each a six-hole pod representing six holes with a combination of time share products and fractional owner homes aligned on both sides of each axis. A large lake could encompass the center to spread out transportation, golf, and pedestrian routes, and would also create a "Central Park" for the project. Golf carts would enter the middle of the lake on elevated golf paths to rotate into the next six-hole golf pod. Each axis will offer different themes, price points, and feature sets, and will include different categories and mixtures of long-term, short-term stays and year-round stay homes, patio homes, and townhomes, all sold through the next time share model focused on these needs.

A sample of possible time share village amenities: Don't forget the millennials, boomers, and Gen X still want a leisure lifestyle. Here are some possibilities:

Frisbee golf: This is a type of poor man's golf but provides many of the same thrills as regular golf.

Drone park: This will soon be a common theme around the country given the projected need and use for drones worldwide.

Cart racing: This type of amenity would draw new customers into the time share model.

The town square: This next-generation mega time share resort could include a complete golf cart path for owners to use to travel throughout the resort. The town square will include a grocery store, pharmacy, movie theater, post office, barbershop, spa, banks, as well as restaurants, coffee shops, and other associated retail.

Off-season travel groups: Long-term stays would allow operators to focus on targeted customers looking to complete a cooking or other class over a 3-month period. They could then book certain target groups into the college on-site. This type of feature would allow for many types of travel groups.

Lower maintenances: Depending on land costs and other features, some owners might prefer a newer design with zeroscape landscaping, no cable or close by park access, and they may give up ownership rights to a number of the timeshare village amenities in exchange for a lower maintenance fee. This could encompass a very small portion of the overall development.

Fractional ownership options: Other owners might opt to purchase a 6-month for even 1-year ownership package that provides trading rights to other projects. Eventually, we predict this model will include year-round residents that want to travel about 3–6 months per year.

Horseback riding: Depending on the climate, some projects could host horseback riding or other types of recreation, like lakes and lake sports, in order to make the project more oriented to entertainment lifestyles with a portion of the customer base looking to remain active.

On-site medical clinic: On-site medical would be a huge benefit to the overall project and would complement a retirement village within the development. This type of development would far surpass the typical nursing home and provide a citylike feel within a nursing home environment.

On-site retail section: This project could easily support an adjacent retail center providing groceries and drugstores, along with typical neighborhood services. Access by golf cart and path lighting could connect these two concepts.

On-site theater, party, and conference center: This type of amenity could host anniversaries and other events to provide a full-scale array of services allowing customers and businesses to operate in a minicity feel without having to leave the development.

Hobby village: A combination of recreational center combined with a hobby or campus set of buildings would allow for the community to benefit from the project while helping draw retail and business customers into the project to maximize sales. A portion of this project could be funded with bond-financed debt to help construct the public amenities.

The assisted living and nursing home pod: The current concept of assisted living is uncomfortable for almost everyone. The problem is complicated by the fact that it is very expensive and emotional to put any parent into either an assisted living facility or nursing home. The process alone leaves families fighting and screaming and eventually just drains family assets over time.

Driving to and from an assisted nursing home, parking, and spending time with a parent can be very stressful. It is as though some sort of clock starts ticking when you walk in. Your parents know you are just there for a temporary visit. The conversation centers on the same questions you asked the last time, just in a different order. You would rather not always be there. They feel like you just dumped them into a home to solve a problem. The parent misses everyone, most likely their deceased spouse, and knows you are watching the clock and hoping to squeeze in the mandatory hour before you are off to dinner or to pick up your child at soccer. In many cases, where dementia has set in, you cannot be sure how much, if any, of your visit will even be remembered. No wonder as you enter and exit the home, you see so many depressed patients, with many folks just hanging on. Some poor patients go years without a visit from anyone. I know. I used to visit them when going to see my mother. If you want to make a difference in the world, go visit a nursing home, get to know someone without family, and then put together a care package that has stuff in it they will enjoy. No amount of church giving will ever compete with this act of kindness.

There is nothing fun about this process, and during the holidays, it is even more stressful when you have to juggle careers, more family in town, and then try to get permission to wheel your loved one out of the home and into yours for a holiday meal, all the while dreading the 2 or 3 hours it will take to reverse the long process of returning your parent back to the nursing home. It is not that you are a bad person. The problem is, both you and your parent are in a difficult environment where feeling good and wanted just works against you both because the environment is awkward for all of the parties involved. If you are young and your parents ask you to visit your grandparents at the local nursing home, it can be equally as stressful when, as young people, you also have school, jobs, and are chasing your own friendship priorities with finals and social media issues occupying your brain.

The time share-assisted living model: There is nothing that aligns more perfectly than a need to purchase lodging by the month or year to help solve a medium-term assisted living challenge. Under today's model, you try to sell the parents' home, call the brothers and sisters to raise cash, fill out all of the government forms, and if, by chance, your parents have a net worth, then your choice is to watch 40 years of hard work go to fund the last 3 years of life for the remaining parent. I watched it happen to my parents, and I have seen it happen over and over to many families.

Why owners and families will spend $350,000-plus on retirement time shares: In today's time share model, owners are asked to go into a 90-minute presentation and spend $50,000 up or down on a vacation model that will fit their lifestyle in the future for vacations. This is a great business and will continue to be a great business. However, those of us born between 1960 and 1980, and beyond, face a new challenge. How do we take care of our kids, and, in many cases, our parents? We do not know how much money it will take to make sure the parents are taken care of, and college for even one child can be a substantial amount of money. If this same person in their 50s goes to a different time share presentation that could be used for retirement, he or she could learn in the future that you can use your vacation or time share points to move you or your mom or dad into an assisted living villa that can be paid for with points, or a combination of points and cash.

Now, instead of the $5,000 to $10,000 per month (or more) options that exist today for nursing care, this option could reduce or eliminate the monthly cost by using points or a combination of points and cash and thereby reduce what is now a huge cost down to a more reasonable bill of $1,000 to $3,000 per month, which could then be funded by the current Medicare and Social Security assignments the way they are used currently. This type of arrangement would be much more affordable than the current solution. The current retirement options for assisted living space or for a nursing home works great if a family has a great deal of money, or is completely broke, where the government steps in to help. The problem is, the 75% caught in the middle who worked a lifetime for a $350,000 nest egg and now have to watch it all go away toward a nursing home.

Most families with at least two kids eventually get together after one parent's spouse dies and talks about how the remaining spouse is going to get along with shopping, doctor appointments, and attend church. All of these things can be built into a megaresort where families could gather in their own luxury villa some or all of the year, but then go visit their loved one by getting in a golf cart and visiting them a short mile away on the other side of the village. In other words, their parent is close but not too close for those families that want or need more separation. This would entice a family to spend $250,000 to $500,000 or more because they are going to spend the money anyway through a combination of liquidating their parents' estate, or by having to advance funds for their parents' final days. Study after study shows that the last 1 to 2 years of life for someone in their 80s consumes 85% of their lifetime medical cost, often wiping out families.

The long-term time share resort that has a built-in section for nursing care and assisted living could help solve this problem because after the parent passes on, the kids know they can use the points for themselves to travel to Paris. All of a sudden, the stress of using family money to extend an in-law or parent's life becomes much easier to handle because the asset stays with the person writing the check. It is a very hard thing to watch $500,000 go out the door to take care of a parent over 5 years. If this could help pay for or offset their retirement living, and then revert back to the owner, many more families would feel much better funding a portion of a vacation plan that includes retirement options, if you need them. Giving up a few trips to Hawaii makes way more sense than having to sell your vacation home to pay for mom or dad. After the parent passes away, they can then use of the points again for family vacations.

It is far more practical for three kids to buy a certain number of points based on their individual financial ability then to have to argue about a will or worry about mortgaging their home, perhaps with a second mortgage. They could pool their points to help with an assisted living or nursing home, and in a way, each person is paying what they can. However, each person also gets the deed to the points, which is a much-better alternative than sending a big check every month to a nursing home. This money is now an investment in the family's well-being and provides a lasting and real solution that will bring much more peace into the current underfunded retirement problem faced by almost every family. This concept would bring millions of families into a time share model, and with the right design, a megaresort could host families in traditional time shares while also managing both the assisted living portion and the long-term time share program. This would allow families to gather at the same resort at various times during the year, and in the process, makes everyone feel much closer and end up much happier.

Why the retirement market will help create a time share revolution: The numbers as measured from almost any reliable source all point to the same thing, and that is, nearly 75% of Americans that are working today cannot afford even a 1-year retirement. The baby boomer generation starts in January of 2017 with over 300,000 boomers retiring every month. This will continue unabated for the next 19 years. The United States retirement model is broken. Social Security was not designed to handle this kind of a problem and has its own fiscal emergency just to avoid collapsing in 2034, when the system as currently managed will run out of money.

The *USA Today* reported on the cover of their January 31, 2017, Money edition, that only 27% of Americans retiring now can fund over 95% of their retirement needs according to Fidelity Investments. This is going to put a huge squeeze on the very same people, now in their prime earning years, to have to not only pay for their own family and kids, but in many cases, their parents.

The market needs a housing solution that can lower the per day cost of ownership for both regular retirees in good shape, and for those that need assistance. The current time share market primarily addresses the general public and has proven it can sell to around 350,000 to 450,000-plus new customers every year. The retirement model is many times large with a very pressing need to find a solution and could add over 200,000 customers a month. Even more amazing is that this new model will require up to $500,000 to finance, well above the average price point for today's traditional vacation time shares currently in the $35,000 to $50,000 range.

The baby boomers in 2017 will be retiring at the rate of 3.6M people per year, although about 50%–65% of them will need to work at least part time past the age of 62 just to make ends meet. The vast majority of these 3.6M new retirees each year need either a neutral or offensive retirement plan that makes more sense than the current "lose everything" model. If the industry were to address just 5% of this market, it could benefit by providing 180,000 villas per year just dedicated to the long-term time share market with an increasing portion of this number going into assisted living and nursing homes. It is not that the assisted living industry is not filling this need, it is that their business model is outpacing most Americans' ability to pay for it. There are no real viable solutions to replace the economics. The problem needs another currency to finance the demand. The demand for retirement living is overwhelming, but the ability to pay for the coming crisis is not there. The time share industry can solve the problem by combining family assets in an orderly way that preserves family wealth rather than the current model that is designed to destroy it.

The new "points-based" retirement model: The time share concept for assisted living or nursing care can be used to arrest the real estate portion of the retirement housing model by issuing fixed point commitments into the future. This model can even be adopted or restricted up to a certain age, say 100 years old, well beyond the average life span for a male at 78 who might be 60 today. One option instead of a deed in perpetuity could be to require a rebate of a portion of the points purchased in lieu of the developer taking on a portion of the actuarial risk. For example, let's say a family spent $500,000 and bought 50,000 vacation points, to make the math simple, and the retirement villa was priced at 60,000 points per year. The age of the retiree enters the retirement villa under an assisted care model that requires a separate upcharge for assisted nursing services in addition to the regular maintenance fee. The retiree moves into the retirement villa at 68 years old. The expected remaining life span is 78, so in a perfect world, this person will pass away in 10 years. The family cannot purchase any more points but will agree to pay the maintenance fee on 60,000 points per year, the actual cost of staying in the retirement villa for 1 year.

The developer agrees to let the retiree live there for life or trade into a like-kind location, but when he or she passes away, the family agrees to rebate 15,000 points back to the developer, and their membership reverts back to 35,000 points. Their maintenance fee also adjusts back to 35,000 points. Now, let's say the retiree lived 10 years. The developer lost 10,000 points per year for 10 years which has a value and costs the developer some money. In 10 years, however, the 15,000 points are now worth $15 a point instead of $10, and the developer can resell those points for $150,000, more than recouping the loss for the use of 10,000 points for 10 years. In other words, the developer can set up an actuarial model that guarantees a retirement for life in a revolving group of retirement homes, and the family knows that Social Security, Medicare, and a small family combination of either points or cash far outweighs the current market solution of $7,500 a month for the next 10 years. They also end up with about $350,000 of their $500,000 membership completely in place for the family to use as it needs for future retirement needs or for more family vacations. This is just an example of the many ways the time share model can work with the retirement model, and in the process, solve a huge problem for the baby boomers caught in the middle.

In this example, the family saved over $90,000 a year or $900,000 in nursing home fees under the current retirement model and ended up only $150,000 out of pocket on the points purchase. This assumption assumes an assignment just like what is done today with a nursing home with the normal Medicare contributions, a small pension check, and Social Security contributions assigned to the developer to help pay for regular maintenance fees and assisted living fees.

Even assuming all of these contributions were still up to $1,750 a month short, the family would have to advance $21,000 a year or $252,000 over 10 years versus two to three times that amount. The traditional model of spending $900,000-plus inflation over 10 years versus absorbing a $500,000 vacation membership and $252,000 in negative cash results in a net savings of $148,000 under the time share model, but the family owns a $350,000 vacation plan in perpetuity and did not take any risk if their parent was to live past 78. This is one of the biggest fears today for both older parents and the kids left to pay for them. The total savings are over $500,000 if the vacation plan is viewed as an asset. In addition, if the parent was to live past 78 for even another 5 years, that would have cost them another $500,000, assuming low inflation risk which is more likely to turn into moderate to higher inflation as we sit today over the next 15 years. In the end, any family could avoid any long life risk and has a plan in place if another relative faces the same retirement challenge under this new time share retirement model. Most of all that money that would have gone to the ABC nursing home now goes to book that trip to Paris after mom passes away.

TIME SHARE VILLAGE OWNERSHIP-REGISTRATION PROCESS

Interested in owning at Time Share Village? We have designed a form on that you can access at MasteringYourTimeShare.com.

Please fill out this form and we will put you on our list to receive any information we have regarding building this first-of-a-kind project. Feel free to share this page with your friends and family. We can create demand for the project by registering on this site. Our goal is to get 1,000,000 users signed up.

We will also pledge that if this project gets built, those that have preregistered on this site will be granted access to a one-time preconstruction pricing discount. Just go to the Web site and hit the "Time Share Village Registration" button and we will include your family on the future information guest list. We expect to report further on this in 2018. Users on this list will receive the first public announcement via e-mail on its design, possible location, and project timeline.

Register to receive the first Time Share Village Brochure. See www.MasteringYourTimeShare.com.

CHAPTER **23**

Time Share Own Versus Rent- An Evaluative 45 Year Shoot-Out.

WE DECIDED TO take a look at what happens to the numbers when comparing a time share investment with the alternative . . . to just renting the same villa for your vacation. I had several people tell me after a time share presentation that while it looked like a good deal, "I am going to have to crunch some numbers and get back to you." Fair enough. That said, it is a good idea to see how the numbers shake out, but the challenge becomes . . . Under what assumptions does one run the numbers? We knew we would have to be very conservative so that our analysis could hold up under heavy scrutiny. We therefore adopted the following assumptions to run our model.

Assumptions used for rent versus own time share comparison

1. That we cannot compete with alternative investments that have large investor risk, where a loss of some, or

all, of the capital is possible. This is not a rational assumption. We therefore chose to invest the money in a tax-free bond at 3.5%, leaving the tax issue out of the equation since the renter investing his/her money in a tax-free bond has no tax.

2. While we believe that certain Category One time shares will outpace other types of real estate over the next 10 years, we declined to grant any special appreciation rights to time shares in this analysis and, therefore, kept the appreciation rate at 3.5%, the same as the appreciation rate for investing in a tax-free bond. This makes it easier to compare the rental stream against the maintenance fees and thereby leaves both the renter and the owner in the exact same place at the end of any time period as to asset value; i.e., the value of the tax-free bond portfolio is equal to the value of the time share. One is in cash, and the other is in a Category One time share asset.
3. We assumed the buyer just paid cash for 2 prime weeks at the beach. Most people know with rental property, you can vastly increase your ROI by simple leveraging your investment with debt financing. Since we are not technically calling the time share an "investment" per se, we did not seek to optimize the ROI with leverage and just used cash. Therefore, both the renter and the buyer invest $75,420 on January 1, 2017; one buys 2 weeks of time share, and the other puts $75,420 into a 3.5% tax-free bond fund.
4. Now, the owner stays 2 weeks every year in the summer on the beach and must pay the maintenance fees. The renter does not have a maintenance fee but must pay the rental rate. We assume a 16% discount from the rack rate. While we have witnessed rental rate

increases averaging between 5% to 10% per year over the **past** 10 years, we have capped the rental increase at 5% per year, given the demand for prime beachfront. We believe this will continue to rise faster than the 5% rate we used.

5. We capped the maintenance fees at a 3.0% increase per year, in line with what has been billed over the past 10 years. We believe if maintenance fees start to rise to 4% or 5% per year, then it is likely rental rates will approach 10%, given the history of the relationship between the two. In any case, we will not use history as a guideline and make the model more conservative.

Rent versus Own- Results

CONCLUSIONS: We noted the following results based on the 45-year analysis below:

	Years 1–15	Years 16–30	Years 31–45
Cost of Rent—Renter	$237,904	$518,947	$1,078,799
Cost of Main Fee—Owner	$88,125	$137,427	$214,111
Cash Out of Pocket—Renter After credit for bond interest	$237,904	$518,947	$1,078,799
Cash Out of Pocket—Owner After paying maintenance fee	$88,215	$137,427	$214,111
Owner Savings:	$149,689	$381,520	$864,688
Total Owner Savings:	**$1,395,897 after 45 years**		

Both the owner and the renter each hold an asset at the end of each 15-, 30-, and 45-year period. One of the assets is in cash valued at $354,651 in 2061, and the other is the time share which, over 45 years, is valued at the same price, $354,651. We assumed both would earn each owner 3.5% a year, one in cash and the other in price appreciation.

These numbers could change dramatically if the assumptions were changed to include much-higher returns on invested cash. The owner could also use a HELOC or other form of financing and show they can pull out all of their net cash in the first 5 to 6 years by putting down $20,000 and securing a 5% loan for $55,000, resulting in a $295 monthly payment. The rental savings of $6,282 the first year would more than offset the loan and still leave $2,742 in cash flow or rental savings in just the first year. It would only take about 5 to 6 years, and the owner would not have any net cash invested into the time share. In this scenario, the owner is saving over $3,500 a year on average the first 6 years after the loan payment and maintenance fees are paid without any net investment into the time share. Over time, this rises to over $77,000 in cash saved per year by the end of the 45-year term, and the loan is paid off, assuming a 30-year amortization. Our conclusion here is that over any long period of time like 20-plus years, the owner will outperform the renter and saves $1,395,897 in rent over 45 years under a conservative model, while many could make the argument they could invest their cash and get better than 3.5% per year, thereby narrowing the rental gap in their favor. Either way, a conservative approach to valuing money and return on safe investments would favor purchasing a time share if you value your time at the beach over the long run. Time share is not supposed to be an investment per se; it is something you buy after you are successful making money at what you are good at doing. Time share is the reward for making money . . . not the tool to do it necessarily.

	Years 1 through 15		**OPPORTUNITY COST OF INVESTING $75,420 AT 3.5% VERSUS BUYING TWO WEEKS OF TIMESHARE**														
			ASSUMPTION ASSUMES RENTAL IS A 2+2 VILLA WITH A PRIME OCEAN VIEW-TOP TIER DEVELOPER														
			RACK RATE FOR THE PER DAY RENTAL WAS $935 BASED ON 2016 ACTUAL, DISCOUNT WAS 16.00%														
		2017	**2018**	**2019**	**2020**	**2021**	**2022**	**2023**	**2024**	**2025**	**2026**	**2027**	**2028**	**2029**	**2030**	**2031**	
Inflation	**Cost of Time Share**	Year 1	Year 2	Year 3	Year 4	Year 5	Year 6	Year 7	Year 8	Year 9	Year 10	Year 11	Year 12	Year 13	Year 14	Year 15	**Value of**
																	Time Share
3.50%	**$75,420**	$78,060	$80,792	$83,620	$86,546	$89,575	$92,710	$95,955	$99,314	$102,790	$106,387	$110,111	$113,965	$117,954	$122,082	$126,355	**$126,355**
Return	**Assumes Tax Free Bond**																**Value of Cash**
3.50%	**$75,420**	**$78,060**	**$80,792**	**$83,620**	**$86,546**	**$89,575**	**$92,710**	**$95,955**	**$99,314**	**$102,790**	**$106,387**	**$110,111**	**$113,965**	**$117,954**	**$122,082**	**$126,355**	**aftertax**
	Interest Earned	**$2,640**	**$2,732**	**$2,828**	**$2,927**	**$3,029**	**$3,135**	**$3,245**	**$3,358**	**$3,476**	**$3,598**	**$3,724**	**$3,854**	**$3,989**	**$4,128**	**$4,273**	**$50,935**
																	$126,355
	2016-Rent per Day																
5.00%	$750	$788	$827	$868	$912	$957	$1,005	$1,055	$1,108	$1,163	$1,222	$1,283	$1,347	$1,414	$1,485	$1,559	**Total Rent**
	Days Per year	14	14	14	14	14	14	14	14	14	14	14	14	14	14	14	
	Total Cost to Rent Villa	$11,025	$11,576	$12,155	$12,763	$13,401	$14,071	$14,775	$15,513	$16,289	$17,103	$17,959	$18,856	$19,799	$20,789	$21,829	**$237,904**
															Renter Cash for Rent		**$237,904**
	Savings from Owning																
	2016-Rent Per Day																
5.00%	$750	$788	$827	$869	$912	$958	$1,006	$1,056	$1,109	$1,164	$1,222	$1,284	$1,348	$1,415	$1,486	$1,560	
	Days Per Year-Vacation	14	14	14	14	14	14	14	14	14	14	14	14	14	14	14	
	Cost if Rented	$11,025	$11,576	$12,155	$12,763	$13,401	$14,071	$14,775	$15,513	$16,289	$17,103	$17,959	$18,856	$19,799	$20,789	$21,829	**$237,904**
3.00%	Maintenance Fee	$4,743	$4,885	$5,032	$5,183	$5,338	$5,498	$5,663	$5,833	$6,008	$6,189	$6,374	$6,565	$6,762	$6,965	$7,174	**$88,215**
	Rental-Rate Ratio-RRC	2.32	2.37	2.42	2.46	2.51	2.56	2.61	2.66	2.71	2.76	2.82	2.87	2.93	2.98	3.04	**Rent Saved**
	Net Savings from Owning	**$6,282**	**$6,691**	**$7,123**	**$7,580**	**$8,063**	**$8,573**	**$9,111**	**$9,680**	**$10,281**	**$10,915**	**$11,584**	**$12,291**	**$13,037**	**$13,824**	**$14,655**	**$149,689**
											RESULT AFTER FIRST 15 YEARS						
2031	**Buyer Owns Time Share worth:**		$126,355		Owner Cash Out of Pocket through 15 years				$88,215		**Winner is Owner**		**$149,689**				
2031	**Renter Sitting on Tax Free Cash of :**		$126,355		Renter Cash Out of Pocket through 15 years				$237,904								

	Years 16 through 30		**OPPORTUNITY COST OF INVESTING $126,200 AT 3.5% VERSUS BUYING TWO WEEKS OF TIMESHARE**														
			ASSUMPTION ASSUMES RENTAL IS A 2+2 VILLA WITH A PRIME OCEAN VIEW-TOP TIER DEVELOPER														
			RACK RATE FOR THE PER DAY RENTAL WAS $1947 BASED ON 2032 ESTIMATE, DISCOUNT WAS 16.00%														
		2032	**2033**	**2034**	**2035**	**2036**	**2037**	**2038**	**2039**	**2040**	**2041**	**2042**	**2043**	**2044**	**2045**	**2046**	
Inflation	**Cost of Time Share**	Year 1	Year 2	Year 3	Year 4	Year 5	Year 6	Year 7	Year 8	Year 9	Year 10	Year 11	Year 12	Year 13	Year 14	Year 15	**Value of**
																	Time Share
3.50%	**$126,200**	$130,777	$135,354	$140,092	$144,995	$150,070	$155,322	$160,758	$166,385	$172,208	$178,236	$184,474	$190,930	$197,613	$204,529	$211,688	**$211,688**
Return	**Assumes Tax Free Bond**																**Value of Cash**
3.50%	**$126,200**	**$130,777**	**$135,354**	**$140,092**	**$144,995**	**$150,070**	**$155,322**	**$160,758**	**$166,385**	**$172,208**	**$178,236**	**$184,474**	**$190,930**	**$197,613**	**$204,529**	**$211,688**	**aftertax**
	Interest Earned	**$4,577**	**$4,737**	**$4,903**	**$5,075**	**$5,252**	**$5,436**	**$5,627**	**$5,823**	**$6,027**	**$6,238**	**$6,457**	**$6,683**	**$6,916**	**$7,159**	**$7,409**	**$80,911**
																	$211,688
	2032-Rent Per Day																
5.00%	$1,636	$1,718	$1,804	$1,894	$1,989	$2,088	$2,192	$2,302	$2,417	$2,538	$2,665	$2,798	$2,938	$3,085	$3,239	$3,401	**Total Rent**
	Days Per year	14	14	14	14	14	14	14	14	14	14	14	14	14	14	14	
	Total Cost to Rent Villa	$24,049	$25,252	$26,514	$27,840	$29,232	$30,694	$32,228	$33,840	$35,532	$37,308	$39,174	$41,132	$43,189	$45,348	$47,616	**$518,947**
														Renter cost to Rent Villa			**$518,947**
	Savings from Owning																
	2032-Rent Per Day																
5.00%	$1,636	$1,718	$1,804	$1,894	$1,989	$2,088	$2,193	$2,302	$2,417	$2,538	$2,665	$2,798	$2,938	$3,085	$3,240	$3,402	
	Days Per Year-Vacation	14	14	14	14	14	14	14	14	14	14	14	14	14	14	14	
	Cost if Rented	$24,049	$25,252	$26,514	$27,840	$29,232	$30,694	$32,228	$33,840	$35,532	$37,308	$39,174	$41,132	$43,189	$45,348	$47,616	**$518,947**
3.00%	Maintenance Fee	$7,389	$7,611	$7,839	$8,074	$8,316	$8,566	$8,823	$9,088	$9,360	$9,641	$9,930	$10,228	$10,535	$10,851	$11,177	**$137,427**
	Rental-Rate Ratio-RRC	3.25	3.32	3.38	3.45	3.51	3.58	3.65	3.72	3.80	3.87	3.94	4.02	4.10	4.18	4.26	**Rent Saved**
	Net Savings from Owning	**$16,660**	**$17,641**	**$18,675**	**$19,766**	**$20,916**	**$22,128**	**$23,405**	**$24,752**	**$26,171**	**$27,667**	**$29,243**	**$30,904**	**$32,654**	**$34,497**	**$36,439**	**$381,520**
														RESULT AFTER 30 YEARS			
										1 thru 15	**16 thru 30**						
2046	Buyer Owns Time Share worth		**$211,688**		Owner Cash Out of Pocket over first 30 years:					$88,215	$137,427	**$225,642**		**Winner is Owner**		**$531,209**	
2046	Renter Sitting on Tax Free Cash		**$211,688**		Renter Cash Out of Pocket over first 30 years:					$237,904	$518,947	**$756,851**					

	Years 31 through 45		**OPPORTUNITY COST OF INVESTING $211,688 AT 3.5% VERSUS BUYING TWO WEEKS OF TIMESHARE**														
			ASSUMPTION ASSUMES RENTAL IS A 2+2 VILLA WITH A PRIME OCEAN VIEW-TOP TIER DEVELOPER														
			RACK RATE FOR THE PER DAY RENTAL WAS $4,250 BASED ON 2047 ESTIMATE, DISCOUNT WAS 16.00%														
		2047	**2048**	**2049**	**2050**	**2051**	**2052**	**2053**	**2054**	**2055**	**2056**	**2057**	**2058**	**2059**	**2060**	**2061**	
Inflation	**Cost of Time Share**	Year 1	Year 2	Year 3	Year 4	Year 5	Year 6	Year 7	Year 8	Year 9	Year 10	Year 11	Year 12	Year 13	Year 14	Year 15	**Value of**
																	Time Share
3.50%	**$211,688**	$219,097	$226,765	$234,702	$242,917	$251,419	$260,219	$269,326	$278,753	$288,509	$298,607	$309,058	$319,875	$331,071	$342,658	$354,651	**$354,651**
Return	**Assumes Tax Free Bond**																**Value of Cash**
3.50%	**$211,688**	**$219,097**	**$226,765**	**$234,702**	**$242,917**	**$251,419**	**$260,219**	**$269,326**	**$278,753**	**$288,509**	**$298,607**	**$309,058**	**$319,875**	**$331,071**	**$342,658**	**$354,651**	**Aftertax**
	Interest Earned	**$7,668**	**$7,937**	**$8,215**	**$8,502**	**$8,800**	**$9,108**	**$9,426**	**$9,756**	**$10,098**	**$10,451**	**$10,817**	**$11,196**	**$11,587**	**$11,993**	**$12,413**	**$135,554**
																	$354,651
	2047 Rent Per Day																
5.00%	$3,401	$3,571	$3,750	$3,937	$4,134	$4,341	$4,558	$4,785	$5,025	$5,276	$5,540	$5,817	$6,108	$6,413	$6,734	$7,070	**Total Rent**
	Days Per year	14	14	14	14	14	14	14	14	14	14	14	14	14	14	14	
	Total Cost to Rent Villa	$49,994	$52,494	$55,118	$57,874	$60,768	$63,806	$66,997	$70,347	$73,864	$77,557	$81,435	$85,507	$89,782	$94,271	$98,985	**$1,078,799**
	Savings from Owning																
	2047 Rent Per Day																
5.00%	$3,401	$3,571	$3,750	$3,937	$4,134	$4,341	$4,558	$4,785	$5,025	$5,276	$5,540	$5,817	$6,108	$6,413	$6,734	$7,070	
	Days Per Year-Vacation	14	14	14	14	14	14	14	14	14	14	14	14	14	14	14	
	Cost if Rented	$49,994	$52,494	$55,118	$57,874	$60,768	$63,806	$66,997	$70,347	$73,864	$77,557	$81,435	$85,507	$89,782	$94,271	$98,985	
3.00%	Maintenance Fee	$11,512	$11,857	$12,213	$12,579	$12,957	$13,346	$13,746	$14,158	$14,583	$15,021	$15,471	$15,935	$16,413	$16,906	$17,413	**$214,111**
	Rental-Rate Ratio-RRC	4.34	4.43	4.51	4.60	4.69	4.78	4.87	4.97	5.07	5.16	5.26	5.37	5.47	5.58	5.68	**Rent Saved**
	Net Savings from Owning	**$38,482**	**$40,636**	**$42,905**	**$45,295**	**$47,811**	**$50,461**	**$53,251**	**$56,188**	**$59,281**	**$62,537**	**$65,964**	**$69,571**	**$73,369**	**$77,365**	**$81,572**	**$864,688**
									1 thru 15	16 thru 30	31 thru 45			**RESULT AFTER 45 YEARS**			
2047	Buyer Owns Time Share Worth		**$354,651**		Owner Cash out of Pocket over 45 years				$88,215	$137,427	$214,111	**$439,753**					
2047	Renter Sitting on Tax Free Cash		**$354,651**		Renter Cash out of Pocket over 45 years				$237,904	$518,947	$1,078,799	**$1,835,650**		Winner is Owner		**$1,395,897**	

CHAPTER **24**

The Ultraluxury Time Share Market—What Is It, and Where Is It Headed?

IS THE DISCOUNTED luxury life for me? The best thing about doing research, and then finding something really special is that the very act of being right creates a paradox. Let's use gold as an example. What if you did a lot of research and traveled to a foreign country, rented a cabin for a few months, and settled in to pan for gold? Over the next few weeks you are up and running—and then you find it. As you pull out what appears to be a large gold nugget, your first reaction is to look around. Is there anyone there? What if someone else finds out about this discovery? Who should I tell? Why would I tell anyone? Moreover, is this act repeatable, or did I just find the only gold nugget in 100 miles?

As I reflect on my childhood, I remember growing up in Beverly Hills and working one block away on Rodeo Drive. I worked for Food King as a grocery clerk. In the 5 years I was there, I never really saw a great deal. Not anywhere. In the decades since, I have yet to really find a consistent, year after year, repeatable bargain. I have seen some great one-time discounts here and there, but generally, I grew believing you pretty much get what you pay for in life. I, of course, used to think that about real estate. I got my first broker's license in California at 20 years old and began my career in real estate. I soon realized, like apples, sometimes real estate gets marked down. This is when life got exciting for me.

I recall the first time I checked into the Ritz Carlton in Vail. I think it was around 2005 or so. I had spent years in my previous time share down the street at the West Vail exit. Nothing wrong with it. It was on the stream, lavishly appointed, and I realized the $300–$400 nightly rental at that time for prime ski season was well above what I would want to pay. I remember my kids running into their bedroom to see who could claim each of the two large queen beds. It soon seemed like this annual vacation rated right up there with Christmas morning for the kids.

I knew I had made some smart time share purchases as the years rolled by. I did not have to worry about prices heading well over $1,000 per night as my kids got older. Then came the Ritz. Being a real estate broker in Colorado, I studied mountain real estate as a hobby. I knew the prices of the homes in Vail by the street, and even the condos and smaller cabins on the edge of town. I spent years looking for a real Vail real estate bargain. I realized after I checked into the Ritz I no longer needed to search for gold. I was living in it. Today, in 2017, large, two-bedroom villas and condominiums routinely sell for around $2.2M a bedroom, so $4.5M for a nice 2+2 villa with ski in/ski out access was very much the norm in Vail in 2017. Some properties in ground-zero locations are priced even higher. Rental rates typically run from $1,000 per night to over $5,000 a night for larger, three- and four-bedrooms in prime seasons.

I have now stayed at this same Ritz for over 12 years. It feels like home when I check in. I know several of the bellboys by name, and I have watched many of them grow up. I have managed my account to the point where my daily maintenance fee is now under $40 a night, and it continues to fall every year. Meanwhile, rental rates for 5-star resorts that include 1,800 square foot villas and higher continue to do nothing but go up, year after year, fetching higher rental rates. Luxury can be affordable with the right vacation plan. It is a matter of understanding all of the options. Many people tell me they are not luxury people and do not need to stay in 5-star properties. I wonder what they really mean by that. I think the real answer is they do not believe it is possible. I did not believe it until I figured it out. All you have to do is follow the path laid out in this book, look for Category One or luxury time shares, and follow the suggestions on how to increase your RRC ratio, and soon, luxury villas at ten cents on the dollar will be yours to enjoy. It is not a matter of spending huge amounts of time, it is not finding an inside deal, it is not about a once-in-a-while bargain. It is about putting knowledge to work.

There are dozens and dozens of prime real locations around the world that can be rented for very little money when you have knowledge on how to do it. When the process involves a different currency like "points," it becomes even easier because the process itself creates "arbitrage" when outside the box trading rules are engaged. That means you make money before you even make your trade. Now, using discount rules, you up trade and make 30% on the up trade, another 30% off with discount rules, and then offset your maintenance fee into a small fraction of what is was per night with just a few strategic rentals during the year. Next thing you know, you are living for ten cents on the dollar in luxury housing. The process is so stable that it can actually work for an entire year. This is very possible in time share and even more so at the luxury end of the rental curve if the principles herein are deployed. They are also highly repeatable without much compromise.

What do New York, Florida, Texas, and California have in common? How do these states define the future of real estate, and what role do they play in time shares? Each of these states draws large population bases, albeit for different reasons. New York is a global financial center, Texas is a very large oil producer, Florida is number one for tourism, and California has an economy larger than many countries. All of these states also offer waterfront real estate, something that is always in demand. People want to access time shares within driving distance of their primary homes in addition to having choices around the world. The cost of land in these areas continues to rise, and with it, the demand for staying in these locations. This is in addition to all of the resort locations already proven to be in high demand, like the Caribbean and Hawaii. We predict the industry will also put more focus into expanding into the larger U.S. cities because the need to have a trusted villa in large cities is increasing faster than the supply. New York City, as an example, is a location that could easily support several more projects if the land or the right renovation could be found. Locations within 45 minutes of these core cities will also make ideal time share facilities because they offer year-round tourism near the major cities. Be sure to write to your time operator if you would like to see a location in a city near you. They pay attention to base customer demand if the demand gets large enough.

What does a $5M to $15M vacation home cost to operate? Most financial experts agree that owning a vacation home will cost between 5% to 10% of its original purchase price per year to maintain, excluding the mortgage. This may seem high, but some resort towns have not only high property taxes, but many command transfer taxes as high as 1% when you sell your vacation home. In addition, insurance, maintenance, utilities, house managers, landscapers, pool service, and reserves will consume a large portion of the ownership budget over time. This means a $5,000,000 home can run up to $250,000 to $500,000, or more, per year, to support the property and the real estate. We predict given the upcoming demographic shift that demand for these homes will not rise faster than the availability except in the top 5% of vacation markets like Vail, Aspen, Jupiter Beach, San Francisco, La Jolla, Boston, New York, etc., where foreign investment along with the sports and entertainment business help support the market. Large homes located over 2 hours away from ground-zero locations are likely to stay at current valuation levels or even decline as interest rates rise. We believe this shift will place more luxury homes into the rental pool, allowing owners to absorb some of the tax and utility increases that will continue.

Some of the current weather patterns that include more extreme heat and cold will further increase exterior vacation home budgets to maintain and replace frozen pipes and stressed-out roofs and exteriors over time. These are now becoming more normal as desert communities continue to see summers peaking above 115 degrees and many states are seeing more frozen rain and snow, increasing budget demands for local municipal communities to acquire snowplows and de-icing machines to maintain and replace frozen power lines. In 2017, 47 of our 48 continental states reported snow and many at record levels. All of these trends are here to stay and will keep the rise in property taxes in the pipeline for the next few decades. Increased cost of ownership, higher interest rates, and fewer buyers in the next-gen and millennial pool of buyers will require more foreign ownership to maintain further price increases. The irony is that these changes will increase demand for luxury time shares when some owners want to continue their vacation patterns, albeit, at a lower cost of ownership. It is the combination of these trend lines that favor a more shared cost of ownership. You can see this in many of the old castles in Europe, particularly in Ireland and France, where many owners have converted into boutique bed and breakfasts and even time shares in order to offset maintenance costs and keep the properties in the family portfolio. This trend will start to emerge in the United States well past 2020, when some listings start to stretch past 24 months without selling. Price reductions of $10M and more will be commonplace with many of these top properties, particularly in top B locations where views and properties are excellent but require 1 hour or more drives outside the major services to get to.

How could I redeploy the family vacation assets? If you own a large vacation home you could consider putting the home into a luxury rental pool to offset costs. Another strategy would be to sell the home while prices are still high and use a small portion of the proceeds to acquire some prime luxury time shares. The top 1% of luxury time shares are actually starting to increase in value. While luxury time shares can include up to four bedrooms, some families will still want to have plenty of land and a place to store the family furniture, artwork, and paintings that occupy a vacation home that has been in the family for generations.

Another strategy is to consider selling a ground-zero location that might fetch that $10–$20M price point and replace the home with the same square footage 45 minutes away at half the price. While this may remove the ground-zero status of a top vacation location, it can cut your cost in half and still allow for many of the prized memories to continue. Lastly, renting large vacation homes for longer periods will become more commonplace, along with the ability to move some furniture and artwork that is part of the vacation experience for some families. Most luxury owners are very understanding, and renting a home for even $75,000 a month or more for 3 to 6 months will still be cheaper than owning the same home. We predict all of these trends will continue, causing more brokerage firms to specialize in luxury rentals, even some for 2 or 3 years, as this shift begins with baby boomers who inherited some of these properties and need to liquidate them or offset increasing budget concerns.

Can I get the same vacation experience in a luxury timeshare? Given the rise in $10M-plus luxury homes hitting the market for rental there is no question that families seeking large luxury compounds in ground-zero locations can enjoy them, often at a significantly lower cost versus owning them. This trend is not only increasing, but it is creating a more vibrant market for the top end of the market and allowing some families to continue to own their prized vacation home. In some cases, the luxury time share exchanges provide currency to use in another home, possibly halfway around the world. Since some families may own three or four luxury homes, the idea of selling one or two is likely to emerge as a popular trend since locating in different cities offering different experiences is a luxury trend that many families are starting to recognize. It also makes sense for family reunions with family spread out all over the country and allows families to trade off each coastline every other year, making it easier for large families.

Spend $250,000 to $350,000 one time and live like a multimillionaire with time share. As a professional real estate broker and agent in Colorado and California, I have observed many real estate trends over the past 3 decades. One thing that I find interesting is that most all time shares have lagged far behind their real estate cousins like full-fee ownership or condo ownership, yet both products offer similar benefits, the only difference being the amount of time spent in one place. As the market trends start to reverse as we predict in Chapter 21, the Beachfront Index, the relationship between a beachfront home and a beachfront time share, there is quite a compelling case that the gap between the two has almost nowhere to go but to narrow, meaning from a pure math point of view, time shares are poised to rise faster in price than their year round counterparts like homes and condominiums. . Common sense will, at some point, take over paying three or four times as much for nothing more than a different version of real estate that essentially delivers the same thing.

This massive price discrepancy is why today for less than a down payment on almost any beachfront home in California, one could acquire enough time share to live at the beach year-round. In many cases, the numbers are so overwhelming it means one could retire, often, at 45, and live at the beach in a time share, or work until 60 to pay for a mortgage to live at the beach. What is 15 years' worth of free time worth at the peak of your career? Since time shares have not appreciated relative to year round housing like homes, it is like going shopping in a grocery store still stuck on prices in the 1970's Many of us would jump at the chance to buy a home at the beach today for what it cost 45 years ago. Well, here is your chance. For about $250,000 to $350,000, you could live on both coastlines year-round in time shares in Mexico and the United States if you know how to acquire the right combination of time shares. As we have also suggested, many people could sell their homes and take the $500,000 in equity and buy a smaller home and spend $75,000 on time shares for 90 days every year. While we believe the baby boomer generation is now retiring without anywhere near the funding levels needed to finance their retirement, , the idea of using alternative forms of housing to lower retirement costs has no where to go but up if the value proposition is significant.

However, when you look at Gen X and Y, followed by the millennials, a very different story emerges. They do not seek large fortunes, don't want large mortgages, love to travel, want to live in different countries, and will likely have eight or nine jobs over the next 35 years, versus a baby boomer's two or three. All of the trends point to a shift in temporary housing. Time shares fit this need like a glove. The time share industry has not even begun to tap this market or the biggest one of all, retirement time shares. When this trend starts to emerge and we see the gap between new and older time shares start to narrow, we will see an explosion of time share appreciation, especially with customers that were smart enough to string together a well thought out vacation portfolio with preferential booking rights, VIP reserve status, and a vast array of luxury choices. We also predict as the average purchase skyrockets from around $35,000 to over $250,000, that mortgage lenders will flood into this market, making interest rates significantly more affordable than today's 500 to 1,000 basis point spreads that are commonplace. I know this trend is in place because I am living in this new world. I cannot remember the last time I had to clean my room or wash my sheets. I am in a new bed every week, often in the same resort. It takes me way less time to move than to wash the sheets.

Making time shares more permanent in your life—just get a PO box and a storage garage: One of the challenges in the time share life is where to have your principal home. This can greatly impact where you live and what your tax bill will be, so it is important to consider having some type of legal address that constitutes your primary residence. Another concern is making sure you are near a large airport, or even two or three. While I often drive to many of my time shares in the Western United States, it is also nice to hop on a plane and be into a new luxury villa the same day. Renting a storage garage also over time lets you realize how unimportant 90% of your stuff really is over the long run. If you are storing anything past 1 year, the reality is, you really don't need it.

Renting out your home and retaining a bedroom or guesthouse is another great method of downsizing your budget and provides flexibility to come and go as you please. Renting a PO box and a storage garage will also give you maximum flexibility until you figure out where to live. I was fortunate to rent out my house and left all of the furniture and a good bit of stuff in the house and in the attic. I am now looking into different states to acquire a small 2,200 square foot home as a permanent residence. I have found a number of new communities that support price points of $250,000 to $400,000, and many of them are gated with attached garages. This makes downsizing a snap and is a perfect complement to 6 months on the road. I have found a whole new life with more energy by forgoing the expensive nightlife every night in place of reading and writing. I have also discovered the joy of the early morning. When you give up a lot of long nights out on the town, you can retire at nine o'clock and sleep in until 6:30 a.m. and have plenty of time to watch the early sun rise on the ocean or on the mountains. The view just never gets old, and with time shares, it is always changing.

Reallocating the family wealth vacation model in the coming decade—why it matters: As we view the economic landscape in early 2017, we see a Republican White House that is moving toward a huge $1B infrastructure plan, a commitment to cut taxes, and a promise to unwind a lot of heavy business regulations. While this combination seems fruitful to many, the reality is that it is likely inflationary and will require the United States to borrow more money. This could have an adverse impact on interest rates as businesses and consumers have to compete with each other and the government to finance their respective objectives.

Given the underlying pyramid of millennials heading into their 30s, 40s, and 50s over the next 2 decades, it suggests there may be a fewer number of buyers interested in acquiring multigenerational vacation homes that require significant maintenance costs every year. We believe that for some families, rebalancing the family vacation portfolio may be a good move for those looking to offset downstream financial burdens on the overall family estate. Clearly, other families have the cash and net worth to handle even decades' worth of turmoil.

The good news is that for those who may be looking to acquire a first, second, or even third vacation home, chances are very good you are going to be able to find a great deal if you are patient.

Fewer buyers, higher interest rates along with higher water, gas, and electrical cost on top of colder and hotter weather patterns will cause overall vacation ownership costs to rise every year over the next decade at rates higher than the past decade. We expect to see increases at or slightly above the rate of inflation for the foreseeable future for vacation homes in the United States. We have already seen a trend toward filing new subdivision maps in some cities to sell off extra ground adjacent to large estates, and in recent years, we predict a new trend toward selling parts of the house and/or selling every other year ownership will start to emerge as some families look at solutions that will allow them to retain some, or most, of their ownership rights.

These types of reactions are reflective of stress cracks in the old family vacation model where legacy families and Internet-dot coms have done the heavy lifting to keep estates intact and prices rising. While this trend will continue, it will start to slow down in 2018, and in the future, the buyer pool for $10M-plus properties will have fewer people relative to the overall population. New technologies will come more and more from the spectrum of emerging technologies already in the hands of a few hundred new tech lords that have endless access to Wall Street if they need more capital. They will eat up many of the new ideas to expand new revenue streams into their own companies. In Silicon Valley, you need a new hit parade every few years to stay in the limelight. If you need any confirmation here, just look at the thousands of companies and patents that Google and Facebook have acquired in the past decade since going public. They have swallowed thousands of entrepreneurs in one check.

We believe the lower end of the luxury market defined as fractional ownership or time share is where the best buys will come from in the form of long-term time shares because they will offer targeted markets like outdoor kitchens, private chefs for small dinner parties, brand fire pits with bar service, and personal services like dry cleaning and limos. This newer breed of luxury time share will have way more appeal to smaller millionaires who want to stay on the move, enjoy life, and finance their next deal at the brandy bar.

The future of luxury time shares: Some of you will remember the phrase "A chicken in every pot, and a car in every garage" from President Roosevelt. We might add a new sentence for what we predict is another new trend in time shares: An outdoor kitchen for every villa, and a BMW in every garage. Today's time share buyers are savvy. They know technology, even though they were not born with cell phones in their hands like the millennials. They also know luxury and how to cook. Next-generation time shares will have a luxury section with a separate pool area and outdoor mini backyards with smaller, private Jacuzzi areas that can be shared or reserved.

These villas will have access to the time share garage. When you want to go out, you just walk in and take any car that is available. Your account will be billed when you leave and clock you in and out as you go. You will also be able to reserve a car for the week you are staying if you like. Perhaps a BMW on Monday through Wednesday, and then a Porsche for the weekend. Your account will be charged so many points a day, just like your villa. This luxury section will have larger units with more details inside. More like home. They will also cost more and demand will explode when the first developer introduces this product. Time share is in an infancy stage, and it is time to move on with next-generation products that save time and make life more enjoyable at lower costs. Pooling these ideas can dramatically lower the per-event cost, making services like limousines, private luxury cars, private chefs, custom outdoor kitchens, and outdoor cigar bars highly efficient and very profitable for the operator while gaining a new breed of customer. In addition, the concept of paying for your parent's nursing care, your own retirement, and still keep those trips to Europe, albeit if only every three years, all in a one stop one shop product will be too cost efficient to ignore. The current industry is just now tapping on the door of a time share revolution. We intend to keep pushing the industry and the consumer closer together to make these products a reality, life more enjoyable, and of course while lowering costs for a more impactful retirement for all of us.

CHAPTER **25**

How to Understand the Time Share Booking Process—Knowing How to Think like Software

LET'S TALK ABOUT your grocery card—what it says about you: How many of us maintain a grocery card that gets scanned when you go to the grocery store so you can get that discount? Under the new grocery model, information has become as profitable as selling groceries. The average large national chain earns two to four cents on the dollar after all expenses have been paid out, making the grocery business one of the most competitive markets to compete in. The good news is that everyone needs to go to the grocery store. These large national chains have figured out that they can sell information they gather at the checkout counter, and even better, it takes very little effort to gather the information. That is all done by computers. Your store knows what you spend per year, when and what you buy, and how often. They may know more about your shopping patterns than you do.

This information is then scanned and sorted into large databases for sale to any company willing to pay for it. Ever actually read the small print on the "Terms of Agreement" for a grocery card? It grants them permission to gather "data" and resell it. This means if you like bacon and buy it every week, and then you want to apply for life insurance, who would pay for that information? People are creatures of habit and tend to repeat certain patterns. That is why groceries now print out coupons based on what you buy. They are literally analyzing you while you are standing in line. No sense giving that pizza roll coupon to the gal whose cart was full of vegetables and fresh fruit. Who would want to guess how long you might live if one cart is full of fruits and vegetables and the other is full of pizza, bacon, and cheese? Which person would you bet on living longer? Well, your new insurance company is willing to pay for that information. While this can be done by zip code, town, and other criteria, remember, they have your name, address, phone, and e-mail. Does that seem like it might match an insurance application? Grocery stores are now so dependent on this income, it is the fastest-growing part of their business, and it can add 30% or more to their profits. Information is power to make more money, and every time an item is scanned into your cart, that information gets populated into dozens of different data banks where it gets data mined. Data mining is the art of reverse engineering future purchase patterns based on existing behavior. Do you know what a luxury retailer might pay to have information on which customers are willing to spend $50 or more on makeup in a single visit? They only want the 1% list.

If you ever want to really know how pervasive this practice is, open a new e-mail account with any large airline company. You will then know the only way you could get an e-mail is from the airline, right? Watch what happens almost overnight. You will see dozens of e-mails headed into your e-mail account when you only used it for one purpose. There is no way you could have received any e-mail other than from just that airline. Check the privacy box but read the fine print. You may have just thought you agreed to total privacy. Apparently, privacy rights are more like a general guideline for junk mail. You may have agreed to only accept future mail that is determined to be in your best interest. Determined by whom?

How products get packaged together: Many time share operators also want to maintain information on your travel patterns, and they keep very advanced records of where and how you travel with them. They know which hotels you prefer, where you like to stay, whether you smoke, how you like to dine, what price points you prefer, how often you travel . . . Get the picture? This is driving the trend toward "packaged deals" in the time share industry. People want to go to Napa to taste wine, so buying a time share trip that includes a vineyard tour makes sense. Grocery stores know there is an 82% chance that, if you buy hot dogs, you are going to buy hot dog buns. Ever see them together? They could put one of the items in the basement or on another floor because they know if you get one, what are the odds you will have to get the other? Put them as far apart as you can because there is a much-better chance you will get something else in between. Why is milk always the furthest from the checkout counter? The answer is, the store wants you to walk past everything else. The time share business needs information to make smart decisions. They know the relationship between airfare costs and the number of trips to Hawaii. They know why a project's inventory should only contain between 10% and 15% of three-bedrooms, the rest being one- and two-bedrooms. They know when the weather will impact pricing. They know that people who spend over $35 for a luxury sunscreen lotion may also be a potential time share customer. Data mining is now a multibillion-dollar business, and companies will pay up for any list that has a great return on investment.

Common sense rules: When informational patterns can be consistently observed, you end up with very valuable information. Time share operators have a vested interest in knowing what you make, how you spend your money, and at what point you need more time shares. This makes complete sense because their goal is to buy property, construct buildings or renovate them, and then sell time shares. Some people might be offended that almost anywhere people are, a computer now tracks you like a stalker. This is the world we live in. When you purchase on the Internet, you are feeding many databases about your choices. I am doing the same thing in this book. I am building databases of people who think that time shares are a great idea for retirement, either for themselves or their parents.

If you sign up to register, you will get that information the first time it is available. The same with the Vagabond travel bag. It is much easier to launch a product if you have a list of people waiting to buy it. The reality is that you may not always realize this information is being gathered, but understanding modern-day marketing, you should come to realize this is how the world works. If you start to understand how the information world gathers and sells your information, you can at least make the world work in your favor. An example: You could have two carts at the grocery store. One for pizza, meats, and cheese. The other for fruits, grains, vegetables, and other healthy products. You could use your grocery card for one but don't use it for the other. Your health library will then score very high. Figure on about 2-plus years for the data to really confirm your trend. This process can be repeated in different forms for every business, including time shares. Simply said, if you want to go the extra mile, you can window-dress your computer profiles to match what you want to be rather than who you are. Most of us really don't bother or don't care what a computer thinks of us. Your life insurance company has a vested interest in you staying alive and is willing to invest in you to understand your habits.

Learn your time share scheduling stack: If you want a room or a particular location in your resort, you should figure out when the rooms get scheduled. This is when 95% of the action takes place. It is usually about 14–30 days before check-in. This is when all of the requests are processed for room allocation. This process could vary, and some resorts may have different time frames. Each resort, however, usually has an exact time when they combine computer reservations, written requests, inbound phone requests, and then use "prior data" to determine your room. You may not care where you stay in a resort. Be careful, though, because if you don't object, the computer will start to build your "vacation pattern" and, based on prior information, will determine what you like and don't like.

This means where you stay in the resort matters to the computer even if it may not matter to you. Try to maintain some consistent travel patterns if certain rooms and views are important to you because computers like to post you into the system first, and then the manager has to allocate the rest. This is where managers may have to override the computer. However, if they have 350 of 400 rooms filled in, then the distribution will more likely occur within the open 50 rooms, leaving the chance of you getting undisturbed even higher. Managers and computers must account for membership status, overbookings, other channels requesting rooms, VIPs, system overrides, and then they must attend to special needs and requests. They do not want to bother with rooms already allocated because it just creates another problem to move a desirable room and guest match into a relatively undesirable room. They also know who is likely to complain by rank, membership status, and by prior visits because they maintain information on preferences. Knowing how and where you fall into your inventory stack will tell you what your odds of upgrading are and how to go about getting it.

Dissecting the resort inventory ratio: I used to attempt to figure out how to get upgraded into top hotels and time shares before I received the top VIP status, where it now happens almost automatically. I discovered many different methods for upgrading "around the rules" when I was younger. It starts with analyzing the resort's overall occupancy. You can hardly expect to get upgraded past your pay grade if the resort is full. Most off-season or shoulder seasons have a few rooms to fill, at least some of the time. The great thing about this time of year is that most of the "normal" rooms fill faster than the Presidential Suites. I always tried to figure out what the resort called the "next best suite." The Presidential Suite is almost always held open until the very last minute, and usually only the top manager can overrule its use by a non-VIP. They seldom allow this. There are two methods for upgrading in this scenario. The first is to upgrade through the computer, and then the front desk. The other is to get upgraded through the management. In some cases, a combination of both methods will likely yield the best result because of gaps in the information process, a key point when upgrading.

The blind computer booking—how I landed a $23,000 suite: I once stayed in a small 5-star resort in Scottsdale, Arizona, known for its movie star and entertainment guest list. This is a small boutique hotel with very high service marks. It has a very nice "Guesthouse" on the property that also comes with a secret limousine entrance and therefore had two front doors, one of them very secret for special guests needing absolute privacy. I had inquired about this special house on prior visits and found out its typical rental was around $9,500 a night. It had two large master suites and a number of rooms, a private kitchen and dining rooms, and three very private outdoor patios. Naturally, my goal was to stay there and pay almost nothing for the Guesthouse. This one required a combination of computers and human interference to make that happen. I received a special promotion coupon from one of my Internet travel companies I used to book resorts. It was a week before prime season was to hit in late February when Scottsdale is about to boom with spring training. The weather is perfect, and hotels run very full for the next 90 days.

I started out booking one of the nicest villas at this small 5-star resort and got 40% off the bill while booking the room online from a very special "2-day only promotion." The villa was the nicest one I could find on the Internet that handled this small boutique hotel's limited pool of rooms. I then called the hotel and discovered they had three other options for rental that are not handled via the Internet. I was told that only the manager can book these upgraded villas usually reserved for their best clientele. I explained I needed something just a little bigger as I was planning a small dinner party. I was, of course, quoted the $9,500 a night "Guesthouse" as a perfect solution. I said that was bit high but did agree to the "Presidential Villa," a private villa with three rooms and a nice private patio. The room was $2,100 a night. The manager on the phone saw that I had booked a regular villa but they did not have access to the coupon information. Her screen just showed the room was paid for through Orbitz. Since the regular rate was $995 a night for my existing villa, I was told I would have to pay $500 a night for the upgrade to the Presidential Villa. I explained this was for an anniversary, and since the room was sitting empty, would they accept $100 per night? They called the next day after the manager approved the deal, and I was now upgraded to the "Presidential Villa," just one shot away now from the Guesthouse. I now knew the main manager, the assistant manager, and the night manager as this process had taken about 45 minutes on the phone over 2 days as I charmed my way through this challenge. My goal was now set to take down the "Guesthouse."

I immediately sent some chocolates overnight to the day manager and explained I was very grateful for the upgrade and if, by chance, the "Guesthouse" was still available, for her to call me. I, naturally, got a call later that day from the third manager, explaining the beautiful Guesthouse was available. She did not see what I was paying for the Presidential upgrade because she was in a different computer program that simply showed what rooms were already booked. She just assumed I was in the $2,100-a-night suite at $2,100 as most guests just pay the rate because there is only one like it, and it rents all the time at that price.

I went on to explain my need to entertain and that I needed to hire the hotel to "decorate my villa" with flowers and balloons. After the decoration discussion, we finally agreed that for $200 a night extra, I could have the Guesthouse. It was now only 3 days before my arrival. I went on to hire the hotel to fill the room with balloons, a chocolate cake, and I also arranged for flower petals placed on the bed and a large floral display around the room. This, of course, was $450, but since I got a $9,500 room for the weekend, I naturally had to spend a few bucks to decorate the place. She agreed when I agreed to hire the hotel to decorate the Presidential Villa that this would work better in the Guesthouse. She became emotionally attached to my reservation request.

By the time the dust settled, I was in the room for about $900 a night, about the price for a regular villa for that weekend. It was one of the best weekends of my life and included several limousine rides to and from the "Guesthouse." I figured the weekend should have cost about $23,000 for just the room with taxes, taking the sting out of my cost of the $2,700 bill for the Guesthouse, including taxes and flowers. The point of this story is that sometimes, it is easier to get an upgrade through three or four steps because the discount for each upgrade gets you closer to just "one more upgrade," where the pricing is based off of **where** you were staying not **what** you were paying. She also knew her friend who owned the "balloon company" would be thrilled to have my decorating order. Many boutique hotels use different inbound reservation software systems that do not communicate with the in-house reservation system, leaving "gaps" in the information pool. By just moving up one step at a time, starting with 40% off, I was able to get a deal that never would have been offered. I have since used this coupon trick on several other trips with similar results. It works particularly well on small, single-owner hotels rated at 4.5 stars or better. Again, this process involved a combination of well-placed phone calls, increased business with each one, and by using blind information, the managers were flying in the dark on the actual pricing, and upgrade choices were based on already having the "next best suite" likely at, or near, the rack rate.

The human approval rationale: It is always best to just assume the manager has the power to grant you any request, and that it is really just a matter of time combined with the approach you are taking to get the request. In general, the more ridiculous your request is, the longer it might take to get approved, given that many managers have to draw the line somewhere, and realizing that over time, your request might not seem that aggressive, particularly if the alternative means the resort makes less money. Taking an approach that gives yourself a week or so to get the deal done means you can make progress along the way toward a better stay. You first have to get the manager on your side as an advocate so they will fight for your deal. Remember, managers have bosses too, and giving away thousands of dollars in concessions does not help their career. Neither does leaving large suites open to gather dust. Try to find a way to help the manager before you ask them to help you. In my case, she got involved with the decorations, probably bought a cake at the local bakery and up-charged me for it, and got her friend a nice account for balloons and flowers. Everybody won, and especially me. I got my cake and got to eat it too.

How to combine time share tours to lower your vacation costs. Time share operators are in love with their customers. They will spend money five or six times to get you back into their resort with all kinds of incentives. Nothing wrong with that. The practice is so common it may as well be a part of your overall strategy. Instead of using your points or weeks to book your reservation, start off with first getting a free tour and the right to stay at the resort for a huge discount. You will need to go on the tour and should remember the people on the tour are there to earn a living. They are not there to hear about your cracked coffeepot, why you don't like your room, and why you had to wait in line too long.

They are there to earn a living, sell you more time shares, and feed their family. Most of the time, share salespeople take the time to treat you well and often have to hear about your problems. I sometimes wanted to remind some rude tour guests, when was the last time *you* spent 90 minutes listening to a stranger tell you about their problems for free? Since I work in this industry, I certainly know what I am talking about. If you think you have problems in your life, try working for 2 or 3 weeks full time without any real pay, a common occurrence in the time share industry. I say this freely because this is my book, and I can say what I want. I want to acknowledge the vast majority of people who went on tours, were really not in a position to buy in many cases, but at least were kind enough to play along and tried to be sincere. That is the proper way to act if you are not there to buy. Many people do change their minds, but in order to get the most out of your tour, you need to listen and ask the right questions. Time share salespeople are not allowed to complain. Nobody there really cares about how bad their personal tour flow was for that day or for that month. It is a tough business, pays well for those who can handle it, and only the best survives it. Treat them well and you will get more out of your tour.

Now then, once you get your 90-minute tour set up, you can then call up and book another 4–10 days using your week or your points and squeeze in some free time. Although the mandatory tour does cost you 90 minutes or so, the extra several days for a small room charge is well worth it. If you want a faster tour, book the last one of the day right before dinner. Salespeople are usually worn out and tend to short-circuit a few minutes here and there unless you really want to purchase. I have stayed until 7:00 p.m. at night to close a 2:00 o'clock tour because that is what it took, and the buyers wanted to feel safe in their purchase and preferred that I be present during the whole process. I had no problem staying late because like most all time share salespeople, we know the product works great and creates great memories.

I have seen these tours go on in prime summer weeks when rack rates pushed over $900 a night and the tour charge was $99 to $199 a night. You can also usually find tours at the same operator in other locations during the same year and thereby also add a few days and nights to your annual time share stays in different locations, including Hawaii and the Caribbean. While any operator maintains the right to deny future tours at any time, if you act and behave well, and even buy a little more time shares here and there, you can end up booking free time year after year for several years. Unfortunately, there are some people who seem to tour for a living, so like everything that may seem easy or unfair, taking too many tours without ever intending to buy hurts the real owners in the long run who are there paying with their points, dollars, and membership in order to be there, so using discretion is the best way to go with this idea. The salespeople know by reading their morning notes whether you are real or not to a large degree. While you are walking away, they are telling their confidants what a yahoo you are, so I suppose everyone pays some kind of price for being too greedy. This, of course, is a very small percentage of the public, but like every well intended promotion, there are people ready to take advantage of the system. Stay reasonable on this one or we will all lose this precious extension treat.

Does cross marketing hotels and time shares help or hurt the time share customer? I often get asked, does it make sense for an owner of a resort hotel to mix their guests with the owners of a time share resort? I have pondered this question for years because I was not sure if competing with hotel guests or vice versa actually made the overall experience a better one. My initial thought was, it may depend on the situation, and in specific cases, that may still be true.

As I continued to observe this practice, I began to realize having different and distinct travel options can only help a time share owner, even though staying in a hotel is very different and can cost a lot more per night. When you look at trying to enhance the overall travel experience, it is logical to have more choice, better travel options, and a vast array of price points. This clearly works in the advantage of the time share owner.

The comparison comes in on how you manage your hotel stays to minimize cost and maximize your overall travel experience. It is not likely you can "stretch" your hotel points, although many hotels offer a free night after so many stays. You are not likely to rent out your hotel room, so there is no way to lower your cost per night. Finally, if you are traveling into a big city like London, Paris, or New York, it can be much harder to find a large two-bedroom suite at anywhere near the price of a time share, luxury appointed or not.

Hotels are not designed to function like time shares. The advantage to having access to thousands of hotels does change, however, once your membership level on the hotel side starts to move at or near the top. Now, luxury suites can be complementary; often, you can have free food and drinks, and you can enjoy late checkouts, and in many cases, early check-ins. These benefits mean a lot if you are traveling over a long period of time and find yourself in a city early in the morning. The key to maximizing the hotel side is to gather your business under one hotel brand and achieve the highest status you can reasonably obtain as the enhanced benefits can be very worthwhile. Some top operators are now offering Presidential or Platinum status for as long as you travel when reaching certain membership levels in their vacation clubs. These are basically lifetime benefits to be treated as their top customer.

There are also some other benefits that may be not as obvious. Many of the top vacation brands offer incentive points or reward points when you stay in their hotels. Some of these programs allow you to book worldwide vacations and receive vouchers for business and first-class travel around the world. If you carefully pay attention to these details, you can acquire a very nice vacation portfolio for around $100,000, but in the bargain, pick up over $60,000 in real travel credits. It may not seem possible, but I can confirm I have done it and also sold this type of package. Since traveling around the world can be expensive, a well-crafted vacation acquisition plan can provide up to three separate trips, just by buying the right time share package. I sold one couple a medium-size vacation package, and they bought it just for the travel perks for first-class travel to Africa. They planned to sell it at a 50% discount in 2 years because, overall, they figured even with a 50% projected loss on the time share, they will save money on the combination of incentive perks and time share use over the 2 years. Far be it from me to argue with math logic. The math was there.

Obtaining a higher reservation priority: If you are able to reach the highest level in both your vacation club and within the hotel company connected to your time share, you will likely be in the top 1% and perhaps in the top 5% of all of their customers. This will provide special marketing to you, and usually results in your automatically getting the best rooms at the best prices. Many of the top operators will allow you to use vacation points to stay in some of their hotels, and in other cases, you can use hotel reward points to stay in their villas. Be careful to pay attention to the exchange rates when crossing hotel points into vacation credits and vice versa. They are generally not very good deals, and you may well be leaving real money on the table. There are exceptions, like trying to book in prime season where you need to use a different inventory bucket to complete a reservation.

These crossovers rarely provide discounts for off-season or short-term stays. These usually need to happen at layer-one transactions where the software does not mix with other credits. Sometimes, you can find certain five-star hotels that routinely charge $800 a night, or more, in major cities that can be had for vacation points that cost you about half in maintenance fees; i.e., in this case, for $400 a night. These are great deals, but you have to search for them. You might find the three closest hotels surrounding the one-five all charge 800 points a night, to use this example, which would equate to $800 a night in maintenance fees, which means you are paying close to or at the rack rate to stay in the hotel. You can usually get a better deal with Triple AAA, or with a senior's discount.

In many cases, you might find that booking worldwide trips using reward points can offer a better exchange rate for economy and first-class travel than if you were just a hotel member. Some programs have different software algorithms for different customers. For example, you might find that it takes, say, 540,000 reward points to travel business class to Rome and stay for a week. That same trip might require 680,000 reward points for a nonvacation time share owner to book the same trip using the same points. In other words, the conversion rates may not be the same. It makes sense to comparison shop, and if you enjoy travel, the right time share can definitely help lower your cost over time. In the time share industry, do not assume an orange is an orange and can be used for a certain value proposition. Understand that pricing models can change and which ones cannot change. This is one of the hidden secrets in time shares. Most all of the large operators now have fixed price points for their vacation plans; that is, the price per night per point stays the same. This may not be true for the hotel side and in particular for airline travel. I have seen airline travel vary significantly over time, often working much better under a land/sea combination package where hotel stays are part of the reservation.

Why Web hits matter. This chapter is about the software booking process and how your membership status can affect your pricing. We have seen examples of how you can route into different software buckets to seek a reservation when some buckets are sold out in the same resort; i.e., see Chapter 17, "Understanding Software Rules and Network Reservations Systems" for more details. We also note that when you are surfing on the Web, remember that as you travel through the Web site, clicking in and out of different Web pages, that information is being gathered on you. This information could impact your next pricing offer. Travel sites know you can comparison shop and purchasing a ticket from Denver to LA has very little room for price discounting beyond a certain point, so airlines want to grab your reservation as soon as possible. When they do not get it, they get cranky and program the reservation software to remember that you wanted to travel to LA. They go back in and see how many times you make that trip per year. If you travel every other week to LA, do you think you might get a better price than if you travel once a year? The computer knows your travel pattern and is trained to follow you if you do not complete your reservation. When I need a ticket for a city in 3 weeks or so, I often go into one of my travel sites and inquire about a ticket. This is a good thing to do because you are telling the computer to look out for future prices in that city around that time. The travel site now knows to send you a discount e-mail if they can find a lower price. This practice sets in motion that you are willing to wait for a better deal. This works with hotels and rent-a-cars as well.

Hit the luxury button: Many times when you are Web surfing for travel plans, you will see some offers to look into special travel destinations. It might be Hawaii or even more exotic places like Bora Bora, or Tahiti. Go ahead and hit that button. Even if just for a moment the travel site will tag you for future promotions to that destination or ones like it. The software will record your interest, and over time, it will send you some offers. Every now and then, I have seen pretty good deals pop up that just feel cheaper than they should be. I am not talking about two- or three-star hotels. These are first-rate hotels that are actually running a promotion. Remember, promotions are where you start to get interested in going somewhere. Getting another 30% off using the techniques in this book is why you book your trip and actually go. Getting huge bargains on travel is like finding the right person or the right job. You have to have a lot of poles in the water. You have to always start with a good deal in order to convert that deal into a *great* deal. That is why letting your software know where you want to travel will pull you to the top of the next promotion list when that bargain trip presents itself.

Understanding airfare software when booking for your family. Don't book at once: I remember the many times I needed to buy airfare to fly my wife and two kids to California from Colorado for one of our family vacations. I would always start shopping for airfare about a month before the trip. I discovered when I started playing around with the booking software something rather amazing happened. It was like trying to buy stock options on the Internet. I do my research, enter a bid, and then the price goes up right before I try to close the trade.

When I was willing to pay a certain price, why did the price for four tickets just go up when I entered four people into the booking software? I don't mean the actual price went up; that is supposed to happen. I mean, why did the *price per ticket* go up? Then it hit me. The software knows that as the remaining seat count goes down, the price for the remaining seats must go up. It was not that I was buying an airline seat, and clearly, there was one more seat gone that was the problem. The problem was now, all of a sudden, four seats are missing and now the pricing is based on the **rate** of decline, not the fact that the seat count itself is declining. I quickly learned to look for the biggest planes leaving Denver for LA. They were likely headed to Hawaii or Asia. If my theory was right, the emptier the seat count when I booked my ticket, the lower the price should be. Also, why would I want to trip the price increase wire by booking four tickets at once? By booking my wife and me on one ticket, I got a lower price per ticket. I then would go right back in and book either my son or daughter. Then I would go back in and buy the last ticket. I discovered the price stayed lower because even though there were fewer seats remaining, I avoided the rate of decline penalty and routinely saved about $120 one way by just booking the tickets separately. Same airline, same flight, even got the same seats although in some cases, I got two in one spot and two seats in another.

Turn the airline cookie monster back on the airline: I like to take the airline cookie monster that comes standard now with most all of the large, public travel sites and make them work for me. I start off asking for three tickets on business class departing to a city I want to travel to in about a month. They will then send me a price which is generally more than I want to pay. No worry, you have just started a game of airline price war. When you decline the first price, go back a few days later or respond to their first attempt to win you back because they "found" a lower fare. *Of course, they found a lower fare*. They were just waiting for you to reject the first one. You are now engaged in what I call "algorithm tag." Now that they know you have not booked your ticket yet, this means you are a serious customer. One that deserves another reduced price. After all, you took the time to inquire again. Now, go ahead and reject the second improved offer. You stand a 50/50 chance of still hitting the discount floor that could be either higher or lower next time. Based on seasonal demands, cancellation rates, price of fuel hedging, and probably the odds of weather disruptions before or after your flight (this means loss of revenue), the airline may send one last offer to you as many as 2 weeks later. When you get this offer, you will have a sense you have hit the low point. Now, go back in and book just one seat. The software has to realize it will still have two more open seats, and that could affect another discount because the computer was playing three-seat war with you. You are now switching to one-seat poker, meaning you are leaving the plane more vacant than before. This means more seats left open closer to the flight, triggering another possible discount because it is better to sell at least one ticket than none at all. I have enjoyed this game for years and even better, you just turned that cookie monster into your personal travel agent, just waiting to contact you with good news. It knows you will only respond to good news since it already provided pricing. If you are really clever, you can try this with a few different sites and you may find that just one takes the bait. Then again, you only ever needed just one seat. Once this trick gets recognized, you will need to use one seat. Artificial intelligence will soon be coming into the airline booking process and the Bot robots will be trained to recognize costly trading patterns that cost the airline money. They will interfere with any pattern that out tricks the airline on a consistent basis, so be sure to mix up your travel strategy so the computer cannot profile your tricks.

Car rental software—dos and do nots: Rental car software can be really fun to play with because the rules for renting a car are pretty simple, so the ways to outprice the system are pretty easy. Most of the price for renting a car is in the real estate where the car sits. If the value of that real estate is high, the cost of renting the car will be higher. Most rent-a-car companies pay within $100 to buy the same car, and they pay within $1 an hour to hire the same person to rent you the car. The only thing left is where they park the car when it is not in use. Renting from an airport can be expensive even for the large national chains. Renting or buying from a lot a mile away can save money since you need shuttle service anyway at many airports. I have often jumped in a cab to the offsite location and still saved hundreds on a long-term rental, more than offsetting the cost of the cab. I also arrive well ahead of the next van loaded with customers. These sites are generally less staffed and run on slightly lower payroll numbers, making the average wait time longer. The key is to know how often the shuttle runs because these smaller chains tend to run fewer shuttles. I then learned in LA I could get on one of the top shuttle buses that ran every 5 to 10 minutes, and then just walk across the street to my off-brand lot. Knowing your territory is key to being a road warrior. Nothing stops a good road warrior, and there is nothing that cannot be worked around. In one area of Newport Beach, I routinely take a cab to the rental office because the shuttle seems to always take 45 minutes. Since I only rent for a week or longer at this company, the cab fare is more than paid for since my weekly rate is about 35% of what the competing on-site companies charge.

Know what your real car rental software covers. I routinely decline coverage because I make sure I have an e-mail from my insurance agent on what I am covered for on a rent-a-car. Don't assume you are covered for rent-a-car damage, and frankly, I would not believe your agent if they struggle with an answer. Have them put it in writing in an e-mail. Make a copy of the e-mail and carry it in your travel briefcase. It will save you a lifetime of hassles if you ever need it. Even better, copy the portion of your policy that covers this item along with the coverage page that shows your name and policy number and put this into your travel bag. In an extreme case like in

Hawaii, this piece of paper may be the reason you are allowed to leave the island. This is even truer with the off-brand rent-a-car companies where an accident on a late-afternoon Friday could have your passport and driver's license revoked until your insurance office opens on Monday morning. If you know your agent well, get his or her cell phone. Although this is not likely to happen on any one trip, it is likely to happen over a lifetime of trips. This small effort could save you a world of pain.

Once you are clear on how you are covered, you can waive the additional insurance charges. I prefer to always rent a car that offers the best value. Sometimes I can upgrade for $20 a week into a really nice midsize or, on occasion, a luxury car. Other times, the rental car company wants $25 a day, or more, for an upgrade. Remember, you have two bites at the apple . . . one when you rent, and the other when you get to the counter.

Managers run out of the lowest-grade cars first so they must offer you the next class of car for free. If you are arriving after 1:00 p.m., you will pretty much get a free upgrade. It also works with a midsize after 4:00 p.m. for a luxury car. I also like to look at the per-week rates of the smaller companies. They tend to keep certain cars on the road because their lots are small, and they don't make money with a car sitting in the lot. I have rented cars by the week that end up costing less than renting for 3 days. The problem lies in how the rental car companies charge for rentals. Renting on noon on Thursday and returning by noon on Friday still counts as 2 days. The 24-hour-cycle clock is only there to work against you, not for you. The worst deal in rent-a-car is for 26 hours. You are past the grace period, and the 1 hour late fee is almost half the daily fee. It is like you rented the car for 3 days with many rental agencies.

Rental discounts and promotional specials work very well with rent-a-car companies because you can book them into the price right on the Internet. The best deals are when rent-a-car lots get the cars back. Usually Sunday night allows you to get anything you want, well before the Monday morning rush. I have also booked the cheapest car on the lot, and then because the price was $189 for a week, I was able to negotiate a luxury car by doubling the price, well below the $650-per-week cost the car was advertised for on the Internet. I have often rented a car for a week, and then bring it back in four days. The cost was still cheaper than a 4-day rental. Rental car companies have different pricing models for 1-week cars versus daily cars. Another trick is to look at which cars just came back onto the lot. The smaller rent-a-car companies will usually let you jump right in almost any upgraded car if your price level is out of cars.

If you have a really good deal on an upgrade but the company is out of cars, ask to jump in one of the return cars sitting in line. Just make sure the car gets checked out to you in your name. Lastly, in the rental car business, you can generally rent a car without having to pay for it at the time you make the reservation. Sometimes it pays to hold a reservation, and then see if the prices drop with another competitor. Large events in town can trigger an early return of hundreds of cars, making that Thursday rental much cheaper on Thursday morning versus the price of the week before. It is all software driven based on actual cars sitting in the lot. If you pull into a lot that is depleted of cars and has a long line, your leverage is gone and getting a no cost upgrade is not likely. Remember, cars do not care who drives them, and computers and managers, in combination, determine our rent-a-car fate. Regardless do not forgo the rental coverage unless you are positive your regular policy will replace the coverage. Sometimes it pays to pay more for extra coverage if just for peace of mind.

The cruise ship—booking tips The best suite I ever booked on a cruise line was because I had asked the travel agent to get me a detailed depiction of the ship. This was a brochure that illustrated the eight different levels on the ship with pretty good details. It was very easy to review what suite was near what pool, and to a certain extent, how big the various suites were. I assumed the brochure was reasonably accurate. After my review, I discovered one level on the back of the ship seemed to have what looked like very large patios. They were about three times the size of the suite they came with. When I inquired, three of the five suites were available and there was no upcharge to have a private patio. These end suites were the same price as the outdoor-facing suites that lined the hallway, yet they had 800 square foot patios that came with them. It was clear no one was really paying attention to this because right before the cruise, I booked one with two more left. Since this was a 17-day cruise, having an outdoor patio that could easily seat 6–8 people seemed like a nice perk. Sure enough, I booked the suite, and my wife and I enjoyed our private patio way more than the room it came with. Just looking at the ship's outlay can really help you make a wise choice.

The best time to book a cruise: Many of the larger cruise lines, like their time share counterparts, are public companies. They have a real need like all public companies to hit or exceed their revenue targets in order to meet Wall Street expectations. Cruises that are selling in the last week of the quarter are the best cruises to book because the cruise lines are under pressure to make sure those ships are as full as possible. While this may be true for every cruise, it is only the last week of the quarter that can help them during the last week. If they were ever going to take lowball offers, this is the best week. While the actual cruise must hit a certain number to make the cruise worthwhile, the cost of an upgrade can be as low as $100 into a much-larger cabin. Taking the $100 is better than letting the larger suite sit empty.

Ask for the moon—it just might be on sale: I remember boarding a flight many years ago, and I was headed into the coach cabin. I always tried to fly business class if the upgrade was not too expensive, but many times, I ended up in coach. On this occasion, as I was boarding, I told the flight attendant to let the captain know if it would help any, I would be happy to move into first class to help load balance the plane—of course, in the name of public safety. She laughed and told me she would indeed pass on the message. Naturally, I had little to no hope of this actually happening. It was like buying a lottery ticket. You can't win if you don't buy a ticket.

The plane was nearly full, and I settled into my aisle seat and put on my headphones. A few minutes into the final boarding call, I saw the flight attendant moving in my direction with a big smile on her face. I just assumed she was going to walk past me and was headed for someone behind me. She stopped in front of me, and I eagerly removed my headset. I thought she was going to tell me a joke. She indicated the captain had asked that I move to first class "at his request." She said it loud enough so many around me heard it. I can't imagine what they must have been thinking. I, of course, replied that I was happy to comply with whatever the captain needed and asked if I may grab my overhead bag. She said no, go ahead and proceed to 4 (A), and she will follow with the bag. I have to say that in all of my years of flying, this only worked once. I have since tried it about 20 times, but I am still 1 for 21. That said, she offered me a drink once seated, and I responded, "When in Rome act Roman," and promptly ordered a drink. I recall that I was in a good mood that day, was unusually full of positive energy, and it seemed I could do no wrong. If you think and act positive, study after study shows that you will be more successful. It sure worked out that day.

I always make a point of looking for luxury cruises that are not sold out or can be booked last minute. I recall a particular cruise to the Baltic Sea where I asked if the cruise line had a suite with a piano in it. I was quite surprised to hear that indeed they had an Owner's Suite that came with a piano. Since I do not even play the piano this might seem a little silly, but I was pretty sure if the suite had a piano, it would likely be a great place to hang out and enjoy the cruise. I spent the first 2 days on the cruise looking for someone who played the piano. By the end of the trip, it was standing room only in my villa as half the ship came by to say hello. Moreover, most everyone brought a bottle of something to drink so I had an open bar for free the whole trip . . . just for sharing my piano. The entertainment was also free. I just placed a tip jar on the piano as a joke, and my piano guy, a semi-retired entertainer never left and came back every night. He told me I paid for his cruise as we laughed our heads off every night.

As it was, it came with two full bathrooms, one for guests that came by for entertainment, and the other was a private bath in the master bedroom, which could be sealed off with two private doors. The suite was like a small apartment and absolutely made the cruise a lot of fun. Through a combination of small strategic upgrades, preciously timed, I ended up in this Owner's Suite for about $5,000 total (my original cruise was only $3,000), well below the $27,500 it went for at their booking rate. I waited patiently and had developed a relationship with the travel agent and had managed to get the e-mail for the ship's purser, who introduced me to the suite manager. Then I was able to get the suite for a $1,000 upgrade after two smaller upgrades costing $500. I recommend always looking at the ship's layout before you make a final choice. Landing in the very front or the very back of a cruise ship is a very special experience that everyone should do at least one time. Bon Voyage!

CHAPTER **26**

Time Share Travel Tricks, Strategies, and Tips That Create Better Results

LEARN WHAT DAY is villa allocation day: We have discussed in this book how important it is to know when your resort actually assigns the rooms for your stay. It will generally be about 2 to 4 weeks prior to your arrival. This means your best chance of getting what you want is 1 day before villa allocation day. The best way to find out is to chat up the manager or at least someone close to the manager that knows when the schedule gets set. These people know everything about the schedule when you are coming in and can make changes up front much easier than on arrival day.

I use to send a card and thank the manager in advance when I was requesting a certain villa location. I almost always got what I wanted, and this was when I was just a 1-week owner, not a multi-month owner like my current status. The fact is . . . niceness counts, and sending in a coffee card or thank-you will more than likely pay off very big for you. There are some locations like Maui, when it gets very competitive for top ocean views. We recommend if a certain location is a favorite, that you consider a fixed week that comes with a fixed unit. It can be very frustrating to try to book that perfect unit year after year, only to be disappointed. In time share, most locations can be managed with ease; however, a top unit in peak season just has too many people often chasing the same thing, and it sets up some disappointments. In some cases, a mixed portfolio of fixed and floating weeks is the perfect solution, depending on your travel needs.

Shipping to your villa for free-when this works best.: If you are heading overseas or just want to avoid the hassle of checking in extra luggage, we recommend you consider sending a care package before you get to your villa. I have done this several times and have never had a problem. I would send a card requesting a certain villa or building, and then ship a large box when the trip was about 5–6 days away. I would pack spices, wines, frozen cheese, crackers, olive oil, tuna, and other can goods that I planned on using in the villa. Since the cost of these items was generally higher because of the resort locations, I saved a little money buying these products at the discount stores and having them a arrive a day before I did. I always took advantage of the "if it fits, it ships" motto the post office used to offer.

Now, they are back to shipping by weight, which can make shipping expensive. That said, some rates that take 7–10 days to arrive work very well. While the cost of shipping adds a small bump to your budget, it is also really nice to have that package show up at your door with all of your favorite items tucked inside. I also threw in my favorite saucepan and cutting knives, and it felt just like home when in the kitchen. It makes shopping much easier, and since you are not likely to spend $50 on spices for just a week or two or longer, sending them in the mail allows you to prepare some really great food. Also most of the internet sites now offer shipping for free so it makes sense to buy these items from Amazon or Walmart and have them delivered for free or at least very low cost. In any case, this beats spending time in a long line at a top destination grocery store when peak season is in full swing.

Here is a sample label:

The RidgeLine Resort
8257 Desert Ridge Road
Valley Oaks, CA 92741
ATTN: John C. Botdorf
Arrival Date: 6-20-2017
Manager: Ted Smith

The Coffee Card: Remember that Ted just got your coffee card and thank-you last week so he now recognizes your name on your package when it comes in. Your package is now in safe hands, and when you pop that favorite champagne and cheese, it will taste all the better knowing you did not overpay for it. Everyone can use a coffee card, but more important, a simple thank-you goes a long way today.

The rolling closet—for early departure(s): I often book three or four reservations together when I am on the time share road show, moving from one resort to another. On occasion when I waited until the last minute, I would end up with two reservations in the same resort and have to check out of one unit and check into another one. I would arrange for a late checkout, and then head over to the bell captain. I would roll my stuff over to the bell captain and let him know I would be gone for the day, but I have a new reservation opening up later that day. I would ask them to deliver the rolling closet into my new unit when it was ready. I have figured out that you can strap just about anything to these rolling closets, making them very useful for moving without much trouble. While it might be inconvenient to move, when you design a method of moving in advance, it makes moving very easy. I start to pack all of my spices and nonfrozen stuff in my travel kitchen bag for three or four meals before I leave.

I always bring a small or not so small cooler when I travel to most of my time shares. This acts as a freezer when I am moving from one villa to another. By using the frozen ice packs on the bottom, you can store frozen food for 1-2 days just in these coolers. This makes moving a freezer pretty easy when moving to the next villa. I throw everything in the cooler that needs to stay chilled for a day or so.. I don't ever even pack my clothes. They hang up on the rolling closet and just move from closet to closet. I keep them in the trunk of my car, and they never leave the car unless I am checking into a resort so I never have to pack for a resort unless I am flying. In that case, I just throw them into a large travel bag. I have my favorite dry cleaners I use and will check in several pieces of clothing into the local dry cleaner before I even check in. They are often ready for the next trip, if not the next day. I often leave at three of four in the morning to avoid freeway traffic and generally arrive at my new destination in late morning.

I have got this system down to about 15 minutes to execute a full move. It is amazing that with a couple of jackets, two sweaters, two pairs of slacks, three bathing suits, two pairs of shorts, and a combination of 10 shirts, you can live anywhere for 6 months by just rotating this small inventory. When you travel with a laptop, you don't need paper. I throw in my kitchen bag with all of my spices ready to go, and it is on to the next pool, ocean, or mountain, often to meet some friends or my family.

Don't forget the artwork: I have on special occasions brought my own artwork when I wanted to add some spice to my villa. Artwork can be very soothing and provides a personal feeling when you are staying somewhere for a month or longer. The small effort to bring in a few pictures or statues is well worth the effort if you enjoy art. I find smaller pieces of art and smaller pictures work really well, and in about 5 minutes, it looks like you own the villa you are staying in. I have had many new friends ask me how or why my unit contains artwork and special family photos. I explain having it makes it feel like home. In my situation, it *is* home since I travel more and more to chase the good weather.

Promotional offers—how existing owners can benefit: Promotional offers are a very good way to extend your vacation, increase your annual RRC, and cut down your payback indicator because you can generally add nights for below your maintenance costs if you are a smaller owner of a time share. This can also be done by staying at a competitor across the street, and then checking into your own resort in situations where the area is populated with many time share resorts. I have seen people stay for 9 or 10 nights, moving from one operator to the next over a 9-day period. While we are not big fans of overtaxing this process, if you never intend to buy, it is a very fair and smart way to see how you might wish to add to your portfolio. Remember, if you book a trip, you will be allocated into the less-desirable units because you are filling tour rooms that are dedicated to the tour process. One way around this is to book your points or weeks first, then add the villa tour. It will likely take a manager or villa scheduler to override the system and let you stay in your owner suite, but you have a good shot at it.

Be sure to bring all of your dirty clothes! I always bring all of my dirty clothes when I head to my next villa reservation.

First, they are very easy to pack. You just dump your dirty clothes hamper into your suitcase. When I walk into the villa, I dump the clothes in the suitcase into the washer, and then hang them up to dry. A few hours later, I have clean clothes for the week. I have not bought laundry soap in years. Not sure I am much richer because of this, but it does add up. I also always take the shampoo and conditioners I have used and have a large bucket of them at home. I travel with them in a plastic bag and never need to worry about what type of product will be at the next resort. One thing about 4 to 5 star resorts is they get shampoo. They take better care of me than I do myself. I suppose if you add all of these together over a year, it probably lowers my cost of time share by $200 a year or so. In the end, it is all about the most amount of fun at the lowest cost per day. I am on my way to living year-round at zero cost per day with a small income from rentals. It makes sense to save as much money as you can because the money for nice dinners has to come from somewhere!

Advance location reservations before you travel—why this matters: I prefer to have reservations in place before I arrive because the more notice the resort has before your arrival, the better chance you have of getting that top corner suite. I do not always know how long I might stay, but I always shoot for making a reservation for a busy weekend as early as possible, with the option of extending my stay as long as needed. Prime weekends can book months ahead of time, so getting an early reservation is well worth the effort.

The odds get better as you approach 24 hours before check-in because many resorts will release rooms based on last-minute cancellations, inventory rebalancing, and late check-in predictions. When rooms do not fill up, the rooms get released on a first-come, first-serve basis. Even though I know I can get into a prime resort most of the time, I still go through the reservation process as early as possible because my membership status does all the talking for me. It can't do that if all of the rooms are taken, so even a small 24-hour window can make a difference. Also, the more the computer records you have in the same villa or suite, the more the resort treats your reservation as sacred. It is not up for debate when someone has to get moved. This is why if you like a resort and prefer a certain location, stay in that building or villa as often as you can, and after a few stays, the software will just start putting you there automatically.

The music matters: The current time share policy on music varies quite a bit as operators struggle with the need to enjoy music versus the owner's right to play. I still bring my own music player when I travel to my time shares. Today's newest products are so small and sound better than most larger more expensive systems. There is no reason to forgo the tunes any longer when on the road. **The Family photo wall** : We will see many high-tech photo walls in next-generation time shares. The always popular "Fish Tank TV" will continue as a digital fish tank, albeit the family photos and digital "Hellos" will become commonplace. In other words, the age of the electronic butler is upon us.

Time share portfolio rotation: As the concepts in this book begin to become commonplace, customers will start to realize that as the times change, so will the need to "rotate" your time share portfolio. It may make sense over the long term to rotate out of some weaker time shares in favor of buying weeks that have more trading power and lower maintenance fees. While most time share plans are likely useful as they are, the time share user looking to extract over 3 months a year has a much-higher vested interest in maximizing how the portfolio is managed. Assembling a larger portfolio is key to having a seamless experience year after year that performs well. A portfolio based on renting, long-term stays, more powerful trading power, and owning "workhorse weeks" that provide solid stays at a good value are all keys to making sure your time share portfolio is finely tuned. In many cases, a good review from a time share expert who is knowledgeable in the entire industry can help fine-tune and improve your financial performance and, in the process, may add extra nights or weeks at little to no cost per year with the right strategy.

Increasing your RRC ratio: The key to lowering your overall time share cost per year is monitoring your RRC ratio and making sure you are getting the proper value out of your portfolio. Since the industry has adopted a number of different booking rules and seasons, it is possible your operator could have four or five ways to book the same vacation. Only one way will give you the highest RRC ratio, so you need to make sure you understand your discount windows, trade up possibilities, know your prime rental windows, and how you can optimize your membership opportunities. It is the combination of these events that optimizes your RRC ratio.

Walmart and Rubbermaid— a perfect combination: Time share travel is very different from hotel or even other types of travel because it offers a different combination of hotel experiences combined with an apartment life. In other words, you have access to a laundry machine and a kitchen which requires a different strategy for packing. I recommend a good set of Rubbermaid Tupperware which can be purchased at Walmart for under $10. When you travel back home from your time share, you will be able to save any food in these containers. If I am traveling a long distance, I have put an inch of water into these Tupperware's and put them in the freezer overnight. You can then load eggs and other deli or cold storage items into each container, and they will stay cold for 1–2 days. If you have any deli products or cheeses, put them into a freezer bag, and then place them on top of the ice. This works very well and keeps your items fresh, even in warmer climates, for the day.

Free shipping to your villa. The Internet is now so competitive it is easy to find free shipping for not only food but also for recreational items, new clothes, sporting equipment, and for materials for your new hobbies. This is always a favorite time for me to ship as I am not wasting time at the post office, nor am I paying for the shipping. Getting a basket of crackers and cheese or even a ham or full meal is now very easy, and the price on some on sale items will save you money compared to what prices cost in beach and ski towns. It also allows you to pack less, and if you time the purchase right, you can pick up your box at the front desk when you check in.

The top 16 spices for life: Get to know how to use these spices and you can create incredible meals, even if you only have a few ingredients in your refrigerator. It is very easy to turn even the plainest types of fish, meats, and vegetables into gourmet dishes if you know how to spice them up and make simple sauces.

1. pure sea salt and a good meat tenderizer
2. ground pepper
3. turmeric, All-Spice, mustard seed
4. cumin, chili powder, paprika
5. basil, tarragon, thyme, rosemary
6. red pepper
7. garlic or/garlic powder
8. five-spice for Chinese food

These spices will allow you to create hundreds of flavors for almost any dish. I routinely carry them in my travel bag that just stays in the car, along with olive oil and several of my top cooking utensils. This saves quite a bit of time moving the same stuff back and forth. I will take it into the house if it gets real hot in the summer. Either way, it saves time every year not having to buy these spices over and over every time you need to cook. These represent the staples of cooking and allow you to make the most of every dish. We are designing the Vagabond Travel Bag that contains a specific bag for transporting spices and kitchen ware. See the Vagabond Travel Bag Advertisement at the end of this book.

Top ten time share complaints and how to solve them:

1. I cannot get a reservation when I want. Computers are already grading humans and monitoring their job performance. See Chapter 17
2. I cannot seem to book the villa I want. See Chapters 17, 25 and 26
3. My maintenance fee is too high. See Chapters 10 and 20
4. I don't have time to rent my villa. See Chapters 20
5. I don't want to burden my kids with maintenance fees. Read the Book
6. I need more flexibility. See Chapter 26
7. I don't like waiting in line to check in . See chapters 25 and 26
8. Time shares are too expensive . See Beachfront Index-Chapter 21
9. I can buy the same thing on the secondary market for a fraction of the cost. See Chapter 18
10. My brother in law says time shares are dumb investments- See below

My brother-in-law says time shares are dumb investments: He probably also says there is no such thing as booking a 1,800 square foot luxury villa that rents for $2,200 a night for less than the tax on the room. Yes, the unexpected does happen. I remember when not a single team in the history of the NFL had ever come back from a 25-point deficit to win a Super Bowl as of 2017. It will never happen. It is not possible because the other team, just by being in the Super Bowl, would be able to win out with this type of lead.

How about a $23,000 guesthouse for 2 nights for $900. Been there, done that. Can you believe some New England fans left the game in the third quarter in the 2017 Super Bowl at the Astrodome in Houston when the Patriots were playing the Falcons? How much luck would any of us had trying to explain something that just does not seem logical, like the Patriots winning the game halfway through the third quarter, losing by 25 points? People steal real estate, companies, artwork, paintings, and automobiles almost every day, acquiring them for pennies on the dollar. Is it that far-fetched to think it cannot be done with travel or retirement living? Hopefully, because this book is almost over, you not only know it is possible but exactly *how* to do it. The tricks and methods are in here. You may need to read the book again and go back to the math. Saving millions of dollars over a lifetime of travel can easily be done if you start early and follow the rules in this book. I do it every day.

I have calculated I will have left over $1M in hotel and resort bills at the front counter with a final bill of zero or under $100 over the past 30 years using the methods in this book. Not sure this is worthy of the Hall of Fame; after all, I don't have the million. Then again, I sure lived like I did. All the money in the world won't replace the decades of memories that will be the only thing I have left on the last day. All of a sudden, that million dollars does not seem like it can compete with a lifetime of first-class trips. It is why I can look at a sunset, a mountain, or an ocean, and remember all of the people that mattered in my life and why sharing this book was important to me. I hope some of you take to the skies and never look back like I did. There is always a new job, a new career, a new family, and new friends, but to figure it all out, you have to travel. Distance makes most things you thought were important not even matter. What matters is how you lived, who you changed, what you changed, and whether you did something in between your first and last day to make a difference. I hope this book will help inspire you to live your dreams and go find your very own Vanden Plas.

Registering for the Vagabond Travel Bag!

CHAPTER 27

The Art of the Time Share Life

CONTROL—CONTROL—CONTROL: WE ALL have heard when looking to buy real estate, always pay attention to location, location, location as the most valuable rule to follow. This is slightly different for time shares since almost all Category One and Two time share products come with location built in because they are at or near ground-zero locations to begin with.

The mantra therefore becomes, how often and how well can you control the villa you want, and how long can you occupy it? The longer the time frame, the more valuable the time share. For example, a block of time controlling a month in a prime resort in high season we predict will be worth more than 1 week times 4 if the weeks can be occupied in a row. In other words, we predict that the markets will pay a premium to have longer-term stays available, like 4 to 12 weeks. The reason for this is that less than 1% of all time shares in Category One can deliver this type of time, therefore, driving up the price for the renter looking for this type of white tiger. This premium is more likely to be reflected in a resale, but under certain conditions may also be present in some prime rentals. This new longer-term trend will also lead to a developer focus on this type of product becoming more commonplace.

The 10-10 rule: Remember, the top 10% of time shares as defined by location, views, overall desirability, amenities like golfing, etc., are highly rentable 10% of the time. Your time share will fall from there depending on how far down your time share is from a top ten. Holiday weeks as a percentage of the year are all less than 10% of the time. Do not assume anything past these windows is automatically rentable. It may not be. Sometimes, supply and demand factors will favor the buyer market with too many choices on the market. If you are looking for rental security, you may wish to stay inside the 10-10 rule by acquiring a time share in a prime location for a major holiday week.

Cash to points to package points to airline points: Multiple conversions may hide benefits. When one trades an apple for a cantaloupe for a tennis racket for a ring for a car for a boat . . . You could end up with a $5,000 asset that started as a $100 asset. I have done it, but it takes patience. The point of this advice is to be wary of multiple trades from one program to another to another; i.e., like trading vacation points for hotel points to buy a hotel/airline package. On the other hand, about 10% of these types of trades actually work in your favor and sometimes to a significant degree because the companies are large global operators moving tens of millions of dollars of inventory, and sometimes, they need to make adjustments to close out their audits or quarters. While changes can be small and quick, stay on top of airline packages that involve luxury locations. You can usually find a bargain if you follow the market. The software rules can vary depending on how you use your points. See our chapter on networking and reservations for more details.

Membership benefits matter: Perhaps one of the best pieces of advice is to understand how all of the membership tiers in your time share work and what levels offer what array of benefits. Time share companies are very good at running the numbers, and often, 80% of the time share membership can help offset the cost of providing "Presidential Status." In many cases, incentives offered are just to help with load balancing and therefore are financed through rooms that might otherwise sit empty. In any case, it is wise to make sure you bump to a level that fits your budget, especially if travel and villa stays are a large portion of your lifestyle.

The art of life with or without a time share—a personal note from the author

We have all seen them. We all know them. Most of us, if only for a moment, would not mind trying their lifestyle. You know what I mean, always traveling off to here and there. Their house is full of items from the Far East, Europe, and the Caribbean. Perhaps you have only known one or two people like this. Are they bad people? Probably not. After all, *you* are at *their* party. Are you really looking at the nice paintings and sculptures, or are you just pretending to care? Perhaps you just think they are rich; after all, they have the newest Audi in the garage. They have the biggest pool or the biggest pool table in the neighborhood. Why is it they always have the nicest Christmas decorations?

Maybe you are them. Well, if you are, welcome to the point of this book. Life is way too short. The only certainty in life is not whether disappointments and challenges will come, but when. In between, it is our job to live life to the fullest and grab all the gusto you can. My mother used to cry after realizing this was my high school year book quote. Four years in an expensive Jesuit prep high school and my graduating words of wisdom were: *"You can only go around once in Life: Go for all the gusto you can"* Source: Burnett Marketing .

I tried to go spiritual with it, but like travel, fun matched with exotic lands seemed more appropriate. New adventures expand our horizons, letting us realize how many millions of people have a fraction of what we have. The poorest 5% of us in the United States would be near the richest 5% in the poorest country. If you were the poorest in our nation now, would you be happy being the richest with the same income in the poorest country? If not, then why are you not happy? You just turned down a chance to be the richest person in a country.

Faraway travel allows us to connect to what happy means and what it is. You have not missed much if you have been to most parts of the world. All of a sudden, the town bridge, waterfall, or river or lake *is more special* than ever before because you can now view it differently. You get it?

It is not where you have been that even matters the most. It is what you got out of going to where you did go. You realize you did not need to drive a $100,000 Rolls-Royce to be complete in life. After all, with a time share mentality, you could have that same Rolls for eight cents on the dollar if you really want it.

I did drive a $100,000 Rolls-Royce when I was 22 years old. I did not have anywhere near $100,000, though. I did, however, have a partner and big dreams to execute on.

The $100,000 Rolls-Royce tale—how I drove this car in college-a true story: There I was drinking beer in my room at age 21 with my good buddy, Robert Rose, a longtime friend of mine to this day. We were open to dreams. We were open to shortcuts. We wanted bigger-than-life experiences, and we wanted it right away. After another one of our highly philosophical discussions on life improvement, we started reading *The Recycler* magazine that specialized in used automobiles. It was as though we felt some divorcee was going to sell her husband's $100,000 Porsche for $8,000 because she was mad. The least we could do was come up with $8,000 to help her out.

And there it was. A 1964 Vanden Plas for sale for $10,000. Just the name sounded like we needed to own one. We were not sure what this was. After a brief "company" meeting (between the two of us), we secured the two votes necessary to call the number and explore this rare find. A commercial pilot answered the phone and explained he had been laid off and needed to sell his prized beauty. While we still had no idea what this was, we knew if it was good enough for a commercial pilot, it seemed good enough for us. After all, we had standards to meet. We had people to impress, mostly girls, but girls, after all, are also people.

We drove down the San Diego freeway all the way to the Venice Beach area from our homes off Mulholland Drive. We finally found the owner and rang his doorbell. He explained his sorrow for having to sell the fine specimen of an automobile as we talked in his living room. We tried to be sympathetic and comforting and agreed that his fortune would soon turn up. Meanwhile, we each had sugarplums dancing in our heads. It was like Christmas. We knew we were getting a present, just no idea what it looked like or drove like.

We knew not to be eager or overly impressed. After all, we were buyers with $10,000 in cash and certainly knew what we were doing. Finally, the moment came. He asked us if we wanted to see the car. This was like asking John Elway if he wanted to play in the Super Bowl. When we entered the garage, we saw it. There it was covered in a huge car blanket, but the hood ornament stood tall, pushing the blanket skyward. We both knew it. How many people could own a car with a real hood ornament? This was no Jaguar hood ornament either. This was a 1964 Vanden Plas , whatever *that* was. We had concerns as well. What if we liked the hood ornament but not the car?

We each gathered around sections of the car like cadet's ready to unfold a Super Bowl flag. Upon waiting for the owner's command, we unfolded the blanket and at long last, we got to see the car. I will never forget the sparkling 20-plus coats of pure lacquer black paint. The car had the most positive energy I had ever seen. Plus, it looked like a pure gangster car. How could anyone not get a date driving this car was one of my first thoughts. We soon noticed the steering wheel was on the right-hand side. No biggie. We just have to reverse everything we knew about driving. Second, it had a hugely pronounced mermaid swimming off the top of its gleaming silver grill. It was as though she could speak to us. Like *I Dream of Jeannie*, she had welcomed us into a future of fame, fortune, and fun. All we had to do was buy the car.

The question was not whether to buy the car, but rather, how could we *not* buy the car? I looked over at Rob, and he had "the grin." I knew the grin. I knew he was up to no good with it. I knew we did not need another voting session. It was as though he had forecasted his approval in his glance back to me, all the trouble we could get into by just owning this fine vessel. This car made a $100,000 Rolls-Royce look like a cheap, distant cousin. I knew I had the right partner, the right car, and between us, almost half the money we needed. We quickly compiled about $150 between us to use as a deposit. After another 30 minutes trying to convince the owner we were just the right derelicts to entrust this museum piece too, we took off up the freeway more lit than a New Orleans drunk. We had negotiated a final price of $8,000 in cash.

We were in the moment, enjoying life, about to buy what looked like a $100,000 car for $2,000 off the $10,000 asking price. . If our car were parked next to similar cars worth $100,000 or more from the same era, it would be hard to tell one from the other if you were not an expert. That is the point of calling it a $100,000 car. We did not know and many people over the years assumed the car was worth well over $100,000. The point is in the end it did not matter. It was what it was. The fun was real and the memories are priceless. All we needed to close our deal was a finance meeting to figure out where we were going to get the other $4,000 we needed in 24 hours since between us we had only $4,000 in cash.Needless to say, we made the purchase the next day. This was the day we learned how to turn credit cards into cash. I could write a book on what happened with the car over the ensuing 4 years. I recall to this day laughing so hard on certain occasions my gut hurt. It hurt badly from the pain of laughing. We had it all. Girls, movie stars, some of the day's top rock 'n' roll artists, police escorts, police pulling us over, police trying to arrest us . . . or the car. We were often pulled over by the police who just wanted to see who was in it. We managed to always come out on top. Worry was not a word in our world, and getting what we wanted, when we wanted it was the order of the day. The Jeannie was very good to us.

By the time we sold the car, we had made more money working as part-time chauffeurs than we paid for the car. We had the joy of being on the front row in all the top restaurants, often out-fronting cars that cost 20 times more than ours. We often got VIP treatment at the hottest clubs in town. Wow, all because we had a mermaid Jeannie as a hood ornament. She was something in all fairness. We imagined the fun before we ever saw the car. Most of all, for eight cents on the dollar, we lived like kings. I imagine today the car is worth over $100,000. I doubt there is even a dozen of them on the road. We installed a full cherry wood bar, complete with additional lantern lights, private "lock-boxes" for our favorite clients, and, of course, a full stereo. It was heaven on wheels. The car was pure gangster, and the places we went and the things that happened with the car allowed us to live life to the fullest.

The Time Share Creed-Summary Conclusion : The point of this story is to make sure you go out and find your own Vanden Plas and make the best of your life. For some, it is about charity; others have hobbies like running marathons or restoring cars or boats; and many of us have dreams and wishes to own a business or travel the world. I hope this book has created some opportunity for you to expand your horizons and consider all of your options. We have a form on the Web site www.masteringyourtimeshare.com that will allow you to calculate your cost per day of your home, and even your second or third home. This can help you start to figure out if a better plan is in store for you. We can also help you build a time share portfolio for your vacations, your business trips, and even your retirement. You can download our four-page questionnaire, and once filled out, it will tell us how to assemble the ideal time share portfolio just for you, which we can likely do for you at significantly lower costs. If you are interested you can fill it out our form, book a meeting on line and we will reduce our $450 Consulting rate to $299 for a one hour meeting on the phone to discuss your plan in detail. Be sure and use the discount code displayed at the end of this book.

Hopefully, you have learned from this book how to manage and create your RRC ratio and estimate your payback ratio. These tools, combined with the other tips in this book, will allow you to more than cover your maintenance fees if you put in the time and effort and own the right time shares. You will then be free to travel the world at little to no cost, for life. What other product can do that for you?

Our goal with this book was to remove the negative stigma that some people have about time shares and present the positives on how this housing model is not only highly worthwhile for most, but will play an increasing role in the future.

We have over 25 years' experience brokering, buying, and selling all types of real estate from major shopping centers, office buildings and large apartment houses, but now focus on just time share consulting and sales. We have a promotional code at the bottom of this page for you. . We will also refund your consulting fee at the closing of the first purchase if you choose to proceed with our representation.

We wish to thank you for all of your future input, thoughts, and support for purchasing our book and hope we have been helpful to you. We will also match your $1.00-dollar contribution when you purchase the book with our own $1.00 if purchased from our website below, and together we will donate the money to the two worthy homeless shelters on our web site, the Denver Rescue Mission and the Friendship house in Laguna to help take more homeless people off the streets. If you liked our book please feel free to send people to our web site and your comments to: www.masteringyourtimeshare.com. Our sincere thanks and wishes for a prosperous life.

Feel free to leave any comments you have at feedback@masteringyourtimeshare.com.

Very kindly,

John C. Botdorf
Chief Entreprenuer—masteringyourtimeshare.com

Discount Consulting Code: HW37809

CPSIA information can be obtained
at www.ICGtesting.com
Printed in the USA
LVOW11s1846150218
566740LV00003B/735/P

9 781478 788768